Prophet
of the
Black Nation

Prophet of the Black Nation

Hiley H. Ward

PILGRIM PRESS
Philadelphia   •   Boston

To my father
Hiley Lemen Ward

O Lord, thou hast overthrown thine enemies and destroyed them. Look down on us from heaven. O Lord, regard the distress of thy people: open the heavens and send us relief: help, help thy servant now, O God! . . .

Then did Elijah the prophet break forth like a fire; his words appeared like burning torches. Mighty kings by him were overthrown. He stood on the mount of Sinai, and heard the judgments of the future.

> —Recitative and chorus from
> scripture texts in Felix
> Mendelssohn's *Elijah*

Contents

Introduction *viii*

1 Paradox in Worship *1*

2 Nation Within a Nation *16*

3 Seedbed of a Militant *34*

4 Apostle of Youth *51*

5 The Monster Schools *72*

6 Neorealism vs. Hope *91*

7 Threshold of Fear *105*

8 Black God, Black Gospel *124*

9 Strife at the Shrine *146*

10 The Rebel Committeeman *161*

11 The Candidate *174*

12 Structure of the Nation *190*

Chart: Black Christian Nationalist Movement *211*

Notes *213*

Introduction

Albert Cleage, pastor of the Shrine of the Black Madonna, Detroit, has said things (and usually does) like:

> —Rap Brown may be 100 percent right. In Detroit, we are trying to see whether the white man has the necessary intelligence to make a transfer of power before the final destruction of America. We are not sure, but we are trying. We do not have too long to see whether or not it can be done.[1]

> —You can make movies with Sidney Poitier marrying white women if you want to, but you cannot resurrect the dream of integration for black people. It doesn't exist.[2]

> —If we decide we want the Promised Land of freedom and equality, we have to make the sacrifice involved. It's too easy to look at America today and see the promised land waiting for us all. But God's word to us is the same as to the Jews: If you don't want to fight, then you'll be banished.[3]

> —The crisis is upon us. No longer are we really necessary for the existence of the white man. The nasty work that he doesn't want to do is being eliminated. Because we are no longer necessary to him, we have become a liability. Rather than feed us and take care of us we can expect that he will find some excuse to kill us as he is systematically killing off our black youth in Vietnam right now.[4]

> —Don't ever forget it. A white man killed Dr. Martin Luther King.[5]

—It is my honest opinion that white people are incapable of facing reality in any consideration of the problem of race.[6]

—[In a letter to Olympic 200-meter gold medalist Tommie Smith and John Carlos, bronze medal winner in the same event, both of whom raised their fists in defiance and bowed their heads in receiving their medals—they received Cleage's Shrine of the Black Madonna first distinguished service award]: Your categorical dismissal from the Olympic games by those counter forces of the Black Revolution can only add impetus to our struggle for justice and freedom as it shows how stupidly white people react when confronted with the accusation of racism.

—Everything about traditional Christianity is false.[7]

—In the New Testament we find a revolutionary message addressed to a Black Nation by a Black Messiah.[8]

No wonder Pastor Cleage is probably the most hated man in Detroit, by all reckoning, including his own. "You won't have any trouble finding my enemies," he advised at his desk at the Shrine, which is affiliated with the United Church of Christ. The desk was a clutter of dusty letters and papers in a long room marked by nearly empty bookshelves with occasional clusters of paper and books. A bare overhead light bulb presided over rickety folding chairs and the unruly desk. Cleage sat in a neatly pressed black suit, with black tie, black socks and loafers, and a black tiki amulet around his neck.

Mention Cleage to almost anyone, from the fellow at work to the man on the street, and you'll get a response and a chain of expletives reserved only for the less desirable of God's creatures. Certain pastors regard Cleage as a threat of some sort or other, one who, they have convinced themselves after hearing one of his unadorned utterings on TV or seeing a sentence-or-two quote from him in a newspaper, would not object to seeing their big structures burned to the ground; or they may just see him as one who threatens their own influence. In the first category is the white suburbia pastor whose members are part of the white hysteria that created an arms race to "get" niggers like Cleage, if he set foot in their territory[9]; and in the second, black pastors who are threatened by Cleage's continuous denouncing of Toms in the pulpit. The Baptist Ministers' Conference, with the Rev. Charles Williams, president, as spokesman, held a press conference declaring black unity and denouncing Cleage's philosophy as "the foolishness of separation."[10]

Cleage scorns all pastors whose main purpose is to satisfy souls and guarantee individual salvation, although he understands them. He says:

> Black churches played a leading role in this escapism (trying to forget brutality and oppression). Once a week we could go to church and find the strength to endure another week. We took delight in contemplating life after death. . . . The church was not our only means of escape. There was sex and alcohol. All these things offered a very necessary psychological relief. They made it possible for us to maintain our sanity.[11]

With some 400 storefront churches and 150 registered denominational black Baptist churches, not to mention pietistic AME, AMEZ, CMC denominations out of the Wesleyan tradition, such sweeping indictments of men dedicated to preaching individual salvation—and their congregations, possibly a majority of Detroit's 660,000 blacks—has not attracted any particular following. Denouncing such piety-religion as a "comfort station" might be one reason for his own sagging attendance. Possibly most people still go to church to get some "individual" comfort or bonus.

Cleage is also caught in the internecine jealousies of blacks, believes Tommy McIntyre, maverick ex-newsman and agent given credit in a book, *Senator Joe McCarthy*, for writing a release under the name of a former Michigan congressman employer of his, denouncing Senator McCarthy. The release probably aided in bringing down McCarthy. McIntyre is now a westside weekly newspaper columnist. Though he is in semi-retirement, he is noted for having his ear to the ground. He says, "This is a gold rush, not a philosophic thing. They (Cleage, etc.) are being treated as traditional revolutionaries. They are not. They are at the Klondike and there is only a need for so many whorehouses." McIntyre spits in a bowl as he talks, in his underwear, before an electric fan at midday during a hot July spell. A black maid brings him a newspaper in his eleventh-floor room of the narrow old Royal Palm Hotel. The room is in total disarray, and you have to sit on a pile of papers in a chair. "Cleage is the kind of guy who arranges to be put on a cross, and when they're not looking, revives . . ."

Despite rank-and-file distaste, without honor in his own milieu, Albert Cleage enjoys considerable national prestige. Whites and blacks, at the very top, sing his praises. He can walk into a national meeting of all the militant blacks of Christian persuasion, the black caucuses, with many able leaders, a session of the National Committee of Black Churchmen in St. Louis, and the conference stands still for him and all the media turn to him. There are interviews on national radio, Night Call, a round of TV press conferences. Officials discuss their new committees in terms of Cleage's own views ("We may not go so far as Cleage on this, but . . . ," they say) and they put him on their key executive committees. In New York, as I did at the NCBC in St. Louis, I've watched his electric influence on the Interreligious Foundation for Community Organization—he sits quietly, and brings up a motion, which is eagerly adopted. He has served on the ad hoc Operation Connection to raise funds as cochairman with the presiding bishop of the Episcopal Church.

Cleage has done little to endear himself to people. He is always late, often misses a speaking engagement altogether—he either forgets or calls up at the last moment to say that he can't make it, with excuses ranging from "too many threatening phone calls" to a late plane arrival. When he speaks he is to the point, preferring to say what he thinks to making friends.

Former parishioners in Detroit and earlier parishes describe him as "tactless" and "blunt." Yet Cleage, whose high forehead, expressionless eyes, and slightly tapered mouth make him resemble an old elk looking out of the forest, has a gentle, winning manner, a warmth about him; he is an easy guy to talk to because he listens, constantly agreeing. "I understand, I understand," he says, disarmingly. He is a man of wit and humor. Says a former girl friend of his student days at Wayne State University, "My girl friends could never understand why I wanted to go with him, but I thought 'Toddy' (a nickname given him by an aunt from Kalamazoo who took to Cleage as a toddler) was funny." Though he is often pictured as a bland, stoneface type, minus antlers, I have seen him warm up and nearly laugh himself sick. One occasion was a little New York Greenwich Village musical, which he and his daughter Kris and myself attended. He chuckled, laughed, slapped his knees, although they couldn't get him or Kris to come on stage or dance in the aisle in the audience participation.

He was divorced by his wife Doris after twelve years of marriage. She married her former beau, Henry, Cleage's attorney brother. Henry continues as Cleage's attorney and the three are often part of a gathering at Cleage's mother's home where Cleage takes many of his meals. He has continued to live alone, until recently in a twelfth-floor, panoramic apartment ($360 a month, two-bedroom) in the exclusive downtown eastside Lafayette Park overlooking the river, Detroit, and Windsor, Canada. His church described his moving there as a security measure, although some regarded this as catering to rather sophisticated tastes. McIntyre: "I imagine his stomach would turn upside down more than mine if someone put chittlings in front of him. Caviar is more his dish. There is none of the worker priest in this man's makeup." Yet McIntyre's sweeping theory is largely discounted by observing Cleage. He seemed, for instance, on new territory when I took him to a sukiyaki restaurant in New York City. He settled for one scotch and soda (as he does in the evening with a guest in his apartment), and when it came to the sukiyaki, preferred a fork, without trying the chopsticks. He was the only non-hep person, besides Kris, at a table that included a team of chopstick-wielding Japanese visitors. His church is ill-kept; in his immaculate apartment two of three paintings remain unhung after a number of months – not a sign of particular interest in the place.

Cleage has always been a riddle to Detroit's black community, denouncing a school tax raise one year, favoring it the next time around; welcoming the most extreme militant Muslims into his church membership while keeping a traditional Christian service; turning down money because of strings attached while other blacks clamored for it, then sitting on predominantly white boards set up by white auto industrialists, such as Accord, Inc., geared to finance-rehabilitated housing. Says Brother Imari (Richard Henry), public relations officer for the Republic of New Africa, the extreme separatist group who want a series of states for their own nation and reparations from the United States government:

> It was with deep shock and dismay that my brother and I, representing the Republic of New Africa, returned to Detroit from conferences in East Africa with black freedom fighters to find that black leaders here [referring to Cleage?], some of whom had identified with the Black Revolution, had joined with the white exploiter in a new approach to exploitation of black people. . . . The difference between Accord, Inc. and the old way is that now the white exploiter is willing to allow a handful of black people to share in the exploitation with him.[12]

Cleage was an enigma to the black community way back in 1962, when the black-edited *Michigan Chronicle* observed:

> Throughout his stormy career as student minister and plain citizen interested in the welfare of others, the Rev. Albert B. Cleage, Jr. has been known as a "loner.". . . Is the Rev. Albert Cleage, Jr. a maverick rabble rouser or a dedicated leader? This is the question being asked in many quarters as the controversial pastor of Central becomes involved in virtually every major public issue. . . .

> Is there any answer to the question? . . . Obviously the Rev. Mr. Cleage will remain an enigma in this area of community leadership. He is making his presence felt.[13]

That in 1962. The paper has not ventured any interpretation since, except to run pro-and-con letters from readers concerning Cleage, and Cleage's own column.

Cleage continued in 1968 to receive national attention, boosted in part by his new book *The Black Messiah* and coverage in many major national magazines, as the one representative of radicalism in the church par excellence. *Ebony Magazine* in its September 1968 issue said the "fiery Rev. Albert B. Cleage, Jr." was "easily the most radical figure among black rebels in white churches."

As Cleage develops his Black Christian Nationalist Movement concepts, which could be the seeds of a major new black Christian grouping or denomination to replace the somewhat foreign Black Muslim influence among US militant religious-minded blacks, he is a man to watch and deserves a studied hearing. Few know anything about him. Few have probed in depth into his thinking. His exposure has been in headlines, two-minute TV interviews, and briskly written paragraphs or full-page-width photographs in *Life Magazine* and other picture media. He told a nearly all-white rally at the University of Detroit in March 1968, "People hate me for what I believe, but practically nobody knows what I believe."[14]

What is the context of this complex man and his thinking? What is he really saying? Why does he say what he does? What does he mean?

This book, we hope, through a study of one black nationalist leader, will offer some insight into the whole movement of black nationalism and where it is going now and in the 70's. It is a look into black leadership—at least one black leader or candidate for leadership. What are the forces shaping this prominent pastor, sophisticated and trained in the best of schools, into a radical black spokesman?

For political analysts, sociologists, and economists, this practical prophet who talks of a revision of society, the economy, and a process, if not dialectic, that does not exclude revolution, must hold some fascination.

To the ecumenist and religious orientated, there are some new, exciting frontiers that transpire doctrine in the name of a new practical unity while maintaining a semblance of traditional ties. To the Protestant watching the annual Consultation on Church Union evolving a plan to work out a 25-million-member federation of nine U.S. denominations, for instance, Cleage's interfaith dynamic — using funds of all churches and mapping his own Black Christian Nationalist Movement, renaming churches from independent backgrounds from other traditions — should help indicate some new vistas.

Cleage has avoided the temptation of clergy to adapt to the ways and language of the institution and its bureaucracies. His language is always simple, non-bureaucratic. Though his bluntness is a handicap in winning and keeping friends, honesty and directness have their values. He is not afraid to let old institutions die; but he is also laying bricks and building for tomorrow. "We are not starting out with the intention of dying. We are starting out with the intention of changing our basic situation."[15]

This book offers no final judgment on Cleage. There is material here to make a judgment and a summing up.

Students of religion will ask whether Cleage is a prophet or not. The prophets of old were generally, if not unlikable, at least unpopular anti-status quo men, who basked in the favor of God if not that of men. Elijah ate in caves from food brought by birds after his bout with the status quo of King Ahab and Queen Jezebel's land. Jeremiah, the agitator, in a conquered Jerusalem under the oppressor, was thrown into a pit. Amos went about at home in Judah, but mostly in Israel among the northern "suburbanites," denouncing their luxuries and summer houses and calling for "justice" to "roll down like waters, and righteousness like an ever-flowing stream" (Amos 5:24).

Elijah, Jeremiah, Amos — very unlikable, and perhaps misunderstood fellows, all, but prophets all. And Albert Cleage?

People react differently when you ask if Cleage could be called a prophet:

McINTYRE: He's not quite as convincing as Joseph Smith. And he did not put any gold tablets together, and he's not as simple or easy to understand as Mrs. Eddy.

PEARL (*Cleage's daughter*): I don't know. He may be a prophet. It's hard to think of him that way. I know him so well. There is no objection to it. It is not a negative concept.

NICHOLAS HOOD (*United Church of Christ minister and Detroit city councilman*): He has been very honest in terms of his concern for the community. In spite of this, I believe he has been very responsible on the crucial issues that are basic, and consistent right down the line. Although he was years ahead, we are getting around closer to his position.

JAMES FARMER (*assistant secretary of Health, Education, and Welfare*): He's [Cleage is] serving a positive function. A kind of symbol around which militants can rally for constructive purpose.

MRS. BETTY SHABAZZ (*widow of Malcom X, and first vice-president of the Republic of New Africa*): I don't know much about what Mr. Cleage is doing, but anyone who has such a beautiful picture of a black woman in his church must be a great man. Anyone with such a painting, that is so beautiful and has such a spiritual quality, I think what he would do would be for the good of black people. As far as I know, he's a fine man and should be congratulated.

JULIAN BOND (*Democratic state representative in Georgia, and first black nominee for Vice President on a major party ticket, in an interview at the Georgia State Capitol*): I have a lot of admiration for Pastor Cleage. I read a lot about him. He does with his church what more ministers ought to do. He has, for lack of a better word, "de-honkified" Christ. When you go to his church, you feel confronted with the social teachings of Jesus.

Bond has been in Cleage's church, a non-churchman himself though his grandfather was a minister, and his father, leading educator and former college president, is active in the United Church of Christ in Atlanta, the same denomination as Cleage.

MILTON HENRY (*Republic of New Africa vice-president*): Cleage is not a prophet. He is a messenger, which is not the same as a prophet. A prophet would ultimately speak in terms of the future. He is clearly a messenger, and unusual, but lacks prophetic vision. Separation—into a state—is prophetic. John in Revelation 18 talked of separation of people, and so did the Old Testament.

WILLIAM H. DANIELS (*chief executive officer of the Detroit Metropolitan Association of the United Church of Christ*): I would hesitate to say that he is a prophet. I personally don't agree with all his theological conclusions but there are other people whose theology and social interpretations I also wouldn't agree with 100 percent. He is a pioneer. The word prophet scares me a little. But as a discerner of the times, as an innovator, going ahead and stirring others into action, I think this is correct.

"Prophet" was used by media for styles of some of the new faces which emerged in the summer of 1969. James Forman, director of the United Black Appeal for the National Black Economic Development Conference, was called a prophet. His style is more of confrontation, but the prophetic tone is similar. Forman looks a prophet, even in blue shirt, tie, and dark suit. I walked down the aisle as a newsman with him in his second appearance at St. George Episcopal Church, New York. He had arrived alone, and continued alone, carrying an African cane like a prophet of old as the choir sang "Hallelujah," and later, "Mine eyes have seen the glory." Though Cleage stayed out of the initial NBEDC development, which was centered in the hands of younger men, he hailed the controversial Black Manifesto of the NBEDC and its demands for funds from churches as "an important document," and said "there is nothing un-Christian about tactics that advance the cause of Christianity and justice."

And Albert Cleage gave his views on the meaning of "prophet" and his answer to "Are you a prophet?"

"Religion has several aspects: (1) priestly and ministerial, and (2) prophetic. Being prophetic is largely to place society under judgment of eternal values. It is a spoken thing—a voice, rather than a person-to-person ministry instead of a sacramental ministry. Just to talk is not a prophetic role. But a prophetic voice indicts, condemns, and brings under judgment of eternal values under the will of God. My ministry is more closely that of a prophetic voice than any other aspect. My ministry is to evaluate social action in the world, to see if it is compatible with what I consider truth, justice.

"Jesus is my favorite prophet, not in a sense of traditional interpretation but in terms of a revolutionary leader, as a black leader as I interpret it, to bring back Israel. He didn't get far toward power. But his was a revolutionary movement, and we are trying to do the same basic thing."

CHAPTER 1

Paradox in Worship

"Lord, I wanna be a Christian . . . ; Lord, I wanna be a Christian . . .

"Lord, I wanna join the nation. . . ."

A broad-shouldered young tenor, light-brown-skinned, with a shadow of a goatee, looked skyward over the heads of his fellow choir members at Detroit's Shrine of the Black Madonna as he belted out the old slave spiritual with the sudden new modern punch line.

A young assistant, deacon Thomas E. Williams, who during the week is a supervisor for the Detroit Water Board, prays: "As we consider our struggle for freedom and self-determination, we also pray that each of us in the nation will see his own place . . . and we pray for growth . . . we pray for brotherly love, and we pray to hold our heads high . . . and for unshakable determination in our struggle for Black Power in light of oppression; we pray for Pastor Cleage—give him the encouragement and strength he needs; and we thank thee for the Black Madonna, sweet and elegant . . . we pray in the name of the Black Messiah who taught his disciples to pray" (and there follows the Lord's prayer).

To be a Christian in Albert Cleage's church is to identify with a "people," in a black people's movement. When it comes to the invitation, Cleage extends a welcome for all those who want to join the nation to come forward. "We open our doors to those without a church home . . . who want to join the nation." Baptism is required; but prior baptism is accepted if one has been baptized somewhere once before, and most adult blacks have, Cleage says. Or baptism can be waived on request with good reason,

1

but so far there have been no such requests. "We baptize into a whole new way of life which Christians have
always said, not a mere cleansing," Cleage says. With each
baptism, sprinkling, usually infants, the pastor gives an
informal statement that "baptism is a symbolic ritual. One
dies to the old way of life. For black people who live in a
hostile nation and identify with the oppressor, one dies to
that. The Shrine is dedicated to the rebuilding – if one
accepts the new way of life, he is dedicated to the building
of the Black Nation." The name of the person being baptized is said aloud. Then reading an amended formula
(Black Nation references added) from the *Manual of the
Congregational Christian Churches*[1] he says, "I baptize
thee into the Nation in the name of the Father, Son, and
Holy Spirit."

Asked if a white person could join his church, he said it
would have to be discussed, but "I don't think it would
work. Hardly anyone just walks in and says the first time
that he's going to join. Very few join outright anyway. It
depends if he gets along and can stand the program. There
is no rule against it (whites joining), but our basic fight is
against white oppression, and for a white person to come
in and join would be peculiar. When black folk join white
churches, this is natural, for he has tried to join white
man's society all his life. We are not preaching integration.
If one overcomes his whiteness and feels alienated enough
(to white society), maybe. Frank Joyce (head of People
Against Racism dealing primarily with whites) is the
closest that I can think of (as a possible white member),
yet he knows it wouldn't be sensible; he'd see the incon-
gruity of it and that he could do more as a white working
with whites."

The prayer for Holy Communion comes out slightly
changed also to fit the emphasis of the new Nation.
Adapting the *Book of Worship for Free Churches*,[2] Cleage
prays:

"Thou who hast consecrated for us a new and living
way, even Jesus Christ our Black Messiah, grant unto
us who are here met, so to partake of this bread and this
cup that our hearts and lives may be truly yielded to the

sway of his revolutionary spirit; and here we offer and present unto thee ourselves, our souls, and bodies as a living sacrifice unto thee. Now as we commemorate his Last Supper with his disciples and his offering of himself in sacrifice for the Black Nation, we humbly beseech thee to grant thy Holy Spirit to sanctify this bread and wine that they may become unto us symbols of the body that was broken, and of his blood that was shed for us. May the acceptance of this sacrifice join us to each other and to the Black Messiah in a renewed dedication to the building of his nation. Amen."

Despite the slight changes to accommodate the traditional faith and ritual to new black militantism, the worship service of the Shrine of the Black Madonna is European, Latin, white in tradition, and hardly African at all.

The all-black audience is decidedly sophisticated— adults are in dark suits and ties, and those who wear their African daishikis and other pullover garments do so over shirts and ties.

Candelabra burn at each end of the altar, lighted candles along with white carnations on the altar, as in any suburban church. At Christmas there's the Christmas tree, at Easter the lilies (at Christmas there were white poinsettias on the altar), at Thanksgiving the pumpkin and cornstalks in typical white rural North American fashion.

There is the traditional order of worship with Latin words used as much as in a sophisticated Protestant white service. First there's an organ prelude (no drums or African melodies), the processional hymn for the choir (usually "Holy, Holy, Holy"), the Te Deum, invocation, Gloria Patri, responsive reading, an old-fashioned gospel hymn, "Jesus Calls Us o'er the Tumult," an anthem, "God Is Still on His Throne," a pastoral prayer which is very formal and traditional, with the "thee's" and "thou's," except for invocation of blessing on the Nation, a choral response, "Hear Our Prayer, O Lord," a spiritual, "I've Been 'Buked (rebuked)," the sermon, followed by a gospel hymn, "Softly and Tenderly Jesus Is Calling."

The service continues with the offertory "Trampin," a

welcome to visitors, a hymn, "Soldiers of Christ Arise," offertory prayer, the Doxology, a recessional hymn, "A Mighty Fortress Is Our God," a benediction, and a choral amen and organ postlude.

This was Sunday, November 24, 1968, just before Thanksgiving. It was like any other service at the Shrine, except that the church had a nearly vacant look compared to a year before when Cleage was riding the tide of post-rebellion Detroit. Then the old-timers, the young extreme nationalists, many of whom favored starting a new country within the United States, the middle-aged—all still uneasy and angry over the white establishment—flocked out to hear the one man of the cloth who insisted on angrily twitting the system from the pulpit. They were with him through the Easter 1968 season, when fifteen hundred people attended two services. They left him afterward, the pious for more individualistic services, the many extremists for less religious gatherings; and the Black Muslims who had come in returned to their mosques.

One of the more celebrated outsiders who swelled the Shrine congregation in the heyday of the church after the 1967 rebellion was Nathan Wright, director of urban work for the Episcopal Diocese of Newark and a former rector in Boston for fourteen years. Dr. Wright, guest preacher, gave a sermon that he told me later was originally written for whites in Concordia College, Moorhead, Minnesota. Certain words had been added to fit it to the black community. Thus "self-respect for black men" was changed for the Shrine audience to "self-respect for us as black men," and "black men must come to respect themselves as black men" became "we who are black men must come to respect ourselves as black men," demonstrating perhaps how much that is said at Cleage's church is the same as said elsewhere. The emphasis in Wright's speech was on "unity" for action. At the end of the sermon, when an invitation for membership was offered to the congregation, Dr. Wright walked down from the chancel to fill out a card. Cleage was away for the day; but an associate pastor, William H. Colquitt, who is also pastor of the Temple of the Black Messiah, Inkster, welcomed the scholarly black

Dr. Wright as a member. "I see no conflict," said Colquitt, who also said he was an ordained Baptist. "I am elated about any growth of the Black Nation."

When I asked Wright afterward about his joining the church, he said, "I felt a divine spirit here which is needed for the salvation of the nation. I am not going to give up my Anglican membership, but widen my membership. Barriers are superfluous between denominations and we must symbolize this new realization." He said he could take communion in either church. "There is no problem. I have opened up communion in my church in the past to other people. This is a forerunner of what must be done." Open communion, in fact, was approved by Episcopalians in their triennial meeting in Seattle in 1967.

During his presentation on "Black Power and Urban Unrest," Wright was applauded frequently, but not nearly so much as a crowd only weeks earlier had interrupted Mrs. Betty Shabazz, widow of Malcolm X, after every phrase in her account of black mothers in history. On that day the church was packed (there were still seats around when Wright spoke).

Mrs. X praised the Shrine as an ideal place to worship and pledged her support of the work of Cleage. Cleage had been an ardent admirer of Malcolm X, a native Michigander, whose autobiography is a ringing indictment of the white man's world particularly in Lansing, state capital seventy-five miles northwest of Detroit, where Malcolm X spent his early years. Cleage's young ushers at this period of time were brusk and aggressive and could not tolerate a white, or anyone standing in the aisles, and I was crowded into one of the few vacant seats in the middle of a pew in the balcony during the speech by Mrs. Shabazz.

Cleage often refers to Brother Malcolm, whom he still admires profoundly; but he has expressed some qualms about the "new Malcolm," who decided just before his death he could work with whites. Cleage appeared with Malcolm on a Sunday in November 1963 at a rally in Detroit's King Solomon Baptist Church. Cleage in an "electrifying" speech, as *The Liberator Magazine* recalls the event, shouted "revolution—real revolution—is for power!"³ Five years later, when he was pressed about Malcolm in a discussion at Madonna College, Livonia, in a classroom of mostly nuns, Cleage was asked, "How strictly do you hold to Malcolm X doctrine?" He replied, "Which doctrine? I accept (1) his going back to African culture, and (2) black people being alienated."

QUESTION: Would you ignore the last part of his life (*a reference to Malcolm's alleged conversion to appreciate white as well as black after a visit to Africa and Mecca*)?

CLEAGE: I would de-emphasize the last year of his life. It has been highly overemphasized. I think he was highly confused in his last years. In talking with African leaders, he was trying to find something meaningful . . . and was overrated. . . . He was not stupid enough to really endorse living with the Arab. The Arabs carried on slavery, and still do. I doubt if he took living with the Arab with any degree of seriousness. I don't believe it. If he really accepted this in his last year . . . well, his life then was meaningful up to a point—you find many meaningful lives up to a point in an insane asylum. . . ."

Such views probably helped to alienate Milton Henry and others who take their Islam and Arab friendships very seriously, as Malcolm did. Henry, when I raised the same contradiction, defended Arab slave trade, "They did not sell people as chattels. They had human slavery as the Romans had it, with rights of men. These were taken away in the United States. The Arabs never dreamed of this."

The African culture emphasis is heavy in the worship of the Shrine of the Black Madonna, though the worship of the church continues Western and largely indistinguishable (except for "Nation" references) from frontier Protestantism, on the one hand, with its gospel hymns and invitation, and on the other hand, big-city formal Protestant ritual patterns. At the center of the chancel in the sanctuary is a thirty-foot-high portrait of a plump, sad-faced Black Madonna in the whites and blues of Africa with a black baby in arm. Mrs. X, herself on the light side, as Cleage is in complexion, in her soft, spiritually confident voice reminiscent of the tragic life of her martyred husband, formed a memorable image beneath the great African madonna.

The gentle, determined Madonna and Child mural was not put there by gentle hands. The artist is Glanton Dowdell, 43, a former convict at Jackson prison where he served ten years on conviction of a second-degree murder charge. In March 1967 Dowdell and one other person were found guilty by Recorder's Court Judge Robert J. Colombo of carrying concealed weapons and ammunition in a car during a miniature eastside rebellion that threatened to become full-scale a year before the major outbreak in Detroit. Dowdell was put on probation in lieu of a five-year prison sentence but was warned the five-year sentence would be imposed if he were brought in again on any other charge than traffic violations. Dowdell has been charged in a federal indictment with others after an alleged attempt to forge and cash stolen bonds.

In Jackson, Dowdell won acclaim for a severe, gray picture, "Southeast Corner of My Cell." He has some studies behind him in art at the Chicago Art Institute and at Arts and Crafts in Detroit, and won an honorable mention in the Michigan Art Show in 1956, and in 1966 the Trade Union Leadership Council award for excellence in art.

Dowdell's Black Madonna was dedicated on Easter Sunday, March 26, 1967. At the same service Cleage issued a call for a "black ecumenical movement," which he dubbed the "Black Christian Nationalist Movement," and asked for a ressurection of "the historic Black Messiah, and to stop worshiping a white Jesus who never existed." "For nearly five hundred years the illusion that Jesus was white dominated the world only because white Europeans dominated the world," said Cleage. "The resurrection which we celebrate today is the resurrection of the historic black Christ and the continuation of his mission. The church which we are building and which we call upon you to build wherever you are, is the church which gives our people, black people, faith in their power to free themselves from bondage, to control their own destiny, and to rebuild the Nation—beginning with those individual followers of a Black Messiah who are ready to break the servile identification of the oppressed with their oppressor."

Since Cleage's installation of Dowdell's Black Madonna, there have been others in Detroit. During the rebellion someone painted black the statue of Jesus on the Sacred Heart Seminary grounds up the street from Cleage's church by a half mile, and the seminary officials left it black. Most recently Father Raymond Ellis, pastor of the inner-city St. Cecilia Roman Catholic Church, had a 24-foot black Christ painted in the dome of his church by black artist Devon Cunningham, a more conventional man than Dowdell. Cunningham is a marketing representative for Detroit Edison. In Cunningham's painting in the stately Romanesque dome, one of the angels is Indian, another oriental, and two are black and two white. Cleage's Black Madonna is not the first in the center of worship in a Detroit black church. United Church of Christ minister Nicholas Hood revealed that Plymouth congregation once attended by Cleage as a youth, has had a three-foot sculpture of a Black Madonna left of the pulpit for over thirty years, although Cleage says, "I doubt if anybody really considered it black."

When Dowdell did the painting for the Shrine, he said the Black Madonna was an extension of himself. "This is me," he said. "I can't divorce the Madonna from black women. I don't think that any of the experiences of the Madonna were more poignant or dramatic than those of any Negro mother, an ADC mother, a mother whose child goes wrong, anyone."[4] His model was Rose Waldon, an attractive young mini-skirted mother with close-cropped hair. Dowdell described his model, and by inference, his Madonna subject, as "self-confident grace."

The chancel before the advent of the mural was dominated by a great window of Pilgrim elder William Brewster getting off ship with a Bible. Some of the old-timers who left the church were outraged by the covering up of that "splendid window." Offended particularly was Mrs. Edward Jandy. She and her husband are now retired and settled in Delphi, Maryland. Mrs. Jandy was the last white member of the Central Church, and she is responsible for the signboard, which curiously still says "everyone invited." On the sign, Cleage has kept "Central United Church of Christ" as a subline under "Shrine of the Black Madonna." Until only recently he kept "Central Church" as the main designation on the signboard, despite the fact that he used Shrine of the Black Madonna on the letterheads. The reason for the long delay in renaming the church on the signboard was to allow for a "transition," he said. It took him a year and five months to change the outside sign to "Shrine of the Black Madonna" after the installation of the Black Madonna painting. The church, before it became Central Church, had been known as the Brewster-Pilgrim Congregational Church—a merger of two struggling old congregations in 1932.

Cleage came on the scene in May 1951, from Springfield, Massachusetts, to serve the St. Mark's United Presbyterian mission in a Twelfth Street building purchased from the Unity Evangelical Lutheran congregation by the former United Presbyterian Church. But soon fed up with people who just wanted to be "pious" on Sunday, he recalls, he led a group of dissidents out in March 1953. They met in a big home and in the Crosman School for five years. Recalls Samuel C. Weir, former national moderator of the old United Presbyterian denomination (now merged with the Presbyterian Church in the U.S.A. to form the United Presbyterian Church in the U.S.A.) and former chief executive of the Michigan Synod of the new united church, "Albert's father and uncle helped organize St. Mark's. Uncle Henry was a postal employee, one of the first elders. Unable to find a Presbyterian-trained pastor, they suggested we interview Albert. The Presbytery did so and he gave the right answers, but he did not work out too well. He had his strong-minded ways. From our standpoint, we did not feel we had the best of cooperation. To some degree, we felt we could not see much accomplished. He was not regular in attending meetings of Presbytery and Synod. . . . He could listen and then do what he wanted to do. Obviously he was not open to Presbyterian procedures. About St. Mark's being too pious, I am sure that would probably be what he would say."

Some years later, in 1967, St. Mark's moved to scrap its community church outlook and lined up foursquare in the Presbyterian camp in regard to organization and polity. It purchased the old Economy Press building just a stone's throw to the south as an educational building and ministerial office. This was the building where the 1967 rebellion started after a police raid, and already a plastic stained-glass window in the remodeled building has had a rock thrown through it.

Cleage was not the only pastor to do a pullout from St. Mark's. Most recent was the forming of the Fellowship Community Church under James Wadsworth, former longtime president of the Detroit branch of the NAACP, St. Mark's pastor who started his own offshoot of St. Mark's with dissident members in 1967.

The Shrine of the Black Madonna has not been overly concerned with mundane things. Tumbleweeds choke one another among high grass and unkept bushes in the little strips of ground next to the red-brick colonial walls of the distinguished church topped by a tall, narrow spire. Inside, there is almost an eeriness. Walls have grown dim, with the exception of the sanctuary which still has a friendliness about it, although the cream-colored walls several stories high might show more need of painting with better lighting. The halls are bare and rickety. A basement chapel is all but stripped except for a worship area with double pulpit, chairs, and a worn carpet. The rest of the room is bare, with folding chairs, as if the old pulpit ensemble and rug were hauled in from some church being demolished. This room is used for meetings of the action councils and other groups during the week, and on Sunday it is the room where all the classes of the church school assemble for opening exercises. They sit with their coats on, but I hung mine in a coatroom nearby with one other coat. The coatroom was a shambles of old counters and posters heaped up, in dust and cobwebs.

Once there were two church school hours (9:30 and 11:15 A.M.), but now there is one because as the church school superintendent, Dave Albert Cleage, a first cousin of the pastor, put it, "Many families have moved out, and there are now many young people, and they don't have families yet." A big, affable man who couldn't get mad at a flea and who apparently loves kids, Dave Cleage, 62, has been a youth leader for Pastor Cleage since the St. Mark's days. Now a deacon, he is still coach of three athletic teams, all which led their leagues in 1969, and gets kids out to church school by insisting they must attend regularly before they can play.

Outside in the hall three or four young teens were mocking Dave Cleage with a bravado rendering of "Old Man Cleage," sung to the tune of "Old Man River." They soon disappeared. The superintendent admonished his charges inside the assembly room to speak up so he could hear them a little better as his hearing battery had gone dead. His only discipline problem was one of the other two teachers, who wanted to lecture on the Emancipation Proclamation when Dave mentioned it in the opening exercises among things to be thankful for. He suggested the teacher might better save the discussion for the individual class instead of the general assembly, which included kids from age four to high school.

Dave Cleage admitted that attendance had dropped from 400 to only 50 — it was more like 30 on this particular Sunday before Thanksgiving. But, as he pointed out, many of the kids elected to go to church instead of Sunday school, and of the 200 persons in the church service with Albert Cleage at the same hour, probably 100 of them were youth — juniors, intermediates, and a sprinkling of high schoolers and other young adults, some in occasional family groups. Regulars say the attendance normally averages around 250 to 350 at the present, subject to larger crowds on special Sundays. On Christmas Day, 1968, with the flu and snow in vogue, I counted barely 70.

Dave Cleage is a pious man who likes his Bible, just as Pastor Cleage relies heavily on the Bible, particularly the Old Testament for his sermons on the Promised Land and freedom. As the kids were studying in church school, Pastor Cleage was preaching on the Psalms about lifting up one's head in Thanksgiving. He talked about the fact that nearly all the blacks at San Francisco State College were among those arrested in demonstrations, a cause of thanksgiving for their involvement, he said. "Two years ago you couldn't get two blacks together on anything on a campus. Then we were just content to get into a white university. Now we have something to be thankful for. And it's not just being thankful for turkey on Thanksgiving Day when we have turkey and other blacks do not. We are thankful for discontent."

Down in the church school room, with the preschoolers moving to their class with their teacher, and the juniors with their teacher, the junior highs and high schoolers moved to one side, about 25 of them, all with their coats still on, and Dave Cleage saw to it that they all had quarterlies, which were the eleven-year-old teacher's edition of *A Life of Jesus* by Henry R. Rust (Pilgrim Press). They were used, he explained to me earlier, instead of newer UCC literature because the "new books are too liberal and lead in the wrong direction and are confusing. They leave out the historical part of the Bible and leave out parts of the teachings of Jesus. Our identification with the Christian religion is left out." The older lessons could be adapted to the doctrines of black messianism more easily than newer lessons that highlight and encourage integration. Since the Shrine is pledged to a people-of-God concept, a covenant of a people, it is easier to teach this on biblical principles than on the rationale of integration, which Pastor Cleage does not buy as an aim and which he says can be found in the Bible only as a misreading of the Old Testament and the Pauline epistles.

In the opening exercises before breaking up into classes, in perfect consistency with the church service, Dave Cleage prayed for "blessings on all and on our nation." He had the kids turn to a responsive reading from Psalm 147 from ragged old Methodist hymnals: "Praise ye the Lord: for it is good to sing praises unto our God; for it is pleasant; and praise is comely. The Lord doth build up Jerusalem: he gathereth together the outcasts of Israel. He healeth the broken in heart, and bindeth up their wounds."

Then Superintendent Cleage, a toolmaker at Ford's, said,

"I am going to read to you from the Bible," and he read conciliatory passages from the Sermon on the Mount, which might have been the first time they were heard in the Shrine of the Black Madonna for many moons: "Ye have heard that it hath been said, An eye for an eye, and a tooth for a tooth: But I say unto you, That ye resist not evil: but whosoever shall smite thee on thy right cheek, turn to him the other also. And if any man will sue thee at the law, and take away thy coat, let him have thy cloke also. And whosoever shall compel thee to go a mile, go with him twain" (Matt. 5: 38–41, KJV).

Said Dave Cleage, "This Thursday is Thanksgiving Day . . . a national holiday," and he told how the Pilgrims came over, and suffered from the cold, and died, but eventually got on their feet with the help of friendly Indians, and how Thanksgiving became a national holiday. "Speaking of celebrating, every nationality has its own day—the Polish have Pulaski Day, the Irish, St. Patrick's Day, the French, Bastille Day. We have none." He suggested the kids think about an appropriate day and suggested January 1, Emancipation Day, as a possibility. He advised them to read a current issue of *Life* magazine with its cover feature of abolitionist Frederick Douglass and Negro history. "We have never been free"—and he told of his own son who was handcuffed, beaten so that he needed nine stitches in his head, only to be released by the police "because he was the wrong guy, and they were looking for a guy with the same kind of shirt." The Pilgrims came "because they wanted freedom . . . they had tried to go to Holland, and the kids had to learn Dutch and they didn't like that, and integration with the Dutch didn't work."

In his little talk Dave Cleage suggested a thankfulness for a ray of hope, "We should be thankful, I don't know what for, but thankful I guess that we were able to make it; we're in bad shape, but we're still here, with the help of God and a few others, things are going to get better. Maybe we do have something to look forward to. There is a great future. Things were closed to me and they told me so. You will have a chance. And as we give thanks, let's not overlook that we must do some things on our own part."

Then he prayed again: "Eternal God who has provided us with deliverance, help us by keeping the commandments of Christ, so we will be free as he is free."

In the class session that followed as the other younger kids went to their two small classes, Dave Cleage discussed the lesson in the book on Jesus about driving the money changers out of the temple. "The raid on the temple," said a subhead in the text. "Jesus did not do everything according to Hoyle, and therefore he was a revolutionary," said Dave Cleage. "Jesus went in and kicked over the tables." He asked the kids who the gentiles were (this took place in the court of the gentiles, according to scripture), and the kids were led to see that gentiles were the Romans who ran over people and oppressed people as blacks are suppressed today, and the Pharisees and priests were "preachers and leaders of the church who hadn't complained and were getting money too. They were fat and greasy and got a rakeoff."

"Jesus came into a big city from a small town, and carrying on like this, what was going to happen?" A youth supplied the answer, "A revolt." "There's the point. He didn't like it and protested. We've heard about protests before. Here's a protest that Jesus did, and they were going to arrest him, but they were afraid of him."

On that Sunday evening at 6:00 P.M. a family ensemble, "Mary Frazier Jones and her daughters, the Jones Sisters" (ages 12, 13, 15), put on a concert called "a black Christian gospel musical." On another Sunday evening, Ed Vaughn, in his cream turtleneck and amulet moderated a program of foreign students and other speakers on Biafra. "The Black Revolution is worldwide," said Vaughn, after he got the sparsely attended service under way. He had led a bull session of a half-dozen young men in the hall by a table where token Biafran flags were sold for a dollar. Blacks fight each other every Saturday night in Detroit, Mississippi, and elsewhere. Receiving (Detroit General) Hospital is filled, and we want to come out from under this. The action groups—a series of ten cell groups or clubs in the church—felt we were not doing our duty if we let this chance to do something for the Biafra situation pass."

He spoke over an open Bible on a pulpit marked by the large words "Love never faileth." Pastor Cleage, who was on hand but stayed in the background, had said in a hand-out for the program, "The tragic moral and human plight that threatens the existence of countless millions of black people in Biafra is of great importance and the deepest concern of Afro-Americans. Our original homeland is threatened by war and famine. Black Americans must respond to this call for help and we at the Shrine of the Black Madonna believe black people will respond in great numbers." The numbers were small, about 30 or so, but they were an intensely concerned group of young men. Vaughn told me later that the collection came to over $300.

Pastor Cleage is giving special attention these days to revamping his very traditional church rite. His own development of the black theology theme, taken over and enhanced by several denominational studies in the making, and his own association with Jewish personalities, especially the winsome and very effective Marc Tanenbaum, on the Interreligious Foundation for Community Organization committee, have not been without influence on Cleage. Tanenbaum's stock, however, began to go down after he searingly denounced the Black Manifesto of the IFCO-spawned National Black Economic Development Conference and was put under instruction to seek possible means of withdrawal of the American Jewish Committee from IFCO. "Up to this point I have not changed the ritual in my church," said Pastor Cleage in the press room of the NCBC in St. Louis. "But soon I expect to experiment with some Jewish forms" (he's been invited by Detroit rabbis to Hanukkah, Passover, and other observances). "Many Jewish holidays should be observed by black people; for example, the Passover from out of bondage would be a meaningful observance."

CHAPTER 2

Nation Within a Nation

When Cleage and Central Church unveiled the painting of the Black Madonna on Easter, March 26, 1967, and the church under its new name, the Shrine of the Black Madonna, issued a call to launch the Black Christian Nationalist Movement, not much was said in the public purview of the plan for a "nation." He had not revealed plans of implementation, and attention in ensuing months centered on Cleage himself, the painting, the struggle for black unity in Detroit. The rebellion of 1967 itself continued to dominate discussion in Detroit and localized the black movement in such a way that the attention of the country and of the world was focused on Detroit. And the forming of the Detroit-based National Black Economic Development Conference took attention.

Still, Albert Cleage continued to maintain a vision of a new black nationalism, peculiarly centered in the church, which would match the nationalistic movements of the past and possibly go far beyond them in actually facing needs and giving blacks an esprit de corps.

Elijah Mohammed, Malcolm X, Wilfred X, and others of the Black Muslims received national attention and did much to unite the rising new black militants, but they were never able to capture the mass black population — "They're all Christian in background and even the most militant Muslim can sing the gospel hymns," Cleage said. Cleage was looking for a religious weltanschauung that was not only more realistic than the foreign Puritanism of the Muslims but also true to Cleage's — and most blacks' — Western Christian orientation. The young militants weren't going to find it in the fading integrationist dream of Martin Luther King and the Southern Christian Leadership Conference.

The molds of the past offered little on which to shape a new separatist nationalism. The most famous nationalist among blacks had been Marcus Garvey, founder of the Universal Negro Improvement Association in 1917, a big, rotund Jamaican who preached "back to Africa," but was deported himself in 1927. His African Orthodox denomination had a Black Madonna and a Black Christ. There had also been earlier abortive nationalist attempts to set up separate black republics in the United States. S. H. Scott, of Fort Smith, Arkansas, in 1885, and Edwin P. McCabe, a former auditor for the state of Kansas, in 1889, worked for establishing separate black territories, McCabe suggesting Oklahoma. In 1815 a successful African Colonization Society had been organized by Paul Cuffe, a well-to-do black Philadelphian merchant. Blacks sent back to Africa through his efforts colonized Monrovia in 1822 and launched Liberia as a republic in 1847. Black "utopian states" were set up in isolated parts of the Midwest in the middle of the nineteenth century and are considered by some as the first organized effort of black self-determination in the United States. Booker T. Washington, though considered by many nowadays a "Tom" because of his white connections, is credited with being a forerunner of black economic power in his launching of the National Negro Business Association at the turn of the century.

Cleage's proposed Black Christian Nationalist Movement was stalled by other factors. The Shrine was undergoing the painful process of changing from a traditional congregation to a revolutionary congregation with no parallel in history. There were confrontations with those who preferred a regular church. Since he had opened his church doors he also had to face up to some of the country's most active black nationalists in his own congregation whose views of implementing black nationalism differed from his. These had flocked to the church in droves after the

1967 rebellion, but their interest in a religious, Christian-based movement was nil – certainly not within the frame-work of denominationalism historically structured and nurtured by whites. Cleage bided his time, hoping to keep the militants loosely united through the Shrine without departing from the traditional denominationalism in which he had been ordained.

The tipping of the precarious balance came when the Henrys – Richard and Milton, both members of Cleage's church – called a press conference in April 1968 to launch the Republic of New Africa, a movement to confront the government and to try to seek to negotiate for land and money which the Henrys and others feel the United States government owes the blacks in reparations. Did not the government make reparations to the Indians in the past? The Henrys talked of black territories to include the states of Mississippi, Alabama, Georgia, Louisiana, and South Carolina. One of the militants, according to one source, dragged his wife out of the Shrine choir.

Milton Henry, a Muslim before he joined Cleage's church, left and attends occasionally, not a black Muslim mosque but the Arabic Islamic Center of Near Eastern Muslims of Lebanese and other descent in Detroit. "I regret we don't have a black Iman," says Henry, a former Baptist who still has a membership at Cleage's Shrine, though he does not attend. This friendly militant extremist was also recently found in the pulpit of St. Cecilia's Roman Catholic Church during dedication of the painting of a Black Jesus in the dome. The pastor there is white.

Milton Henry is an urbane, good-looking, sharp dresser in dark suit and tie, and interested in the good things of life. As he chats in the car driven by a legal partner on the way to lunch at Joe Muer's, one of his favorite spots, a sea-food oasis of charm and elegance in Detroit, his talk turns readily to mundane things such as acquiring a little-used Cadillac at a very low price. Henry is one of the best lawyers in the game – I remember seeing him demolish the testi-mony of policemen in a trial of a bearded youth accused of shooting and wounding several policemen. One of the other lawyers present told him, "You're a hell of a good lawyer. I may not agree with you, but I'd hate to be up against you."

Over lunch, Henry, who when he is with the officials of the Republic of New Africa is known as Abiodun Gaidi Obadele (Swahili for "joy in house" and "son of God"), outlined the differences of his separatist state nationalism from Cleage's more mystical grouping of a Nation within a nation. "With Cleage, we're friends, but our ideology is different," he said, eating red-tinged whitefish in sauce. "Cleage is a real leaven—the black church is always a force. He has had a function but I would like for it to be better than it is. The Black Power of Cleage is unrealistic."

Henry can't see Cleage's working within the system, but believes even the Constitution would have to be new for the RNA. "If a nation is to be a nation, it would be like another nation, like Liberia, a country of its own. There just isn't enough (money, time, opportunities) to build black co-ops and economic power. Cleage is doing a lot of good, but he is no revolutionary. . . . He doesn't see that God requires physical separation sometimes."

The rejection of the system means a rejection of Western economics—capitalism also. In Henry's view there would be a classless society, one great participatory co-op or group of co-ops. Such leanings toward communalism— along with bitter resentment of the American way of life that has kept blacks suppressed—accounts for some occasional interest of black extremists in the Red Chinese experiment or in nationalistic communism. Unlike classical Marxism, the black struggle is not one of economic class struggle or one of an emergent dialectic and eventual utopia. The blacks do not talk of classism, or the classless state as such. They accept revolution, but also talk of direct results in a monolithic racial state. While classic theory is missing, so is the concept of a comintern or ideological internationalism so prevelant in Soviet nationalistic expansionism.

"Whites could live and function in the Republic of New Africa, but nobody owns property," says Henry. "Cleage's Nation within a nation is private property." How about Cleage receiving white money? "That's OK, we can take whitey's land also."

Cleage has been increasingly taking the militant geographical separatist and the "militant Molotov cocktail" crowd to task, although he has no real objection to the separate state and is also well schooled in the reasons for Molotov cocktails and revolutions in changing society. He feels, however, that these extreme black separatists are too isolated and talking to themselves at times.

"In regard to the black militant," Cleage says, "it is more important for him to keep his roots and develop roots in a black community than to maintain a little fraternity of black militants. They are often leaders, but it's a leadership without communication. There is a growing sense of unity. If he (the black extremist) wants to get so far out with absolutes, which is his greatest danger, he leaves the total black community which is not ready to die for absolutes. There is the progressive, on the one hand, and the completely frustrated who want change now, on the other. You see both in all communities. It is necessary to communicate, if there is to be struggle for survival."

At another time in our talks, Cleage put it this way: "There are two extremes in the black community—the guerrilla warriors and the bourgeoisie who identify with the whites. I have no argument with either extreme, but I don't see solutions coming out of either extreme—not out of the black bourgeoisie waiting to see which way things flap, or one who says development and controls by blacks are impossible (in the system)."

Cleage has gone easy on the cultural aspect of the Black Revolution. He has his African education classes, sells daishikis at the congregation's inspired Black-Star Co-op store, distributes African emblems in church, and has Black Madonnas and daishiki-draped body guards. But he is a consistent dresser in a dark suit and white shirt. Only once—in his apartment—have I seen him without a tie, but he still had his black suit and coat, and white shirt, unbuttoned at the collar. His concession to the cultural phase is the small amulet around his neck, its smallness underlining his greater interest in the economic and power revolution within the system. He appears to be critical of black nationalists getting too hung up on culture. To him culture developments are part of the whole picture; over-emphasis or sole emphasis on culture becomes an escapism, in Garvey style, and does not meet present realities. He says:

> Culture grows out of struggle. In China the Red Guards fought in the streets against those who were taking on Western ways, not because they thought Chinese people looked more beautiful in Chinese dress, but because they knew that Western ideas and dress were weakening the power of China. It was a power struggle. We have made an artificial separation between the cultural revolution and the power struggle. They are more excited about culture than they are excited about the struggle for power, because it is easier to put on African clothes than it is to struggle and sacrifice.[1]

The same point is emphasized by Larry Neal, a black film-maker from New York. In understanding Black Power, black nationalism, and Black Revolution, he says, "The black artist is not interested in 'art for art's sake.' He is not interested in aesthetics without ethics. He wants to arouse and motivate his people into action against the oppressor. If he does not address himself to this idea, then his art is as useless and decadent as Western art." Citing playwright Leroi Jones as an example, Neal said, "Art and life must be unified; there can be no separation." Neal said Jones' poetry "does not exist outside of the social realm for which it was intended. . . . Black art is social and spiritual. . . . The very purpose of black art is to motivate the masses of black people against that which is wrong in their environment through the beauty of black art forms."[2] Cleage would argue this is best achieved in the reality of a present struggle, not in a strict idealization of Africa as a dream home or in separate apartheid states in the United States. Culture and struggle for him cannot be separated, nor one idealized above the other. They exist together in a pragmatic tension.

There are all kinds of definitions of black nationalism. Many have taken a stab at defining it, blacks and whites. White reporters particularly have tried to elicit definitions.

Philip Meyer, Knight Newspaper writer and researcher in social and political affairs, notes that "religious people tend toward Black Power. Those who are alienated from religion tend toward black nationalism."[3] Concludes Meyer, "Black nationalism may be a kind of substitute for religion." Many separatists, even Eldridge Cleaver, minister of information for the Black Panther Party for Self Defense, passed through a "conversion" and baptism and confirmation sequence in prison, on their way to revolutionary black nationalist politics.[4] Cleage's nationalism comes as a substitute for a more intense pietistic religion. One observer has said Cleage could never quite solve the "salvation" crisis in his youth. He yearned to accept the warm conservative doctrine, but his own intellect warred against it. Not making the salvation trail, and keenly conscious of social ills, Cleage to a degree could indeed see nationalism as a substitute for traditional white religion on his part.

Religious qualities carry over into black nationalism. This is obvious when we remember that much of black nationalism has been expressed in the Black Muslim movement for the past fifty years since Timothy Drew Ali founded the first of a series of Moorish-American temples in Newark, New Jersey. W. D. Fard and the subsequent Black Muslim movement followed. E. U. Essien-Udom, of the University of Ibadan, Nigeria, in his book on black nationalism in the United States, after noting the common elements of nationalistic movements of blacks in the United States—"cultural alienation," "social estrangement," "disillusionment," "overwhelmed by a feeling of total powerlessness"—cited their common religious themes. He wrote:

> Concern with racial redemption is an important esoteric component of nationalism. The nationalists tend to perceive black redemption as a struggle between "good" and "evil" in which God is on their side. . . . The nationalists' emphasis on racial redemption and reclamation of the "fallen" calls for a messianic style of leadership. The leader is a national Messiah.[5]

Black nationalism is seen in less depth when whites are asked to say what it is. A young Michigan State journalism student, Eric Pianin, interning on the *Michigan Chronicle,* did a front page report on suburban attitudes of whites concerning black nationalism. When asked by Pianin "What is black nationalism?" whites in Royal Oak, South-field, Dearborn, and Redford said:

— [It's] a country run by blacks.

— It's a calculated attempt to form a cohesive group among blacks.

— Black nationalism is the belief that they are no longer second-class citizens.

— It's something that reduces the defensive mechanism of blacks.

— The colored feel they don't belong anywhere. They are seeking an identity and feel they have to stand up and fight. They are saying, "We are a group of people; we are a nation; we belong." It's a matter of returning to what they came from. They are just as proud to be from Africa as I am coming from England.

— Black nationalists are the extremists, the bigots, who want to isolate themselves from us.

— I don't know what black nationalism is, frankly.

— Black nationalism is what Stokely Carmichael preaches. It's someone who is talking down to the whites. Someone who doesn't want to believe what we say. Someone who wants to take over. It's the same as Black Power.

Pianin found attitudes concerning Black Power were much less charitable:

— There is something sinister about it. It's power trying to disrupt and corrupt.

— Wealth is power in this country. They're banding together to get wealth and power.

— Black Power is frightening. It sounds frightening. It's forcing or trying to force something upon the Negroes and trying to get around whites in an under-handed way.

— When I think of the effects of Black Power, I

always think of a speech I heard by the Rev. Albert Cleage about it. He said, "When we take over, don't worry. We'll treat you like you treated us."[6]

In some respects, Cleage's definitions have some affinity with the white concepts on black nationalism and Black Power. His nationalism poses no innate threat for it is in the system. His main thrust is with Black Power which hits the whites more directly in their own backyard and at the office. Money, jobs, opportunities of all sorts are channeled to blacks, most certainly in all black areas. His nationalism is understood only in connection with his concept of economic power. Further, he does not raise the specter of messianic leadership as the Muslims and Moors have done. In this matter-of-fact approach, he sees the struggle in less redemptive terms. He doesn't like the word redemption, and I have heard him use it only in scoring King's idea of suffering nonviolent redemption. Cleage has room for a messianic emphasis; but it is historical, in terms of the Messiah of the Gospels, again an affinity with white traditionalism in the United States; he keeps the historical Messiah of Christianity, although he colors the Messiah differently from the whites of suburban Detroit and elsewhere.

Cleage has defined black nationalism, emphasizing in turn its origin, its purpose, its nature, its methods, its goals. Back in 1962, he was already talking black nationalism in his *Illustrated News*. Black nationalism had a strong cultural, visual quality in this early definition (more of the emphasis of a W. E. B. DuBois earlier in the century, on cultural unity). Vocalist Abbey Lincoln and her musician husband, Max Roach, were on hand at the Central Church for a discussion on "Black Nationalism in Jazz." Wrote Cleage:

Abbey Lincoln, who readily admitted that she is a beautiful black woman, wore the "natural" hair style which is becoming increasingly popular among "Black Nationalists," and explained that she has the courage to reject the white man's standards of beauty because her husband has rejected them and she is

not forced to try to look like Elizabeth Taylor to keep
him happy. Even those who were not yet ready to
follow her example were forced to admit that "Black
Nationalism" looked good on Abbey, and no one was
inclined to argue the point when she suggested that
Hollywood would have been closer to realism if she
had been selected to play the black queen, Cleo-
patra. . . . The Negro is beginning to wake up. . . . We
are a people looking for a philosophy.[7]

The origin of the "Nation" is forged by whites, not blacks,
Cleage makes clear. He reminds those who don't like the
idea of black nationhood that the whites forced the blacks
into it for 400 years.

The white man has done too good a job. I was
separated from the day I was born. Every area of
my life has been separate. . . . Essentially all the
people I know are black. You can't ask me if I'm
advocating separation. I don't know anything else.
I know all about separation. But I didn't do it. I
just inherited it.[8]

And further:

I use the concept of a "Nation within a nation" to
describe the separation that's enforced on black
people. I personally do not advocate a "back to Africa"
or geographic separation beyond the separation that
already exists in urban ghettos of the North or rural
ghettos of the South. But black people living in the
separate ghettos to which they have been forced
have a common bond by virtue of their history,
culture, and common oppression. Certainly we can
think of ourselves as being a Nation within a nation.[9]

In a conversation Cleage put it this way, pegging "nationalism" into a process, "The Nation within a nation
is a concept rather than a geography. It's a Nation in a
sense of a group of people united with a common purpose
and who are forced together. Nationalism refers to the
coming of a group unity—in a separate community,
rather than moving to a geographical nation. Yet, black

community is not quite synonymous with Black Nation within a nation. 'Nation' has the implication of severing the old slave identity and recognizing the deep roots by which we are separate. With a Nation within a nation you cease to have a sense of regret or shame for separateness and accept it with pride. . . . It is an active stance, rather than a passive one. It exists rather than being a group trying to be accepted. It is a complete concept." He outlined a four-part process in achieving a black nationhood — within the Nation: "(1) black consciousness; (2) black pride, which requires a little more in analysis to rediscover the black past; (3) unity, which began to be observed as nationalism, as various groups and movements and individuals began to think in solidarity — where there is individualism, there is no solidarity; and (4) self-determination for blacks." Black Power is the transition vehicle between "unity" or cooperative work and control of the destiny of blacks. "Nationalism is meaningless unless there is power, structural power."

Cleage believes no community has reached this fourth stage. As for Gary and Cleveland, which have black mayors: "These are developments outside the progression to self-determination. They are almost counterrevolutionary. The mayors in these cities are not elected solely by blacks. They are representatives of the whites — they are still in a pre-black consciousness. They still have a 'dream' (as King did)."

The Nation concept has with it the concept of citizenship, of responsibility, and involvement. In his earlier writings on black nationalism, five years ago, Cleage used "black nationalism" as synonymous with "black brotherhood," and hasn't departed too far from this idea, for he allowed segments of the 1964 writings associating nationalism with brotherhood to be reported as his "message to the Black Nation" in September 1968 in the *Michigan Chronicle*.

"Black nationalism," or "black brotherhood," offers the framework within which the black man must wage his continuing freedom struggle in America. He must unite and organize to oppose a common white enemy. There is no escape from this interminable conflict. He must undertake such actions as are required in this struggle realizing that he must somehow manage to derive a livelihood from a system which threatens to strangle him economically, even while he seeks to build a separate cooperative black economy. "Black nationalism," or "black brotherhood," offers a powerful weapon ready at hand because it has been forged by the chains and shackles of oppression. Every hand which has been raised to strike a black man down has driven all black men closer together. . . . So the white man's hatred has fashioned a Black Nation within a nation. A black brotherhood of necessity in which black men must unite and love each other if they are to survive. United opposition to a common white enemy becomes the black man's very reason for being. . . . The white man's enmity is not related to the philosophy he espouses, the religion he embraces, or the economic system he supports. He hates black men because they are black. . . . He feels the same way whether or not he lives under capitalism, socialism, or communism. Everywhere white men fight black men because they are black. The Negro, then, fights the white man because he is white. So by necessity black men are a "Black Nation" and by choice they must become a "black brotherhood" united in everything which makes for their mutual benefit and advancement. . . . As a Black Nation and a black brotherhood the Negro must vote black, buy black, and most important, he must build black cooperative economic enterprises.[10]

Cleage has on occasion compared the Black Nation idea to the solidarity of various immigrant groups. They, too, came dispossessed, at the lower rung of the economic scale. The metropolitan Detroit area has an estimated 400,000 persons of Polish descent. There is still a Polish newspaper. The Poles stand out by their names, their churches, and still, their language – just as blacks stand out in color, in a white-dominated society. The Italians and the Irish, and the nationalities of the Balkan states, stand out still in the urban communities, and there are in the United States the Chinatowns and the Spanish Harlems. In cities with a ward system, such as Chicago, some, particularly the older immigrant groups, control their own constituency. And the course for ghetto recognition and self-determination has been violent. Dennis Clark, writing on urban violence in *America* magazine, said:

> There is in the American past a record of group violence that is an astonishing parallel to current black belligerence. The word hooligan is not a derivative from Swahili. It is the Irish who wrote the script for American violence, and the black terrorists have not added anything particularly new. . . . The tradition of Irish urban violence disappeared as a result of economic gains, education, and social mobility.[11]

It has been difficult for militants, however, to sell black nationalism to all of the black community as it has been difficult to sell it to many whites. The dream of instant integration, on the part of many, shared with white liberals, no doubt is a factor. Among the experts, Harvard's Thomas F. Pettigrew says, "To prescribe more separation because of discomfort, racism, conflict, or the need for autonomy is like getting drunk again to cure a hangover."[12]

Among black traditional leaders, educator Benjamin Mays laments the divisiveness of black nationalism.

> Now we are doing exactly what some white people want us to do — fight among ourselves. . . . From those who talk about "black nationalism" I have heard of no reasonable plan to achieve a black curriculum, black teachers, black students, black trustees, and money. I have heard of no plan whereby such a university would be financed. Negro support of higher education in this country is not too good.[13]

Joseph H. Jackson, president of the National Baptist Convention, believes black young people who are separatists preach the same gospel that the Ku-Klux Klan has preached.

An editorial in the *Michigan Chronicle,* which runs Cleage's weekly column, strongly criticized black separatists.

The idea of racial separation now being espoused by so-called Negro militants is a dangerous one. It is an idea which runs against the grain of everything multimillions have dreamed of, lived for, and fought for through countless years of American history. The so-called militants have in no way proved to us that they are smarter than all of the Negroes who have lived before them. The idea of "black separation" is exactly the same idea that white bigots have attempted to promote down through the years. It is an impractical idea, an unwise idea, a step backward into the dark ages of time.[14]

W. H. Ferry, former Detroit reporter *(Detroit Free Press)* and past vice-president of the Center for the Study of Democratic Institutions, outlined in *The Center Magazine* a plan by which the Nation-within-a-nation concept could be wholly compatible with the Constitution in the United States system. The contribution of his article perhaps is the greater for providing a means of linking Cleage's somewhat mystic economic brotherhood with the geographic separatists, the Henry's.

Ferry develops the concept of "blacktown" rather than nation. Now a town is geographic. It is also a component of a nation. Assuming that time is short, that integration is a passé idea, and assuming there is some form of "creative federalism" to permit blacktown to coexist with whitetown within constitutional guarantees for local government, Ferry believes there are possibilities for "tacit consent." "By this I mean that blacktown and whitetown may, by a series of unacknowledged steps, arrive at a mutual and unstated understanding of the main conditions for maintaining an ethnically divided society. It was tacit consent that until quite recently kept the situation relatively quiet and peaceful." Ferry suggests first, a pact—or an "agreement"—by which a whitetown would first "banish integration from the lips of whitetown reformers and politicians and from the expectations of blacktown";

second, the agreement would work out guarantees "against humiliation on the one side and disturbance on the other"; and third, there

> would be increased political autonomy for blacktown, accompanied by markedly stepped-up subsidies from whitetown, which will see blacktown's needs for supplementary help to be at least as important as those of the shipping industry, the corporate farmers, and other veterans of the subsidy trough. . . . The requirement is to agree on the terms of peaceful co-existence. Unless we can find them, the second Civil War is inevitable. We shall make a great error if we seek these terms amongst the fragments of the integrationist dream. If we in whitetown had ever really wanted integration we would have rushed to achieve it.[15]

There are many problems with this suggestion. Who would negotiate the multiple-town concepts? How are we to be sure that whites can be talked into giving in on a negotiated settlement other than traditional handouts when integration, which is a pact or an agreement de facto, didn't work. Nevertheless, Ferry's framework for "coexistence" not only takes into account present realities but also offers an area in which a meaningful relationship can be worked out between white and black extremists, in the great middle ground between the quietly hostile on both sides, and between the economic Nation within a nation and the system at large.

Ferry has some fingers crossed concerning his own mediating suggestion that recognition be given to the existence of blacktowns and whitetowns, with negotiated working arrangements. He anticipates reaction to any solution suggested by whites, but nevertheless believes the separatism which exists — on a town-and-community, or ghetto-suburb level — is indeed a present reality that all parties can and will learn one way or another to acknowledge. "A political theory that will embrace our dilemma and provide satisfactory terms for coexistence is not outside our reach. . . . We shall have to learn how to run a separated society, without the sacrifice of freedom and justice for any man. Since we cannot have integration, we must have something."[16]

I asked both Milton Henry and Albert Cleage about Ferry's article. Henry called a blacktown concept "dangerous." "Look, we are confronted with men like Wallace (this was a month before the November 1968 election). Wallace is no more cracked than Hitler. In Germany, there were many parties and people thought Hitler was an idiot, but he came to power legally." Henry will have nothing to do with recommending continuing under the United States Constitution, and he refuses even to vote in the system which could always produce a Wallace or Hitler to get genocide going. His geographical nationalism has to be outside the present system and have its own constitution.

Cleage would accept a blacktown concept, if blacktowns are not fragmentized and isolated, but a cohesion of blacktowns and areas across the nation is allowed. "It's OK," he says, "only if it coordinates all blacktowns and black rural counties," and "there is a cooperative program between the blacktowns in politics, education, and culture. Ferry has some very valid concepts. I go along with him. There is the fact that blacks are separated by the system, and we have to deal with this as such."

Cleage also acknowledged that the blacktown concept—which he can agree to under certain conditions—does have its geographic connotations. Which is to say that Cleage's Nation within a nation must not be viewed as strictly mystical—although he has used the word mystical in reference to it—or as a movement merely, but in terms of geography. This gives him an affinity with Henry and the Republic of New Africa, although Henry prefers to keep his geography outside the system, as strictly a separate nation and not a Nation within a nation.

Edward Vaughn, Cleage's close aide, owner of the only comprehensive exclusive black bookstore in town, is head of a heritage committee of the Shrine and as such has been entrusted with working on a "code of conduct" for a proposed new manual for the Shrine and other

churches across the United States that join the Black
Christian Nationalist Movement. In his draft material,
which is tentative and subject to change, Vaughn, 34, a
native of Dothan, Alabama, and a graduate of Fisk University, has proposed a pledge of allegiance and a list of
suggestions or commandments to follow in living the up-
right life in the Nation.

I pledge my allegiance and true loyalty to the Black
Nation, the Shrine of the Black Madonna. I will dedi-
cate my life and energies to the work we are about
and to the goals we pursue. I will never participate
in anything or belong to any group that is opposed to
the best interests of the Black Nation. I will do this
because we are the Black Messiah's Chosen People
and this is his will.

Among the proposed conduct guidelines or commandments are:

1. Never do anything that will bring shame on the
Nation.
2. Love all brothers and sisters even when it is
difficult to do so. Walk the second mile or turn the
other cheek when a brother or sister is involved.
3. Honor and respect our elders. If you don't think
they've done anything—take a second look, brother—
we have survived!
4. Honor and respect black women. In the tradition
of our Black Madonna, they are the foundation of the
Nation, the Mothers of Mankind. Respect them at all
times.
5. Consider all black children as your very own. In
the African tribe there was no such thing as an
illegitimate child. They all belonged to the tribe. So
it is in the Nation. Talk to the children, lead them
and guide them. . . . They are our future leaders.
6. Respect the Nation and yourself through your
dress. The Nation will move to a standard mode of
dress, but we will evolve to that standard. So don't
get hung up on what style of clothing is worn. If a
member wears African dress, that's beautiful—don't

knock it. . . . By the same token, if one wears Western dress, don't knock that. . . . One of the problems in relationship to African dress is that most garments are not made for zero temperatures, so whatever a member wears is not as important as what he is doing. We don't get freedom through what we wear.

7. Your clothing and your body should be clean at all times — without exception. We expect cleanliness. This is evidence of your respect for the Black Nation.

8. Black people in the Nation must treat whites as whites treat them. Show him you can be just as courteous as he is and still be for Black Power as he is for white power. He can put on this act because he feels sure of himself. Show him we are just as sure of ourselves. This is what black pride means. Don't ever lose sight of the goals, Black Power, Self-Determination, and the Rebuilding of the Black Nation.

Now, we realize that some brothers and sisters can't return this courteousness and for very good reason. In a situation like this, the brother or sister should simply ignore the Caucasian. Your role is "don't be a Tom but also don't try to heckle or attack every white person you meet."

CHAPTER 3

Seedbed of a Militant

For all outward appearances, the *enfant terrible* of the black nationalist clergy is a "white" man. "I didn't even know he was a Negro, until somebody told me," said one of Cleage's former professors at Wayne State University, Detroit.

Albert Cleage is nearly as light as any man with skin weathered by age or outdoor exposure. A bit sickly in color, he is certainly not black and hardly "nonwhite," which he tends to equate with blackness when he discusses all Near Eastern people as black.

He is a man plagued with a lifelong identity crisis, said the retired professor who is now living in the East. "He is confused with his identity, which is very important to remember. He must have faced a number of crises in which he has had to redefine himself. His marriage and divorce would call for a man to redefine himself; then when he saw he could have power—in the black community—he redefined himself, and now in another shifting role, he faces another redefinition."

The identity crisis, if the professor is correct, may go back to childhood in a family where the father was appointed the first black city physician by a white mayor, a mayor whom rumors linked with the Ku-Klux Klan. The family elected to live in a changing neighborhood that was going black on the fringe of the black ghetto and attend a high school where blacks were for a time a minority and where teachers allegedly discriminated against anyone who looked or owned up to being "colored." With his father, Albert, Sr., clearly black, and one of the sons, Hugh, darker than the others, Albert, though he could slip by as white, was cast in the role of black and took his lumps for it. There was likely a continuous identity crisis, in the younger years at least, for Pastor Cleage himself remembers being accepted by the white students at Northwestern High, who invited him to their homes (although he didn't go), and the teachers were very color conscious and discriminating in race.

Albert Buford Cleage, Jr. was born in Indianapolis on June 13, 1911, and when he was fifteen months old his physician father and the family moved to Kalamazoo where there were aunts and uncles and cousins. Green's *Negro History in Michigan* carries a handsome photograph of the older Cleage, smooth bronze skin, with straight nose and medium lips. Green's paragraph on the older Cleage centers in Kalamazoo before the Detroit days:

> Albert B. Cleage, Sr. – M.D., born in Loudon, Tennessee, May 15, 1883. Graduated Henderson Normal and Industrial College, 1902; Knoxville College, in 1906; Indiana School of Medicine, in 1910. Dr. Cleage won second-highest position in the competitive examination, with all white applicants, in 1910, for appointment as intern at the city dispensary at Indianapolis, where he served as house physician and ambulance (driver). Began private practice in Kalamazoo in 1912, where he has become highly successful as a doctor of medicine and surgery.[1]

Albert, Sr. stayed with his brother-in-law, James, a teacher at Henderson Normal, while studying there.

The Cleage family tree traces back to Athens, Tennessee, between Knoxville and Chattanooga in southeast Tennessee, near the Smokies. This is a hilly, sleeping, well-to-do town of pines and magnolia trees, with a busy town square and constant flow of traffic. I walked up the brief south hill from the square on Jackson Street to the town's only historic plaque on a small three-story red brick building covered with brittle autumn ivy. The building has an anachronistic sign – "The Hut, American-Italian Fine Foods – Diner – Fountain – Carry Outs." The plaque, black-edged with embossed letters on a painted silver-gray background said:

> *Samuel Cleage:*
> This was one of the houses built by this itinerant contractor, who left Botetourt County, Va., in 1823 and made his way south building houses, taking pay in "gold, notes, or Negroes." In 1836, it was the central office for the Hiwassee R.R., which in 1837 became the East Tennessee and Georgia R.R., one of the progenitors of the Southern Railroad System.

A bookstore owner knew of only two Cleages, both white. Two black garbage collectors, dumping garbage into a truck driven by a white man, said they had never heard of the name Cleage. Cleage still has cousins in Athens, but by other names.

Samuel Cleage, the white man and slave owner, whose name his slaves and others adopted as was the custom, was born of Alexander and Susannah Moore Clegg, in Lancaster County, Pennsylvania, in 1781. "He possessed unusual business ability and accumulated considerable property before his father's death in 1822. He was a contractor and built up a large fortune by building brick mansion houses for the landed gentry on the frontier who felt they had outgrown their primitive log cabins," according to a newspaper account of the Cleage history in the *Chattanooga Times* thirty-five years ago. Sarah Moore Cleage, daughter of Samuel Cleage (Clegg), married a Thomas Crutchfield. One of their sons was a representative in the Forty-third Congress, and another, William, was mayor of Chattanooga two times. William also had a fabulous plantation, "Amnicola," north of Chattanooga, and built the "Crutchfield House," Chattanooga's classiest hotel before the Civil War.

"Cleage" is a spelling of Clegg adopted by Alexander Cleage (Jr.), a son of Samuel Cleage (Clegg). The name apparently traces back to the English "Clough" meaning "a break in the hillside." There is a Cleage Ridge near Chattanooga. Nicholas and Mathew de Clegg are listed in a record in Lancastershire, England, dated 1260.

Samuel Clegg took his son-in-law Thomas Crutchfield as his partner and among their many buildings are nine courthouses in East Tennessee, a host of churches, hotels, and other buildings. One person told me Samuel was an abolitionist and took slaves so he could free them and send them to school. Old Samuel was quite a charmer:

> After the death of his mother in 1823, Samuel Clegg sold his property in Botetourt county and moved to Tennessee, as the new state offered a profitable field for the contracting business. He owned a number of slaves, whom he had taught the art of making and laying brick; and it is told of him that as he journeyed from his home on James river to Tennessee, he would stop along the way whenever he came to a fine farm where the mistress was domiciled in a log house and with his Irish gift of speech inspire the wife of the owner with a desire for a larger and more permanent brick dwelling, for which he would draw the plans and then erect with the help of his slaves. Often he took his pay in slaves or teams, thus adding to the facilities for his business. On reaching Mouse Creek valley, in McMinn county, Tennessee, Samuel Clegg recognized the desirability of such a beautiful location for a home and bought an extensive farm about three miles southwest of the present town of Niota. Here, in 1825, he built for himself a comfortable brick house which is still standing.[2]

A relative of Pastor Cleage points out that Athens in the old days was an unusual place, with no discrimination to speak of and no separate facilities for "colored"; and intermarriage was also acceptable and officially blessed, on occasion, in church. Cleage's father, Albert, Sr., was the youngest of five sons (there was also a sister) of Louis Cleage. Nothing is known of the background of Louis Cleage, a black ex-slave, except after the Civil War he drifted into Athens as a section hand and assumed the name Cleage because it was so prominent there. He later moved north toward Loudon, where he was a farmhand on a black-owned farm, and then came back to Athens. He took off again as a railroad section hand and eventually divorced his wife, Celie, pastor Cleage's grandmother. Celie's mother was a slave girl, and her father was a white slaveowner, Pastor Cleage's great-grandfather.

Mrs. Pearl Reed Cleage, who is white in appearance and thin-featured, is a tiny dynamo of a woman, five feet, three inches, slim and a bit stooped with her age, but at 81 still the very regal personality that has left her imprint on all the Cleage children. "My grandmother was a Cherokee Indian, my father was a mulatto, and my mother was a very fair lady," she recalls. She met Pastor Cleage's father at the United Witherspoon Presbyterian Church, in Indianapolis, where she sang in the choir. "We met and fell in love and were married." She got up from one of the two rows of sofas in the neat living room, walked over to the fireplace, and took down a picture of her husband. "He began practice in Indianapolis, but when he heard of a doctor who had died in Kalamazoo, we moved there. He was the first colored doctor in town.

"My husband was quite a rarity for quite a while in Kalamazoo. They grew to love him. And it was heart-breaking when we left. . . . Albert had a friend in college at Knoxville, Ernest Johnson, who was a dentist in Detroit, and he suggested we come to Detroit. . . . You know when you are married to a man you care about, you go where you do the most good, and should be satisfied."

Albert, Sr., who died in 1957 shortly after retirement, had been a city physician for Detroit, the first black named to such an appointment, for sixteen years. "He ran his own practice at the same time. This is hard on any man. . . . I'd go with him many a time, and on Sunday afternoon through Polish, Irish, and other districts, and people would call out and hold out their babies which he had brought into the world and say, 'See how much they like you.'

"He was overworked, and one day he rather fainted, and word was sent. Louis went down, and saw he was overworked and over-worrying, that he tried to do too much, and Albert listened. He resigned. He developed heart trouble." Albert, Sr., a charter member of St. John's Presbyterian Church and active in the St. Antoine YMCA, was a founder of the Dunbar Hospital (now Parkside Hospital), the first black hospital in Detroit. "There was a lot of argument about starting it, but he insisted on a colored hospital where he could be treated with dignity."

The elder Cleage received his appointment from Mayor Charles Bowles in June 1930, on the heels of a controversy where dismissed employees of the garbage department said they were let go so that they might be replaced by blacks ready to serve the city political machine being oiled by John Gillespie, commissioner of public works. Cleage, Sr. was given a $3,000 salary from the city, plus an automobile. The appointment was justified by the welfare commission because 80 percent of welfare cases were black. The fired garbage employees accused Cleage of collusion with a black druggist, Aaron C. Toodle, in order to control placements in city positions on behalf of blacks. Toodle was to provide city jobs on the east side, and Cleage on the west side, they charged. Gillespie denied any such roles were to be played by Cleage or Gillespie or that he had anything to do with the Cleage appointment.

Mayor Bowles himself soon ran into trouble as a result of graft in his administration and apparent collusion with organized crime (his hand-picked police commissioner, Thomas Wilcox, later was sentenced to prison). Bowles was recalled by the voters six months after he started his term in January 1930. Mrs. Cleage remembers Bowles as "a worthwhile and reputable man, who saw the fallacious way whites treated blacks, and he was going to try to rectify the situation." She said there were many lies about Bowles, a former motorman, including a Ku-Klux Klan association charge. "So many picked up lies and believed them—they were started by envious, ugly-minded white people who wanted to kill the man's influence."

Thomas McIntyre, the crusty westside *Courier* columnist, had another opinion, "I was assigned to Bowles in Kentucky (attending the Kentucky Derby) when he was double-crossed, and the booking establishment was raided here (Bowles fired his police commissioner for making the raid, and put in Wilcox who raided only empty buildings thereafter). The Klan was owned by the Mafia. . . . People were stirred up about Al Smith and Hoover. . . . Bowles was the Klan man, but he did not know what he was trying to do. He was a big slob, nothing vicious about him."

The support of Bowles posed problems for the younger Cleages. "This was kind of unfortunate for me," recalls Pastor Cleage. "I had to fight my way home from school every day. This was the time when everybody put the pictures of whom they supported in their windows."

Oscar Hand, 54, choir director, financial secretary, deacon, and trustee for the Shrine of the Black Madonna, and childhood friend of Cleage, Jr., recalls the Bowles controversy. "Cleage and his brothers and I were walking together near 25th and Warren. The city was up in the air about Mayor Bowles. 'I wish they'd get that Bowles out of there,' I remember saying. 'Why?' Al Cleage, Jr. said. 'He ain't no good.' 'What you got against him?' 'He's Ku-Klux Klan,' I said, but I had only read it some place. 'I don't see how you say that – he's done more for the colored people . . . like work . . . he gave my father a job.' I stood and looked at him, and I said 'That ain't nothin.' " And Hand ponders nearly forty years later, "It always stuck in my mind – 'he helped colored people and gave his father a job.' "

"We used to ride with his father on calls," Hand recalls – a pastime that could stir a young black to empathy, and to social concern over injustices and inequities, and toward the ministry and toward a militant black nationalist position in later years as times themselves evolved. "We would sit in the back of the car. His father would call on the indigent people. At dinnertime he would call in. He would go to a police box with a key – this was quite the thing. Black people never seen a man in a suit using the box.

"His father would try to get black people organized. For example, I remember a political rally at the Samson School – I remember what he said, but I forget the issue, 'If we could all stick together – I can't get people to do so . . .' His father was a very militant black person. I can understand how Rev. Cleage is the same way. His father tried to organize black people long before anyone thought of organization. . . . They were Republican in Abe Lincoln tradition.

"Cleage and his father used to argue all the time, and they'd get into some doozy arguments. His father was testing the validity of the young man's arguments. At the house, they would argue about the merits of Republicans over Democrats. It was always based on the fact that the Democrats would disenfranchise the South, and the Republicans did not have the opportunity to show what they would do. . . ." Mrs. Cleage confirmed there were often lively father-and-son "debates." "Sometimes my son would not have the same faith in the same candidates. He had a mind of his own, even disagreeing with his father, as much as he loved his father." Another, close to the family, remembers in Albert, Jr.'s earlier days, "His father was very anxious that he go out and mingle with others, but he would not have anything to do with anyone. He was a peculiar youngster."

Mrs. Cleage, Sr. saw her late husband as a great crusader for the black man, a point that is challenged by some of the old-timers still around. However, he was in the spotlight for his efforts; according to a *Detroit Free Press* clipping on December 3, 1934 more than 350 "representatives of Negro organizations in Detroit and Michigan" were to "attend a testimonial dinner" at a local YMCA "in honor of Dr. A. B. Cleage, Detroit Negro physician, and Judge Charles Willis, Negro, of South Bend, Indiana." The purpose of the gathering, the clipping said, was "to impress on the Negro the need for banding together for the good of the race." Mayor Frank Couzens and other Detroit officials were listed as speakers.

Louis E. Martin, 56, deputy national chairman of the Democratic party, and vice-president of the *Michigan Chronicle* and one of its founders, said, "I don't recall any activity on the part of the Cleages. We put William Sherrill in the race (for council) and he got 26,000 votes, which was good at the time. The Cleages were very middle-class and removed." He noted also they were "not in the labor fight that really racked the Negro community." There were 5,000 blacks, all nonunion, in the Ford plant in the early 40's. "Our concept was that the values and seniority should be shared by the Negro too." Remus Robinson, M.D., long-term member of the Detroit school board, who has been severely criticized by Pastor Cleage, recalls only that "Cleage, Sr. was a rather proud man who worked as a physician for the city, but I do not know of anything he did."

One of the grand old black clergymen in Detroit who was also a neighbor of the Cleages is Charles Hill, 75, one of the most outspoken liberal clergymen of the 20's, 30's, and 40's.[3] Now retired after serving the Hartford Baptist Church for forty-eight years, seeing it grow from 35 to 1,500, Hill seems a bit pained because he is told that Pastor Cleage regards him as an Uncle Tom. The contrary is nearer the truth. Although he may disregard Hill's integrationist views and the emphasis on spirituality in Hill's social action, Pastor Cleage nevertheless cites Hill as one of two men who shaped his life the most. Cleage attended meetings in Hill's church, and appreciated his "protest" and "radicalism," but scored what he called his lack of courage on Sundays. "He would become evangelical on Sunday morning."

The other influential cleric was the late Dr. Horace White, minister of the Plymouth Congregational Church from 1936 until his death in 1958. White was a member of the Detroit Housing Commission and once led a march of 1,000 on city hall to demand integration of city projects. Cleage, who was active in the Plymouth youth group, noted, "Horace White was concerned with the emerging labor movement and political action. He was liberal rather than radical, but he brought it into church. His was all one religion—weekdays and Sundays. This is also my preference—all one faith. He did not make concessions." Recalls Martin, "Horace White worked with me as a columnist. Both of us were kind of radical. I knew the Cleages at that time—1936 to 1946. They were the fair, mulatto type, not too interested in unions. The young boy, however, took interest. Horace was radical as any—very radical it was then to champion the CIO. The Negro establishment was

anti-union. They felt they should get letters from preachers to get jobs—and Horace was against this system."

"The kind of experience Cleage had as a young person
at Plymouth Church has helped to shape his ministry,"
says Nicholas Hood, current Plymouth minister. "Horace
White was twenty years ahead of his time." White had
political influence and was elected as a Democrat to the
state legislature, 1941–42, and also was on the Wayne
County Board of Supervisors. An accredited psychiatric
social worker at the University of Michigan, White had
helped found the Lapeer Parents Association, the first
of a series of organizations under the Michigan Association for Retarded Children. Cleage, majoring in psychology
at Wayne State University, tried his hand at social case
work in 1936 when he had completed most of his WSU
work, but got fed up with both the hopelessness of his
"band-aid" task and the limits of it.

"Cleage's ambition was to succeed White," says Al
Dunmore, former editor of the *Michigan Chronicle*, now
a troubleshooter in urban affairs at Chrysler. "But splits
at Central and the reaction of his congregation prevented
Plymouth tapping him. His hopes were to go there or to
bring Central up to the same leadership."

On Charles Hill, Horace White once wrote in the *Chronicle* (later to be reprinted in part in Ralph Lord Roy's
Communism and the Churches): "The Rev. Mr. Charles
Hill has been used by the Communist forces for a number
of years. He is just thoughtless in attempting to meet the
many problems which confront the Negro population in
America." Comparing himself to White, Hill told me, "I
went to more of the different groups than White. I went to
them all. I am not a Communist, and never was, and never
had any Communist speakers in the church, although I
knew one or two, but I did not let them in any meeting.
Many called me a Communist hoping I'd quit talking during the week and on Sunday." Part of the Communist
charge came out of his association with immigrant union-
izers in his battle, with White and others, to get blacks
into auto unions. "I feel my ministry was consistent. I told
folks on Sunday they got to do something, not just pray

when they were too lazy to use their influence. We were opposed to discrimination and segregation. I don't believe in Black Power, but God power. Our neighborhood — and Cleage's — was nine-tenths white."

Hill does not remember the younger Cleage in his church, and when it comes to Cleage, Sr. remembers him with little fondness. "He (Cleage, Sr.) set up a grocery store (in the early 20's), and I could not agree with the prices he was charging. (Albert Cleage, Jr. said his father only owned the building and on no occasion ran the store, but it was run by Uncle Henry, who had several grocery outlets.) He was not much interested in helping others as I was. I told him when you help others, you help yourself. If he thought it helped him a little financially, he'd do it, but not for benefit of others. He gave up the store when his doctor's work became too much."

Hill was the first black appointed to Mayor Edward Jeffries' interracial committee (later abolished after Hill demanded a grand jury investigation of the 1943 race riot when police accused blacks of starting the riot). He remembers getting into one particularly heated argument with Albert Cleage, Sr. "I ran for Common Council five times and once for Congress. But he never took a stand when I ran. He was never much concerned. He'd say there was no hope, but one year I got 15,000 votes which showed how many were interested in voting." About the Cleages in general he remembers, "We didn't mix too much." On Albert, Jr., "He followed the example of his father over the years. I don't remember him taking a definite stand on joining with any groups."

The Cleage family, despite a certain independence and hard work on the part of the father, appears to have been a strong matriarchy. This is evident now in the constant devotion of the three boys and two daughters to Mrs. Cleage, Sr., as two of the boys, Louis and Hugh, live there, the daughters are often there, and Albert, Jr. eats more suppers there than in his own apartment. Pastor Cleage shuttles his mother around to UCC Detroit district meetings, and she is faithfully in her pew, the only person in the solid black nationalist church that looks white — unless you count her son in this category, as many tend to do at first glance. But even in the early 20's, as a young mother, she enjoyed almost magical powers with her brood. "I remember her coming out on her porch at their home on the corner of Scotten and Moore Place. The children were so well trained and so obedient," said Mrs. Charles Hill. "They would go out and play at the Wingert school a block away. She never screamed or yelled. When she appeared on the porch they just came. She would go to a PTA meeting, and I'd ask if she wanted a ride. 'No,' she'd say, 'my boys will come for me,' and they did. She never had to tell them. It was all very wonderful."

Mrs. Hill applied this "dominance" of the mother in understanding Pastor Cleage's militancy. "Sometimes people get frustrated when they are too obedient as children. Sometimes even a wife or husband, if henpecked, will express himself away from home in business activity as very dominant. It could be the same with children, and in the case of Albert Cleage."

Mrs. Cleage sat in her black lace dress, with her gray and white hair in a sort of bun, slim, lean-faced, pleasant. She reported she had talked with Albert, Jr., earlier, who had told her, "Mother, don't tell him anything foolish." But she did tell me some foolish little things that revealed the warmth and love and closeness of this family with the controversial son.

"I want to say to you, there was nothing funny when he was a small boy," said Mrs. Cleage. "He was a serious little boy. He wore little white blouses and trousers, and was always with a book. The others were excavating the backyard, or wiring the back porch, or Louis would be greasing up something, and Albert reading. He was never happy-go-lucky."

Why? "That's the way God made him." And for another reason she suggested, "It might be that at a tender age when he should be happy, he saw practices concerning colored children and it took all the jolliness out of him." His sister Barbara, who had come into the room, noted that experiences of seating in the predominantly white schools "were shattering, because they were usually asked to sit in the back of the room," as Cleage himself recalls, and said Barbara, "there were the lynching pictures in *Crisis* magazine – all had an effect on him." They noted that Louis was a great builder and Albert, in "his white shirt and tie, and book under his arm, was good at art."

Mrs. Cleage, asked if God had "anointed" her boy in some small way for a special mission in life as God had tapped the boy Samuel, said, "My dear, when he was a little boy, I always told stories – I took them through the Bible – Mary's flight into Egypt, and others. This day, he stood there, his eye level with the table: 'Tell me a story,' he said. 'Not today, I am so busy,' I said; 'you tell me a story!' His face was blush red, and mad; it was not for him to tell a story. 'Sure, you know stories,' I said. He didn't talk very plain. He began telling the whole story of Joseph, sold into Egypt. He dumbfounded me. The poor tiny boy held all that together in his mind.

"And there was the time, I'd be running the carpet sweeper, and he'd be saying, 'Sit down and I make a talk.' 'You go ahead, I hear it.' 'No, sit down and I make a talk.' He'd stand on the second step, and he did not talk plain, and talked and talked and talked, and the perspiration would run down. I clapped . . . 'wonderful' . . . and he blushed. In church, they used to demand for his father to speak. His father would walk to the rostrum and the boy would slide down in the pew, the top of his head showing. When his dad would come back to the pew, he would say, 'Ol' man, you kind of ashamed of me.' . . . He (Al, Jr.) was shy and he'd 'make talk' to imitate his dad. He wanted to speak to people – he felt at a tender age when other kids played on the floor, he would make talk. . . ." Barbara interrupted to say that in Cleage's days at Wayne State University, the late John Dancy who headed the Urban League would send word down to "tell Cleage to break up the discussion around the radiators." "He'd begin talking," she said, "and the first thing you'd know, people would be gathering around him. Most had the image that Al and all Negroes should be charming and have their lips pursed. . . ."

"He's not the loudest talker in the house . . . Henry and Louis are, rather," the mother continued. She reminisced about Hugh, who started out in education, then took up agriculture at Michigan State University, "and we bought him a farm at Mt. Clemens." But then "Henry in law school worried about little Hugh down on the farm, so he left law and went to work on the (180-acre) farm for six years. I felt it was very hard on little Hugh and he left the farm, and I felt Henry should finish law. So we sold the farm, and little Hugh came back into town." Today Hugh is a printer, Louis is a medical doctor, and Henry, an attorney. The sisters are Barbara Martin (divorced) who helps to coordinate the Shrine's Economic Development Corp. office and the clothing factory of the Shrine's Black Star Co-op Services; Mrs. Gladys Evans, a teacher; and Mrs. Anna Shreve, a pharmacist, all in the Detroit area.

The family went into publishing, as Gladys Evans, who came into the room, said, "Friends and associates decided to put out a good black paper, more of a general newspaper but born of the idea to give an objective intelligent outlook"—*The Illustrated News,* in appearance a ghastly eight-page ink blur, attempting to print pictures directly without halftones. "It was started," said Mrs. Cleage, "because my sons felt black people should have a newspaper and to tell the truth about black people." Added Gladys, "And also to tell the truth about white people who need to be told the truth for the benefit of black people." Reaching a free circulation of 35,000, "it became so much trouble to cope with, and we got tired and ran out of money," said Barbara. "But we have talked about another paper," added Gladys.

Pastor Cleage derives a keen religious sense not only from his faithful Presbyterian father but also from his mother, who was always schooling him in the exercise of faith. "The advice I had for him is the same for all his life, was to take your troubles to God," she said. "Don't think you can decide anything by yourself. We, your father and I, lived by this teaching . . . and when others lost all, we, with seven children, we had not lost anything—we trust in God, and he takes care of us. God will hear you, if you hear right. Solomon asked for wisdom to guide him and God made him the wisest man who ever lived."

Oscar Hand, the multi-faceted church official who is

custodian for the Birney Annex school and tries his hand occasionally in politics on a school or county ballot, unsuccessfully, knew the Cleages since 1920. At 6 feet, 265 pounds, he is a generous man in build and spirit. It is more of a compliment than an insult when Cleage's enemies, dissidents from his church, brush Hand off as "Cleage's big fat flunkie." He *is* a very close and loyal friend.

Recalling their childhood (they lived two blocks apart, the Cleages at Scotten and Moore Place and the Hands at Hartford and Stanford), "Toddy never played, never engaged in sport activity with us. Henry was the athlete. I don't remember Toddy participating in the games we did. There was never a reason why he didn't play games—he was probably just not interested; he was always reading and always making plans for something for us to do.

"In the backyard we used to have a carnival, and all the Cleage brothers took part in it. Dr. (Louis) Cleage had a penny machine then; you paid to see how much shock you could take when you held on to a certain part of the car." Then there was a marbles game. "If you grabbed the right marble, you won a pair of ice skates. Nobody would win; the marble was in the pocket. One big white boy wanted to win so badly he substituted one just like it as he pulled his hand out of the jar. We just about had a fight on the corner." Cleage, who was lighter in weight than Oscar (Cleage is now 5 feet, 10½ inches, 185 pounds, adding some weight after giving up smoking), used to challenge Oscar to a race and "he'd run faster, then sit on the porch to prove the point."

Albert grew a moustache, which he still has. "I grew it when I was first able to get one," he says. "If the razor slips, then it is small, if not, then high." With moustache and all, Albert tried his hand at the drums, publishing, and writing saucy little yarns for print. With Oscar, he helped a Mrs. Beulah Young, whose physician husband Cleage, Sr. helped get a job, put out the *Detroit People News*. Cleage, Oscar, and their college chums did most of the work from editing to linotyping. "She'd always put something silly in," Oscar recalls. "She had us put in that a real estate man who was in an auto accident had been killed. There was no confirmation, and we found out later he wasn't dead, and she tried to buy back the papers, and it all reached a point where we couldn't do anything with her putting in those silly, screaming headlines.

"Toddy wrote a story, 'Born Bad,' and put my name on it. It had a suggestion of sex in it, and was about poor people in the South. A little girl in the South wanted to be rich. She was very poor. She came to the big city—all I remember, she tramped the street, barefooted, winter, in blood-red shoes. He never finished the story. In the story, there were some relations in the hay in the country, and things she looked for on the streets, she didn't find."

Oscar recalls that the story by Cleage with Oscar's by-line on it gave Oscar instant "success." "Oh, shucks, I got status. First of all, parents didn't want their teens to read it—it was too sexy. It was just suggestive, but not profane. I felt so good about it, I did not say too much. . . . I was also a gossip columnist.

"Toddy (Pastor Cleage) wrote our themes for us in high school—one paper he wrote for me had opening lines like: All wars are an outgrowth of political and economic conflict." Oscar said the teacher at Northwestern High "suggested I didn't write it, but I defended it so nice. As I look at it today, what he wrote is actually the truth. I got an A, but she wondered if I wrote it."

The Cleage boys, Oscar, and others picked up a little money when Franklin Roosevelt was elected and with the repeal of the Eighteenth Amendment, "Every hole in the wall was opened up. We organized a combination to work a gig (or job)."

Al "had a booking agency and booked combinations in various beer gardens. He was a drummer and played when necessary. His cousins from Benton Harbor also came over on the trombone, sax, and drums. I also played the drums. Frankly, neither one of us were any good." They had the usual snare drums, base drums, with brushes.

Oscar said the most fun was when they played at the Bluebird Inn (it was the DuBois Club then). Cleage was on the drums, his brother Henry on the sax, and there was a pianist by the name of John Hicks. They played Friday and Saturday from 8:00 or 9:00 P.M. to 2:00 A.M. "None of us drank—if we wanted to, we would be the worst drunks in the world. The best part of the evening was not playing, but the fellowship afterward. There was a place on Warren called Slimy Joe's Coney Island, which had chili and hot dogs.... He was always very witty—he always teased people he liked. We would save up money to go to a show; $1.50 or maybe $2.50 we received at a good gig, or 75 cents, or you played for the kitty, and people came up and requested songs and put coins in a box." He couldn't say if Cleage had changed in forty years. "When you work with a person forty years, you are not totally aware of change. You change along with him.

"Once we were in the basement, playing records. The police used to harass the Cleage family, and they'd come and act like something was going on. We were playing a Duke Ellington record, and two big policemen knocked at the door. Rev. Cleage answered. They were going to barge in. It was the first time in my life I saw how mad he could get. The police had come to the side entrance of the house, and would have to go up or down. The police were coming in, trying to, and tried to tear down the door. When Cleage opened the door, they tried to push the door down. Cleage shouted, 'This is what you always do—walk in a black house, and all over . . . you are not going to do it here!' I suspect the neighbors had complained—there were a lot of us over there all the time—seven children of the Cleages and add us to it. Rev. Cleage was really mad and raised so much hell that if they had come in, I think he would have killed them."

CHAPTER 4

Apostle of Youth

When the Rev. Albert Cleage, Jr. was called to Springfield, Massachusetts, as pastor of one of the most historic
of black churches in New England, where John Brown
had worshiped and abolitionist Frederick Douglass had attended, the 124-year-old St. John's Congregational Church,
he told a newspaper reporter he had three emphases:

> Religiously I feel that preaching should be based
> upon the Bible insofar as possible, and at the same
> time should have significant current application to
> the problems of the world in which we live. I place
> considerable emphasis upon those aspects of the
> church program which touch children and young
> people.[1]

Later, as he was beginning to dominate the new wave
of black militancy in Detroit, at the time of a selective
buying boycott, Pastor Cleage was quoted by the *Michigan
Chronicle*: "When first-class citizenship is achieved, I
can go back to pastoring and working with young people."[2]

The special continuing emphasis on youth in all of his
career—and his success with youth—is a distinguishing
quality of his ministry and a factor not to be overlooked in
understanding the development of his hard-line black
militancy.

His main outside activity as a college student at Wayne
State University while attending the Plymouth Church
was working with youth. For a year in high school, he
recalls, he was chairman of a youth group at St. Cyprian's
Episcopal Church. "I was a sort of assistant at Plymouth,"

he said. "Whatever youth work they wanted done, I did."
Mostly this was helping along the discussions and programming of the Plymouth League of young adults. Here
he also met his wife-to-be, Doris.

Cleage had a sporadic college career that spanned thirteen years at Wayne State, starting in 1929, taking only
courses he liked – nearly all in sociology and psychology,
bugging out to attend Fisk University in Nashville, Tennessee, for one year (1931–32), in sociology. Then he decided it was just as easy to go to Wayne (perhaps a bit
homesick for the closely knit Cleage clan), reentered
Wayne in 1932, and in the 1934–35 academic year worked
as a student assistant in the WSU sociology department
under the late professor Maud Fiero. Donald Marsh, WSU
psychology professor, remembers Cleage as "very good in
class in raising questions, a good sociological student
who sought to find how the world ticked," while another
professor in sociology remembers Cleage as a "run-of-
mine student." His first years at Wayne found him by and
large a B student in editorial writing, literature, and
rhetoric, but with no credit in a number of courses for
which he enrolled, among them zoology, European history, several courses in rhetoric, and Spanish. He was
practically a straight A in sociology courses; and by the
time he settled down as a serious student in 1935, mixing
graduate courses with undergraduate, he was making
three or four A's each semester out of five or six courses,
with the one or two other grades being B. He got an A in
state and local administration, and the Russian Revolution,
U.S. politics, social foundations of education, races and
nationalities, principles of economics, local government,
case-work principles, contemporary U.S. problems, Western civilization. In one Wayne project he did a "racial
attitude inventory" with twenty questions, such as "Negroes are dumb, Yes or No," and had "practically every
kid in the neighborhood going around with it."

It was in the interim from 1929 to 1931, between high
school and college, that he ran his combo-booking agency,
booking his own little group and others, such as a group
headed by Glostter Currant, who became head of the na-

tional youth council of the NAACP and director of the branches of NAACP. For over a year between 1936 and 1938, while he was putting a lot of time in at the Plymouth Church, he worked as social caseworker for the Detroit Department of Public Health. Without completing his degree work at WSU (he needed only four more hours in language – he had already had some Spanish and German), he enrolled in the Oberlin Graduate School of Theology in Oberlin, Ohio, in 1938.

While at Oberlin he was a student pastor for two years in the Union Congregational Church at Painesville, Ohio. In 1940–41 he studied in the graduate school program in sociology at Wayne State. In 1942 he finally took his four hours of language (German), received his B.A. degree, and was off for Oberlin again for the 1942–43 year, receiving his Bachelor of Divinity degree in May 1943, with a major in religious education. And the next month he married Doris at the Plymouth Church, where they had met. He was also ordained that summer.

Recalled a classmate, "When Cleage was ordained, the ordination people contacted the school, and said, 'What kind of people are you turning out?' The kinds of answers Cleage gave to their (examining) committee motivated them to ask the school such questions." About his life at the seminary, "Cleage was able to intellectualize on many theological concepts, and it's fair to say that among the students he was considered an intellectual, or rather, a sophisticate, and they respected his point of view. At that time there was a lot of discussion concerning the Central (segregated) Jurisdiction in the Methodist Church. He thought it was the Christian direction to do away with it (i.e., to integrate the black and white geographic jurisdictions in Methodism)." Another Oberlin classmate, Cleage's white roommate, Clark R. Cooper, now a partner in a law firm in Medina, Ohio, said, "Albert lived like an ascetic, and did not run around. The only vice he had was smoking (he has since quit that). He liked to listen to others but was quite brilliant in his own views. He was always reading." Cooper recalls stumbling onto one of Cleage's term papers graded by the late Douglas Horton, leading ecumenist and former moderator of the International Congregational Council. "Al would never have shown it to me. It had A and three pluses after it."

Cleage accepted a call to the Chandler Memorial Congregational Church in Lexington, Kentucky, in 1943, and within the year he had a call to serve as interim pastor with a noted professor at the newly organized San Francisco Church for the Fellowship of All Peoples, a project with much national interest and encouragement from such notables as Mrs. Franklin Roosevelt. His colleague was Alfred G. Fisk, a Presbyterian professor of philosophy at San Francisco State College, who had been active in a number of rights movements including a nucleus of young adults called the Sakai group, which met in a house owned by the Sakai family. All were Japanese-Americans forcibly displaced during World War II. Out of this group grew the idea of a special congregation emphasizing practical brotherhood of all people. Fisk, who was white, and Cleage were to serve until the first full-time pastor, Howard Thurman, prolific author who has been ranked as one of the nation's ten top preachers, could arrive. Thurman was then a professor at Howard University and had to finish his commitments there. He wrote in his book on the new Fellowship Church of All Peoples:

> During the interval between my agreement to come and the beginning of my leave from the university, Dr. Fisk and I agreed to invite a young Negro clergyman, Albert Cleage, from the East who was available for the six-month period ending July 1, 1944. He was recommended by the late Charles S. Johnson, of Fisk University, who had spent some time in San Francisco making one of the community surveys for which he was internationally known. Mrs. Thurman, our daughters, and I arrived in San Francisco, in July 1944.[3]

Reached by letter at his home in San Francisco, Dr. Thurman, now dean emeritus of Marsh Chapel, Boston University, said of Cleage, "It is impossible for me to give any personal testimony as to his service in connection with the Church for the Fellowship of All Peoples. Unfortunately, I only know the Reverend Albert Cleage by reputation." He did, however, wish for me "success in writing an interpretation of the significant contribution of Mr. Cleage." Dr. Fisk died of cancer in 1959; and Mrs. Fisk, now also living in San Francisco, referring me to the Thurman book also, wrote: "Mr. and Mrs. Cleage were guests in our home until their apartment could be made ready. During their brief stay in San Francisco, we were impressed by Albert Cleage's brilliant mind and his intense dedication to the cause of freedom and social justice for the Negro. He was a 'militant' even in those early days."

Cleage does not remember his work with the famous Fellowship Church of All Peoples with any fondness. The new congregation, which had about fifty members when he was there, was a contrived, artificial affair, he says. "An interracial church is a monstrosity and an impossibility," he said. "The whites who came, came as sort of missionaries. They wanted to do something meaningful, but this was not really their church. The blacks regarded it as experimental too, or were brainwashed to think that it was something superior." He called his white counterpart, Dr. Fisk, "well-meaning," and said Fisk thought he (Fisk) was doing a great work, but had no understanding of tension and power. He felt the Lord looked in favor on this work, and any whites that joined him were headed for glory. He hated to have problems mentioned. Problems included the property left deteriorating after the Japanese were moved out, and the boilermakers' union "which set up separate auxiliary units for blacks so they could discontinue the units after the war." Cleage joined in with NAACP efforts to get at these injustices. He was told he could stay at the Fellowship Church of All Peoples if he wanted to, and he said "they were nice people, but it did not seem to me it was a significant ministry." About Fisk, he said, "He talked of the glorious fellowship washed in the blood of the Lamb; I talked about hell on the alternate Sundays. He felt upset about my preaching, but he didn't want to raise racial tension in his heaven."

Still interested in religious education and new techniques, Cleage enrolled at the University of Southern California in Los Angeles for the graduate program in visual education in the cinema department, "considering a doctorate in visual education as it applies to religious education." Here he produced films, usually of a short nature, using campus and downtown scenes, following through with the projects from camera work through lab work. The assignments, he recalls, were mostly to develop and test phases of technical know-how, such as proper exposure and cutting. He had a seminar course with Cecil B. DeMille on cinematology. "It was all very interesting," he recalls, "but I decided against three or four years of study. Other things were more pressing; and I had learned all I needed to know, and if I were going to use it, I was ready to do so. . . . I was interested in religious filming, in trying to find a way to touch the black man en masse"; but film-making, he discovered was "too expensive." During his USC studies, he worked nights as a darkroom developer in a local black nightclub, where various celebrities, including some whites, hung out. He also did some preaching in and around Los Angeles. In LA, he received his call to St. John's, Springfield.

I had not thought of Albert Cleage as a youth leader until I went to Springfield, Massachusetts, to check on his ministry there — his longest and most immediate before coming to Detroit. His commitment and dedication to youth stood out all over the place. I was prepared to find similar patterns of his militancy and controversies in Springfield as in Detroit. It was the same Cleage that was to stir storms in Detroit, and in Springfield the dark thunderclouds hung over his head as he called down lightning and hail on issues. But in Springfield he was specially concerned with youth. As chairman of the Springfield NAACP Redress Committee, he sat in with others in city officials' offices on five occasions pushing for hearings on police brutality cases against blacks, most of them teens. Concerning the beating of a young man, Ralph Hefner, in 1946, Lindsay B. Johnson (LBJ), chairman of the Springfield Park Commission, close associate of

Cleage's in the church as youth director and treasurer (he still is treasurer, more than twenty years in the post now), said, "We sat down in the mayor's office, and all Rev. Cleage said, was, 'I think we should have a public hearing.' It was the first time anybody raised a voice. They did the same when a boy, Franklin Jackson, was beat up and on several other occasions."

Johnson, who was praised in warm terms by the managing editor of *Springfield Evening News*, Richard C. Garvey, in a chat in Garvey's office noted also how Cleage had "fought successfully for securing the first Negro principal in the school system (East Union) near the church, and every time there was a school board meeting would sit down at the meeting and make his request known."

Johnson sat in his windbreaker, sports shirt, and trim trousers and loafers on one of the Danish modern sofas amid orange bucket chairs before a giant stone fireplace, with Japanese ceramic accents. He leaned over toward the glass coffee table as he talked in the hillside home which has a vista-vision window that looks out over a cluster of trees in the backyard. He had had his own battle, according to newspaper clips, with a neighbor, who claimed a driveway right of access was trespassing on his property. Court action upheld Johnson, and he is best of friends now with his white Italian neighbor.

Lindsay told how Cleage once pitched in with $20 from his own pocket, to match $20 from Lindsay to rent the Eli Brookin School gym for St. John's teams, and how:

—When two boys were beat up and came to him, he gave them the last cents out of his pockets and got them home.

—The boys of the Jinx bar across the street from the church all said he was the only man they could call on day or night.

—When a family broke up, he kept the daughter, Carrie, in his own home.

—When one night the four of us, Cleage, myself, and our wives were having coffee, he got a call from the police about two runaway girls; he went down there at once, brought them home, and got in touch with their parents.

—When two girls from our group in church went into the Massasay café and were told they could not be served because the space was reserved, Cleage brought charges, and the judge told him he would levy a fine on the restaurant; Cleage said he didn't want a fine. The café eventually went out of business.

—On trips, he'd practically give the shirt off his back, his last dollar. He made sure every kid had enough money.

—He used to rent buses to go to Boston and New Haven for basketball games. He made up songs for cheerleaders and mostly cheers.

Cleage has been universally described by his old cronies and associates as a "nonathlete." A great book man, though, Lindsay remembers how he got out books and read up on basketball while at St. John's, and "when we'd drill the kids, he got to be pretty good himself. We'd listen to all the ball games, and we'd go to Holy Cross and Long Island to see Bob Cousy play. Cleage did more for basketball in the high school here by developing black athletes. . . every school with a black athlete—the athlete came out of his church."

Johnson is purchasing manager for the Eastern Division of Agway, largest feed co-op in the world, a firm he's been with for thirty years. He is also member of the Springfield Planning board, the YMCA board, Springfield Community Council, and current president of the Springfield area interchurch recreation council of the YMCA.

At a big youth conference, Lindsay recalls, Cleage "gave a talk I will never forget. Cleage made Charles Lee, director of the YMCA, very unhappy. Cleage had said that he would never under any circumstances testify against another black man. I found him very warm, and so did the kids, and they loved him, but the adults felt he was cold."

The image of Detroit's slightly aging Black Power Albert Cleage as basically a youth leader was underscored in random interviews around St. John's on a sunny Saturday afternoon and inside the dark-shingle church on a sunny, fall Sunday morning.

An elderly lady, who had been a caretaker at the church

for years, stood on her second-floor porch on Quincy behind the church, peering over the bannister, and said,
"Cleage had young ideas. Cobb (Dr. Charles, Cleage's
successor at St. John's and now head of the Committee
for Racial Justice Now of the UCC, in New York) was
more political. Cleage was more interested in athletic
programs. I liked Cobb well, but I do not like any church
to be in politics."

Mrs. Fanny Billups, who runs the Fanny's Luncheonette
across the street and several doors up, said of Cleage, "He
was a very dynamic speaker and worked with young
people." Mrs. Billups' children were in Cleage's St. John's
church programs. She said, "The main thing I really like,
he took kids out into the street and had a carnival and there
would be ice cream and record-playing — he'd just walk up
and down among the people and greet them." Contrasting
Cleage and his successor, who was active in city politics
and other areas, "It'd take a great man to surpass him
(Cobb)," and "I feel Cobb got in the limelight more. If
Cleage had been here (in later years), he'd probably have
done the same things."

Burke Johnson, the neighborhood barber on the corner
across the street from the church, remembers Cleage as
"a nice young minister. He was very, very popular. He is
the type of fellow that is interested in every individual."
But he was not a talker. "When he came in here, he'd just
sit there and take a book and not say a word. He never had
anything to say; but in the chair he always talked, but
nothing particular to say." On black nationalism, "In those
days they did not talk that stuff; that's new. I'm not interested, to tell the truth (in black nationalism)." He recalls Cleage as a "very religious fellow, who never had
anything to say at all, and the way I figured it, he had a lot
on his mind. He always got a plain trim, like this one," as
he worked on a teen-ager getting a close, lay-down crop.

The barber's son, Rodney Chester Johnson, 32, picked
up his ears and soon came over with a pamphlet. "Look
at this," he said. On the cover of the pamphlet was a picture of junior-age boys, eyes full of mischief and the future, all in their Sunday best at church. "That's me," said

Rodney Chester pointing to one handsome youth. Rodney had sung in the choir when Cleage was pastor and remembers him as "keeping teens out of trouble" and "a man of integrity who tried to help" and one "who has the right to be in his own orbit (of black nationalism)" now if he wants to. "Here, read this pamphlet, it'll tell you all you want to know," said Rodney, who didn't seem to like to be talking to a white man; and he leaned back in his chair and snoozed as I looked over the pamphlet with his picture that he had cherished for nearly twenty years.

Edited by Cleage, the pamphlet was "An Open Letter to the Citizens of Springfield" concerning the Springfield Housing Authority and its policy of racial segregation in public housing. Cleage wrote the pamphlet, published by the NAACP, as chairman of the NAACP housing committee. At issue was a new multiple-housing project, which Cleage and the NAACP were alleging discriminated against blacks. The *Springfield Daily News* of April 26, 1950 quoted John I. Robinson, chairman of the Springfield Housing Authority, as saying in a Kiwanis speech about the Reed Village project where Negroes were being assigned to live next to Negroes: "Those who make an issue of limited racial segregation in public-housing give aid and comfort to those who by every means at their disposal are trying to block a slum clearance and low-income housing program here under the Federal Housing Act of 1949."

Cleage's position was that powerful real estate interests were fighting hard against public-housing at all levels. Robinson, according to the *Daily News* article, admitted that blacks were not integrating with whites throughout the local housing project, but he denied that the SHA was sanctioning segregation within the meaning of the law. He said the policy of the SHA was justified on a "realistic approach." According to the *Daily News,* Robinson said "a policy at this time of integrating the colored with the white would, in my opinion, furnish fuel to the fire of helping to beat down the public-housing program and be to the detriment of the colored as well as the whites." Cleage's answer to Robinson in the pamphlet, under the heading "First Things First":

Mr. John I. Robinson's long-awaited Kiwanis club address has done little to either clarify or explain his policy of segregation in public-housing. His feeble apologetic has served but to reveal the inner confusions of a man who knows what is right and yet stands stubbornly committed to a policy of wrong.

In contending that those who make an issue of racial segregation give aid and comfort to those who would block all public-housing, and afford these interests an additional emotional and racial weapon which may well swing the fight their way, Mr. Robinson recognizes the existence of a powerful and growing public opinion against segregation. He unwittingly admits his fear that many friends of slum clearances and low-income housing may not feel inclined to support nonsegregated public-housing.

Mr. Robinson's remarks concerning the practical expediency of segregation do not merit serious consideration. His efforts to justify his policy of segregation as "a very realistic approach to the overall housing program" sound disgustingly like Hitler's clarification of his policy of anti-Semitism as "a very realistic approach to the overall problem confronting Germany."

In Mr. Robinson's own words, "Any policy of segregation, however limited, cannot be justified on any moral grounds"! How, then, can individuals for whom moral values are important support any public program however necessary if that program is to be administered with a cynical disregard for moral values?

The greatest problem now confronting this community is the moral question involved in the SHA policy of racial segregation. Conceivably, the problem should come first in the minds of Springfield citizens.

Cleage became involved in another housing controversy in an effort to provide more adequate construction for a new school. The city was balking at tearing down adjacent houses to provide sufficient rooms for the new school, Cleage maintained. Cleage offered to take the buildings on the building site of the school off the hands of the city and move them. Cleage, with others, presented a plan to have St. John's buy the eleven dwellings housing twenty-two black families for $1 each, but bear the cost of moving the homes and providing lots for the relocation. Once the selected site at Harvey and Berkshire was revealed, some 300 members of the neighborhood's Boston Road improvement society filed a protest before the city council to block the removal of the homes to their neighborhood. Their objection was twofold: the homes being moved were two-family duplexes, and "disproportionate expense for sewage that the city would face in having to extend a sewer line 600 feet."

"That is not very important and I don't think the City Council will pay any attention to the petition," Cleage told a *Springfield Union* reporter. However, Cleage and St. John's began to retreat over the "excessive costs" of moving to the Harvey and Berkshire site. Then, "while he did not make a flat declaration, Rev. Albert B. Cleage, Jr. admitted" that the church had all but abandoned the moving of the eleven houses, and instead planned to move only some of the houses to a site closer to the school. The city sat in suspense as Cleage and St. John's pondered the next move. "Some Council members wondered if another storm of protest will arise when the new site of the homes to be moved by St. John's church is disclosed," began a *Union* article.[4]

In three days, Cleage was suggesting a temporary removal of some of the tenants into four vacant houses at Union and Monroe until they could find other quarters. Meanwhile, the plan to move the houses met one more snag after another—that fire hydrants would have to be moved, a large number of trees cut down to move the houses; a complex rewiring scheme would also be involved. All hopes of relocating temporarily evicted tenants in unused buildings later to be demolished for the construction were finally dashed when the associate city solicitor ruled that tenancy in any of the houses slated to come down would constitute legally establishing at least one-year tenancy and the demolition might be blocked. The matter was thus theoretically settled, as Cleage was working to secure the adjacent school construction space, and he did not attend a final confrontation arranged by Mayor Brunton. St. John's member, Paul Mason, black councilman who made the proposals for relocation with Cleage and others, let the houses all revert back to the city so that they could come down and construction get under way.

Cleage's biggest controversy at St. John's was trying to rectify a very delicate but deeply rooted quarrel which had been growing in the church for over twenty years before he came. Granddaddy of all the pastors of St. John's was William N. DeBerry, who became pastor in 1899, the year he was ordained, and continued as pastor until 1930. Under DeBerry the church was erected (in 1911) and the St. John's Institutional Services launched right afterward. The social program, the most ambitious of any church, white or black, in Springfield, spawned a parish home for working girls, a Boys' Club, Men's Service League, night school, free employment bureau, band, and other projects. The programs were stretched out into a half-dozen former residential duplexes, and eventually the institutional services bought an eight-apartment building for low-income families and a farm for a campsite.

Seeds of the controversy that was to involve Cleage were planted in 1924 when DeBerry decided to separate the institutional activities from the church itself. He also revealed his intention of resigning as pastor, but continuing as director of the institutional activities and related properties. All but two members of the church in a meeting approved the move. For a while there was harmony between the church and the small empire it had created as the St. John's Institutional Services, later renamed the Dunbar Community League. The trauma and completeness of the separation was felt keenly with the naming of the Rev. Roland T. Heacock as pastor in 1930 when DeBerry finally let go of the pastoral reins. The church was faced with limited income and the shock of having to start anew with its own social programs. The church acquired several houses and tried to lease a camp in Belchertown, Massachusetts, but lacked sufficient funds.

When Cleage came to St. John's in 1945, its seventh minister, he found the controversy coming to a head. The Dunbar Community League was putting up for sale several of its buildings, and the church officials immediately huddled to consider buying the parcels. But the question was raised, why buy the properties when, after legal investigation initiated by Cleage, it was found the properties had been given to the church in the name of the church prior to the separating of the institutional program from the parish church by DeBerry. Involved were a dozen buildings. "The cleavage, begun by Dr. DeBerry in 1924, with the separation from the church of the St. John's institutional activities with its own board, was now complete," says a history of St. John's published by the church.

The sides were inalterably drawn up, and the ensuing lawsuit became a bitter contest. Doubly tragic was the fact that within the church, particularly among the older members who knew him so well, Dr. DeBerry had a loyal and very vocal following who forsook their present minister and conferred their allegiance on the former pastor who, from 1931, headed an organization now fighting St. John's Church.[5]

By 1948 a settlement was reached with the church paying $11,500 to the Dunbar League for deeds to the parish house and lot next to the church, the houses and lots at three sites on Quincy behind the church, and a corner lot at Hancock and Quincy. "So bitter had been the feelings and so sharply had the lines been drawn, that when Dr. DeBerry had tragically died on January 21, 1948, he was buried from South Congregational Church" with James Gordon Gilkey, minister of the South Church and longtime friend of DeBerry, conducting the services.

Cleage, in one of the properties acquired back from the Dunbar League, mapped "a series of athletic contests and classes," also "an intercultural workshop" and a community program similar to a settlement house.[6]

Cleage also stirred up some other financial dandruff

when he insisted the historic church, which in spite of its historical reputation with John Brown and other abolitionists active in it in the early days, had never had a parish status but was a mission of the Congregational Christian churches, become self-sustaining. "He didn't want support of 'white power,' " Lindsay Johnson recalls. The history of the church records that several influential persons fought this move.

Cleage's work was appraised in retrospect by the church historians in the commemorative volume *The History of St. John's Congregational Church* in 1962, more than a decade after he returned to Detroit. At the outset of Cleage's ministry at St. John's, it was noted:

> Mr. Cleage soon inaugurated a strong youth program for the church. Membership in St. John's Pilgrim Fellowship and College Forum was greatly sought after and attendance at the Sunday discussions, panels, and lectures of these groups grew each week. Included among the popular activities begun by Mr. Cleage were the junior and senior dramatic workshops.
>
> A vigorous church athletic program that produced winning basketball teams coached by Mr. Cleage and Mr. Lindsay B. Johnson, Jr. was another product of the new minister's youth program. During this period, a Brownie Scout group was organized under the leadership of Miss Adele Pickens, a Springfield schoolteacher.
>
> Mr. Cleage was also a courageous fighter for equal opportunities for Negroes in the field of employment, and he did much during his ministry at St. John's to open up new avenues of work for qualified job applicants, particularly in the downtown stores of the city. In addition, Mr. Cleage spearheaded many interracial city-wide youth conferences.[7] He also wrote dramas; one of them coauthored with four others recalled "eighty years of progress" since Emancipation and "the significant role the Negro played in our country's history." The church, during Cleage's

pastorate, voted to stay out of the Evangelical and Reformed-Congregational merger that formed the UCC because it did not "satisfactorily guarantee the traditional and cherished Congregational principle of autonomy of the local church," but expressed "deep and sincere regret" for having to make the choice.[8] In Detroit, Cleage brought his Central (Shrine) Church into the UCC.

In the final assessment of the "Years of Transition and Trial," the *History* says:

> In the five years that Mr. Cleage was at St. John's he increased the church membership and the value of the church property, and enlarged and expanded the community service activities by establishing the St. John's Community House at 643 Union Street with a completely equipped settlement house plant.
>
> While in Springfield, Mr. Cleage was active in civic affairs, serving on the Executive Committee, the Legal Redress Committee, and the Housing Committee of the NAACP, and participating in the Round Table of the Conference of Christians and Jews, the YMCA, and the American Red Cross. He inaugurated Sunday Cultural Vesper Services and programs. At one of these, Langston Hughes was presented. Mr. Cleage was also a popular speaker and lecturer on New England college campuses.
>
> With the death of Dr. DeBerry and the departure of Mr. Cleage a turbulent period in the history of St. John's Church came to an end, and once again the church set about the task of finding a new minister, one who, perhaps, could close the breach that still divided the congregation.[9]

Mrs. Eleanor Clinton, who teaches eighth-and ninth-graders at St. John's nowadays, recalled Cleage as "very aggressive, which is good. Whatever he started, he accomplished. He got the young people and youth forum going. He was militant at that time, and would not let anyone talk him down."

"Of all the pastors here, he was as far as influence goes out in front," said one member, Marvin Jacobs, 44, a plant layout analyst who's been St. John's church school superintendent for the past nine years. "He was not athletically inclined but learned enough basketball to get the youngsters to the New England finals. He gave them something that is missing now."

Jacobs said Cleage set about attacking the "establishment," and when one member "excitedly accused him of being stupid, he brushed off the remarks and said 'pardon my stupidity' and went on." Jacobs said he "only saw Pastor Cleage actually angry once. It was at a local NAACP youth council meeting, and "one local politician came and gave us one of those asinine talk-downs—he represented the 'good people.' It disturbed Cleage and he looked exasperated and invited the man to go to an adjoining room to learn a bit." Jacobs, as others, was impressed that Cleage never owned a car in Springfield—the pastoral salary was never high. Cleage received around $4,000, plus housing, annuity, etc. Jacobs noted that Cleage visited various stores, seeking changes in hiring policies. This was the time that the Springfield Plan, a non-discrimination job placement program tied in with the high school curriculum (now standard practice in most schools), was receiving national attention[10]; but as Lindsay Johnson points out, the Springfield Plan was inadequate at the time for it lacked the full apparatus and community consensus to guarantee hiring.

Mrs. Lillian Myers, who was sitting in one of the pews in St. John's before the morning service, said, "I liked Pastor Cleage's appearance and the way he greeted his members. Some ministers go right out but he shook hands and had a pleasant word." A woman who didn't want to be identified said, "He's all right; he had his ways. A nice man, maybe a little ahead of his time to my way of thinking. He was a little blunt, but maybe that is necessary and maybe that is what we need."

"He was always a very aggressive man on things he felt deeply about," said Albert C. Pryor, professor of sociology at Western New England College, Springfield. Dr.

Pryor, a deacon in St. John's, was married by Cleage, in a ceremony in which Pryor remembers Cleage "didn't embellish it very much but it was a nice ceremony."

Said Dr. Pryor in an interview in the narthex of St. John's, "Cleage developed the leadership of the youth. He had no faith in the old and not much faith in whites. He recognized and fought the system by which whites controlled blacks. Gilkey was the big white god, and DeBerry was a big black god and ran much of the town. You couldn't get a job washing dishes unless DeBerry said so. Cleage stood up in one ministerial society meeting and said the whole system irked him. . . . DeBerry was the type of yesteryear leader with the ear of the white community, and white leaders used him to keep Negroes in line. . . . DeBerry often opposed development of other leaders. There are people in this church today who should be better educated, but he did not want them to grow up in his shadow." Another deacon recalled Cleage simply "as a little way out" but who "did a lot of good things."

The current pastor at St. John's, Vernie L. Bolden, represents a more moderate or conservative bent in the church than Cleage or Cobb. "I reject separateness in developing a black society as nonsense," he said in an interview. "We already have this kind of thing in South Africa and it doesn't solve problems." He said "black nationalism" has its place in a pluralistic society but "integration is not dead. It's never been tried. I see it (integration) as the only realistic goal." Scoring the excessive preoccupation of black nationalists with African culture and history, Pastor Bolden said "no society long existed which emphasized its own tradition and living apart from others," and he cited the Samaritans, the now nearly forgotten people in Bible times. He also saw no advantage in a "Black Madonna" and regarded it as "an element of extremism" and "further frustration." The youth program has fallen back at St. John's; but Bolden, who is new on the job, said he hoped to get a youth program going. "There are no athletics now," he said, and "there is a different emphasis, and not just recreation."

Cleage, who still regards St. John's with considerable affection, returned in February 1967 as a guest speaker, and gave his former parishioners, whom he pastored in a pre-black nationalist era, a taste of his views today, in reality not too different from what he was saying and doing back in the old days. Promoting a national strike in support of Adam Clayton Powell as a new method in the black freedom movement, he talked of the limitations of a march that he regarded as "a small protest." But an organized strike in 200 cities "could be coordinated from the grass roots of individual communities. The very fact the strike would require a degree of sacrifice, in which even children kept home from school can become part of the national struggle, will bring us more power than anything we ever had before."[11]

I asked Cleage, at the Feenjon expresso coffeehouse in the Village in New York, what he thought was the most dominant note in what I found in Springfield, Massachusetts. He didn't know, but suggested that it might be in connection with his NAACP work there, and possibly with police brutality cases. I suggested there were aspects of city involvement, but one thing people mentioned with most consistency was his work with youth.

"Are you still a youth leader, in your estimation?" I asked. "Whatever we do," he said, "it's validity is in terms of the ability to translate it to youth. So if you do not have a basis of youth, then you fail." He noted that a characteristic of youth is change and methods of meeting such characteristics change. Perhaps if there is any change in Albert Cleage, who has a startling record of consistency in his attitude toward whites, Black Power, and black dignity, it is more in methods, which in reality are keyed to changing attitudes of black youths, attitudes toward which he has helped to contribute as well as to reflect. "There are different kinds of youth," he said. "Youth change faster than the church. The NAACP is gradually decreasing. SNCC was ideal for black youth in college (the Student Nonviolent Coordinating Committee was organized by black students at Shaw University in Raleigh, North Carolina, in 1960). The current wave, the Black Panthers, more action and politics orientated than protest orientated, are largely youth-based."

Daughter Kris, who had been listening pensively to the

eerie Near Eastern music, suddenly came alive and said, "Youth should be left to do what they want to do . . . and support should be there when youth want it." Said Cleage, "I do (youth work) within some limitations . . . (such as) making (church) available for independent groups. . . and get adults to accept this." In his concept of youth work nowadays, he said, are such things as getting youths into motorcades for blacks, voter registration activity, school struggles, and the Inner City Youth Organization, a group of about thirty kids meeting on Sunday afternoon from various high schools. He acknowledged that he once had one of the biggest youth programs in Detroit at Central, a fact acknowledged also by dissidents who left the church. But growing disillusioned about all traditionalism that does not get down to the heart of the matter of building the "Nation," a new dynamic people of God, he says of the more traditional youth programs, "They didn't have the content necessary and didn't build philosophy for participation in the world. The effort now is to relate to the Black Revolution and to fit youth into a black action organization."

Earlier in the evening, we – Kris, Cleage, and myself – had watched from the front row "Walk Down Mah Street," a rather amateur Greenwich Village production more in line with the annual skit type of program you might see on the college stage. But it was youthful and in that respect refreshing. Said Kris, a graduate in art from Wayne State (she was a chief artist for the controversial South End WSU newspaper, doing thin pen-lined caricatures on the paper's front page cover – she has since gone to San Francisco to study art, and returned), "I thought it pretty good. I liked it when it got loud. They didn't say anything really new, so I couldn't say if I liked it or not." Cleage, who really enjoyed the show in progress, said in retrospect, "It was bearable, sort of naive," and "it had American youth. In conception, it was the typical, undisciplined young person, which made up for what it lacked in discipline. I think the theme was done for the white American audience, dealing (with race) in two ways – to shock and to keep a constant confrontation."

With a mixed cast, which included a black fellow and a light-skinned Negro girl, the pitch was integration with a militant, can't-wait flavor: "Walk down mah street, the power is in our hand—each step you take along the way, sweep out every ugly yesterday.... Walk down mah street, all you who want us to be free, come move next door to me.... Freedom is not a fashion, we wear it on our skin. You keep moving from us and we'll run this town and have a celebration." She (white): "I love you, Kenneth" (with flower). He (black): "You can't love me" (socks her). And so the little fun show with a youthful flavor by Norman Curtis and Patricia Taylor Curtis went.

Said Cleage, "If this had been done for a black audience, it would have been different ... in terms of black consciousness and 'black is beautiful.' There was no real black girl in it, for instance ... and there would have been emphasis on what people are going to do. It's an old liberal idea: walk in my shoes and see how we live. A black audience does not just want to hear the complaints. Even 'burn, baby, burn' would have been better. It was a commentary and they were crying about it rather than dealing with strategy and what to do." Regarding a minstrel scene in which there is a change in self-image and a lead-in to be free and a rejection of minstrel caricatures as such: "This would have passed with a black audience." But Al Cleage, despite judging that the musical variety play was the old white stuff all over again, for the most part, found it had values, which the old militant, still young at heart and capable of letting his hair down, could enjoy. He said several times, "It was really good; it had some good laughs and songs, and really good."

CHAPTER 5

The Monster Schools

The atmosphere was electric. Three hundred teachers were crammed into a side room of the board of education conference room in Detroit, singing "Solidarity Forever." The Detroit Federation of Teachers were present as an extension of their picketing outside the schools' Center Building to step up their demand for a contract before school closed for the summer of 1967.

Adding to the noise, the Rev. Albert Cleage was soon in a shouting match with board member A. L. Zwerdling. Cleage had come to outline the demands of his parents group, the Inner-city Parents' Council. Also on hand were the Urban League officials with a general outline of ideas, some of them very theoretical, on how to move toward integration. Cleage discounted the goal of integration and called for immediate new black successes in control of black and predominantly black schools.

Caught in the middle was Remus Robinson, M.D., black board member since 1955. A longtime object of criticism from Cleage, Robinson said Cleage was moving to "the kind of thinking that has been at the root of the problems you have defined." Robinson said the board had been consistent and was not apologetic for the past. "I reject the implied suggestion that the all-Negro schools of the South are superior to Detroit schools," he said. Cleage continued in the vein that the board should apologize for its past and then move on to new plans. Zwerdling tried to interrupt him, but Cleage only got louder. Zwerdling started pounding on the table and shouted, "Be quiet and let someone else talk!" Cleage shouted back, "I'm talking! You listen for a moment . . . this is a big liberal here, but he doesn't want to listen to a black man." Before he stopped, Cleage warned, "We will be back in September; and if you don't do something, you will have the biggest problem any school system ever had." Cleage started to get up to leave, but Zwerdling said, "I don't know why Rev. Cleage is leaving. We want to discuss the problem." Cleage stayed. Zwerdling, in a calmer tone, still got in a few interjections of his own. Insisting the board would not back up on its goal of integration, he said, "Let's talk about the real problem instead of the phony issue of deliberate discrimination. . . . Let's cut out the demagogic nonsense."[1]

Before the fracas, Cleage said the Detroit school system was trying to impose a white middle-class outlook on black pupils. He also charged that white officials block blacks from promotion to top school jobs. He compared the starting of blacks in school with cultural handicaps with "nazi-like theories of racial inferiority." To correct the situation, Cleage asked that all vacant administrative posts, among them nine new regional assistantships, be filled right away with blacks. He called for at least a matching of the proportion of black administrators with the 67 percent of the student population in Detroit which is black.

A year later, on April 27, 1968, Cleage turned the barrels of his education guns on blacks as well as whites. Looking out over 300 participants in a Black Ministers-Teachers Conference at the University of Detroit, he asked, "How many monsters did you create today?" He answered his own question and said monsters are any persons who prey on others because they have no sense of social or human identity.

"Both the schools and churches have created these monsters. They have taught black children to hate black people and therefore to hate themselves. Now that they have seen what white people are like, they also hate white people and have abandoned the integration dream which sustained the older generation. With nothing to attach themselves to, a whole generation of lonely, vicious youth is now running up and down the streets, grabbing pocketbooks, knocking down old women, taking anything they can lay their hands on, concerned only with their individual selves. Unless the black church can give these young people a positive self-image and something to attach themselves to, they will destroy not only themselves but all of us." The conference was sponsored by the Black Teachers Workshop (a caucus) and the Interfaith Committee of Concerned Black Churchmen. Other speakers included Preston Wilcox, "strategist" of the Harlem I.S. 201 struggle, who said that "blacks must live by the slogan B.E.D. (Black Every Day)."

The conference adopted a "declaration of black teachers," with demands along the lines of Cleage's thinking. "We maintain that the present system of education is not organized for the benefit of black youth," they said. And among ten commandments that they recommended to "all black teachers": "We shall know no other loyalty than to the children we teach," and "we shall not covet that status in society which will serve to isolate us from our goals and those of the black community."

Calling the conference a milestone, Cleage in the *Michigan Chronicle* a week later noted that more black teachers took part in the meeting than black ministers. Missing from the roster of participating black cleric sponsors were some very big names, although the list included a cross section of black leaders such as the Rev. Hubert Locke, former high-ranking administrative aide to the Detroit police commissioner, and Charles Hill, and key black denominational representatives. But Cleage was not too disappointed at the lack of wider support from clergy. "This is as it might have been expected because black churches do not play any important part in the education of black children other than the destructive one of handing down the white supremacy power symbols of a white Jesus and a white God."[2]

His other observations on the meeting: "The many teachers and the few preachers who were at the conference were overly optimistic about black parents. . . . Perhaps the most pitiful thing is the fact that many black parents still believe that white folks know best how to educate black children. . . . Basically, the problem is with us. We cannot expect white folks to be seriously concerned about educating black children. Why should we expect them to be? We know how they treat us in employment— keeping us in the poorly paid jobs at the bottom."

Cleage's passion for sweeping the slate clean and putting in blacks is punctuated in another column:

We feel that most ghetto schools today destroy children rather than educate them. The teachers and administrators serve as power symbols and kill a black child's self-image. Their influence, their lack of concern, and in many instances their contempt make it impossible for a black child to learn.

So, we are insisting more and more that a school for black children have black teachers, black principals, and black administrators; that its curriculum be re-orientated to cover the culture of black people; that the present textbooks, which are essentially lies, particularly in the area of social science and history, be thrown out and that textbooks explaining the history and cultural background of black people be substituted. We are not insisting that white schools teach the truth, but we do insist that schools in black ghettos teach the truth.[3]

A survey of history books used in Michigan schools, in implementing the Michigan Social Studies Textbook Act of 1966, conducted by the State Department of Education 1967–68, showed that the history textbooks used by Michigan school children are "historically inaccurate," full of prejudice, and perpetuate racism. A national panel of historians made the evaluation. "The Negro does not exist in these books," the panel noted, and they found attitudes of sanctioning oppression in the books; when, for example, in a passing mention of "slaves" in the story of the Civil War, one book recalled the "shouting and singing" of the slaves at work and suggested that the class sing spirituals to recall "the happier aspects of plantation life."

Cleage, who attended Detroit public schools, draws some of his militantism on schools from his own experiences with discrimination back in the 20's, particularly his high school, Northwestern, which was nearly all white at that time but is nearly solid black now. He remembers, "I didn't like anything about it. There were all kinds of discrimination." The school clubs were closed to blacks, he says. "It was a horrible atmosphere, and I took part in as little as possible." He recalls that the teachers would always put the black youths at the back of the classroom. "It was dismal. My parents would go up and raise enough donnybrook and hell to take care of the situation (classroom seating, etc.)"; but, he says, they were powerless to penetrate the fabric of discrimination by the white teachers and administration. "It wasn't the students, so much as the administration." Cleage took a try at the 440 in track, which by his own admission was "nothing great," and he says several black students were able with much effort to break into the predominantly white school's team sports. His brother Henry, now an attorney for the Neighborhood Legal Services, was "first cellist in the school orchestra; but every time they had a concert they tried to place him so it would appear that he was not the first cellist. This was trivial, but . . ."

Cleage's sister Gladys remembers how her father helped form the Wingert school PTA and was instrumental in getting the first black teacher by means of a petition. "He would argue with the school board and everybody else." Concerning Northwestern High, Mr. and Mrs. Edward Jandy—she was the white who stayed on in Cleage's church only to join their black friends who later quit the church—confirmed the continuation of prejudice as the number of blacks increased in the school. The Jandys had wanted to integrate the old Brewster-Pilgrim congregation before the church gave up and sold to blacks. Both Jandy daughters went to Northwestern before Dr. Jandy took a three-year leave in 1950 to work with the United States embassy in Addis Ababa, Ethiopia, and later to lecture for a year as a Fullbright scholar in the University of Karachi, Pakistan. Said Mrs. Jandy, "It used to burn me up, they would never serve refreshments at the PTA because they didn't want to break bread with Negroes."

Cleage's mother said of the schools her boys attended (Wingert Elementary and Northwestern), "I had to fight for them all the way through, for I knew a mistreated child could have a blight for years . . . if a child said he was having trouble, naturally, I'd go up to see about it."

Albert "is a great talker now," she said, "but in high school he was not much of a talker unless he had something specific to say." She remembers going in to see one English teacher who told her, "Albert doesn't smile or talk much." "And I said, 'Is there anything to smile or talk about?' She had sent him down to the principal to see if the principal could make him talk, and the principal said, 'Well, Albert, you are not much of a talker,' and sent him back. The English teacher talked about grades. I said, 'He came to you with an A. Send down to the office and see the record for yourself, and you keep him to a C — ridiculous! I say he's an A student! If he doesn't work, you can still hold him to a C. But I thought you graded on work.' She was foolish. Another teacher said his papers were too lengthy. But God does not make us all alike. God made some minds to be emphatic. . . . Louis — now the M.D. — could write short papers. Louis just put it down, but you can't grade this son by his younger brother's method."

Mrs. Cleage, the 81-year-old matriarch, watched me closely as I wrote down her words. "I feel sorry for parents raising colored children," she said, "for so many don't have the fight like I do." Perhaps I grinned a little at this point, in admiration of the energy of this tremendous lady still full of the old vinegar for her sons. "You smile, but you don't know," she said. "You have to do something in a country like the United States."

She did the same with all her youngsters. "Louis was brokenhearted when he got a C in chemistry. So I went to his counselor. 'You come with me,' I told him. 'I'm taking him out of that class. I can't have a child ruined by a man who hates colored people.' I took him to another class, and the new teacher was amazed — he was an A student all along." Daughter Barbara recalled that "there was a teacher who opened the door by the top where no 'colored' child touches the door." She recalls her mother telling the principal, "I can't stand this. This girl and other children are too fine. Take that polluted woman out."

Cleage's now defunct *Illustrated News* carried an anonymous exposé by a Northwestern High teacher on "What's Wrong with Our Schools." It rapped the new black-board-jungle atmosphere of the school, the lack of any cafeteria for the 3,000 students, "hardly any extracur-ricular activities," "no marching band," only one dance a year, and pervading "low" and "no" academic standards with teachers instructed to go easy and avoid failures. The teacher wrote:

> This no-standards policy, we must remember, is favored by the people who believe that Negro chil-dren are inferior as students so there is no sense in spending a lot of public money trying to educate them as white students are educated. . . . Parents, who are very concerned with getting the best pos-sible education for their children, quite naturally try to send their kids to Cass. . . . Believe me, one of the best things that could happen to Northwestern would be for Cass (high school) to burn to the ground. Then our community school would have to educate all of the community's children.[4]

Walkouts are common in many of the black high schools, with recent walkouts at Mackenzie High on the northwest side, and Martin Luther King on the east side (formerly Eastern High). Cleage joined with others in pushing the Northern High walkout in 1967, which eventually saw a black principal replace an elderly Irishman.

Discrimination in Detroit and Michigan education is an acknowledged fact still. Detroit schools, 60 percent black, have considerable overcrowding compared to other schools. The Michigan School Finance Study shows that 53 percent of Detroit elementary schools reported some primary classrooms with more than 35 students, com-pared to 14 percent in other cities. Quality achievement levels in black schools are lower than in white schools. In the Iowa test, Ford High School with only 3.6 percent blacks was at the top; Redford, with 1.3 percent black, second; and Cody, with 4.4 percent black, third. At the bottom of the 21 schools rated in 1965 was Eastern (now MLK), which is 94.1 percent black; next, Northwestern, 88.6 percent black; and third from the bottom, Northern, with 98.4 percent black. As Marvin Tableman, head of the equal opportunity office of the Michigan Board of Education, pointed out: "Even black schools controlled by black people will not make it possible for the needed resources to go into the area. To redress some of the injustice, to provide equal opportunity for blacks, there is needed an unequal allocation of resources. What is coming through from Rev. Cleage and black militancy is compatible with what we are doing. It's a reaction really to the fact in the past, and in the present we are not doing a good job with these youngsters. To develop pride and confidence you have to have successful models, but I don't particularly buy the fact that a total black setting is necessary to transmit this." Tableman's office put out a racial census of Michigan's schools in 1967 which noted that of 1.8 million pupils registered, 1.5 million, or 85.8 percent, were white and 250,609, or 13.7 percent, were black. But of 63,469 classroom teachers, 57,000, or nearly 90 percent, were white, and 5,000, or 8 percent, were black; and of 3,374 principals, nearly 3,300, or 97.3 percent, were white, and 89, or 2.6 percent, were black. Dropout rates were higher with blacks; 15.3 percent of the elementary school population were black, but this was down to 10.2 percent in the high school population.

A survey put out in December 1968 by the Michigan Civil Rights Commission showed that the typical black college student in Michigan is female, older than the white female student, and more likely to drop out. The survey also showed that although blacks make up 9 percent of the population they account for only 4 percent of college enrollment. The MCRC also found that "there are proportionately no more Negroes in higher education than there were in 1960."

The Detroit Board of Education did some surveying of its own following the dramatic Northern High walkout two years ago when white and black churches became "freedom" schools for youths who would not return until they got their demands. The blue-ribbon committee of some 350 citizens found conditions pretty much as Cleage's *Illustrated News* had described them earlier. The report criticized the pass-all-the-students approach as a "disservice" to the black youth, and identified the main problem as "an attitude among most teachers that reflects frustration, despair, and low expectations of students and of themselves." One of the cochairmen of the study, Edward Cushman, executive vice-president of Wayne State University and former American Motors vice-president, concluded, "Our high schools are appallingly inadequate, a disgrace to the community and a tragedy for the thousands of young men and women whom we compel and cajole to sit in them."[5]

The activist Cleage can always be found in the center of a school controversy. One that was particularly heated and dragged on until a federal court in 1965 finally got an agreement of "indefinite adjournment" pending acceptable efforts of desegregation and equalizing opportunities, involved the protest of 300 Sherrill Elementary School parents about efforts of Detroit Board of Education members to redistrict the school, on the border line of two districts, moving it into the lower, closer-to-downtown district from the more affluent west district where it had been. The fight which began in January 1962 when the suit was originally filed, was triggered by a routine announcement by the Sherrill principal, Mr. Kojesky, that "due to overcrowded conditions, all children enrolled in the eighth grade will be transferred to the Clippert school beginning with the new semester." The decision to move the Sherrill school "to the racially mixed and educationally inferior Southwest School district" was made a year previously with notice to Sherrill parents, Cleage argued. The west district was 93 percent white, and the southwest was about half and half, 41 percent black. Said Cleage in one of his first articles on the controversy, in *The Illustrated News:*

The absurdity of the new district boundaries, obviously gerrymandered for the sole purpose of taking

the Sherrill school out of the west district, clearly
reveals the intention of the board of education. Parents correctly interpreted the action as a maneuver to
strengthen the board's policy of racial segregation.[6]

Cleage was named chairman of the Sherrill Parents
Committee, a dissident group of parents who dissociated
themselves from the Sherrill PTA. The group's initiating
of court action brought charges by board member Leonard
Kasle that the suit was "the work of professional pro-
vocateurs." The *Michigan Chronicle,* looking back later in
the year at the Sherrill controversy, noted: "He (Cleage)
more than any other individual, has been identified as the
catalyst which resulted in court action against the board of
education in the Sherrill school dispute."

During the dispute later in 1962 the Citizens' Advisory
Committee on Equal Educational Opportunities issued a
report that had been two years in the making. Among 153
recommendations of the 32-member committee of leading
Detroit citizens was a strong request that a study of
school boundaries be initiated with full appreciation of
ethnic compositions as well as other factors in getting at
roots of unequal education. The school board had not kept
a racial count of pupils before. The report said, in what
Cleage considered a general vindication of his fight at
Sherrill: "While the great traditions of public education in
America have upheld the belief that the inclusion of all
children of varying backgrounds within a school district
strengthens democracy, it is a fact that in the past, school
boundaries in Detroit have been used to further racial and
social class segregation." The report also urged the policy
of "open transfer" of students to other schools that have
the space. Cleage had criticized overcrowding in Detroit
black schools; for instance, he said, black parents at
Northwestern High, which has 3,800 students, 2,100 more
than it was built for, could not transfer to Mackenzie,
"which is only slightly overcrowded." He championed the
mobility of students to schools best equipped to receive
them regardless of race.[7]

Black nationalist and separatist Albert Cleage, back
in 1962, thus came out foursquare for desegregation and

an end to racial discrimination in Detroit's schools. This was similar to his push for removing restrictions against blacks implied in new housing in Springfield, Massachusetts, while heading the NAACP redress committee there. At the time of the Sherrill fight in Detroit he was a member of the desegregation-committed NAACP executive board, and a decade earlier, in 1952, had been chairman of the NAACP Detroit branch membership campaign. He still apparently had a degree of faith in the school system as such, and hope concerning whites, attitudes not totally absent now despite his clear avowal of separatism. He was action-centered, aiming at avoiding the inferiority involved in a lingering "separate but equal" mentality.

He condemned past policies of "establishing Jim Crow districts, Jim Crow curricula, and Jim Crow schools."[8] His "desegregation," however, sounds less on the side of increasing balanced quota enrollments than providing the best quality education for blacks as well as whites, whether it brings the two together or not.

Cleage wrote:

The school report would already be as dead as a dinosaur if it weren't for the Sherrill School Parents' bias suit! No one seems ready, even now, to face the fact that racial segregation and discrimination do exist in the Detroit school system. Neither the board of education nor Mr. (Samuel) Brownell (school superintendent now retired) have issued any public apology for breaking the highest law of the land. Why does everyone try to pretend that the report will automatically correct the injustices which it clearly points out? . . . Have we sunk so low that we accept segregation and discrimination as normal aspects of American life? . . . Idiotic pundits (editorial writers and columnists) throughout the city do not seem to realize that the complete desegregation of the Detroit public school system is the business at hand! The school board should be in sackcloth and ashes until this job is finished. Thank God the Sherrill School Parents will not permit the board to forget its responsibilities.

The school board will either begin desegregation now, or it will desegregate under court order! . . .

One important fact which the dailies have deliberately ignored, is the fact that Detroit must stop its segregated construction program immediately. . . . All new schools must be built to serve an integrated student body. Sites not so located will have to be used for parks and play fields. . . . The board must stop the building program at once, and undertake a comprehensive reevaluation of all proposed building sites in the light of whether or not they contribute to desegregation.[9]

Cleage was often personal in his charges. Besides incessantly asking for school superintendent Samuel Brownell to step aside (he did, at age 67, in 1967, after ten years as superintendent), Cleage directed much of his ire toward board member Remus Robinson. Back in 1962, Cleage wrote a cover article in his *Illustrated News* on "The Strange Role of Dr. Remus Robinson on the School Board" in a series on "Our Leaders." Cleage said:

Even if Dr. Robinson was completely ignorant of what was going on in the Detroit schools — and even if he dismissed the Sherrill Parents as liars, and the Negro community as overly sensitive, what has he said in protest since he read the (Citizens' Advisory Committee on Equal Education Opportunities) report? Nothing — nothing at all. Obviously Dr. Robinson does not represent the Negro community which elected him to office. Now that he knows that he is responsible for racial segregation and discrimination, he is still reluctant to act.[10]

The attacks on Robinson angered a number of prominent black leaders and they conducted their own boycott of Cleage. Ramon Scruggs and Damon Keith — then an attorney and now United States district judge — withdrew from a panel in which they were to appear with Cleage to discuss "Is There Equality in Detroit Public Schools?" at a Booker T. Washington Business Association luncheon club. In a letter to the chairman of the association's program committee, the two said they were refusing to come because of "the unwarranted attacks" by the Rev. Mr. Cleage on Dr. Remus Robinson, member of the board of education and the NAACP, among other reasons. Both men had been on the Citizens' Advisory Committee on Equal Education. The two said they did not want to involve the committee's report on inequities in the Detroit school system "by taking part in an atmosphere of irresponsibility and a program that would divide the community."

Cleage, who later developed the knack of bowing out of panels himself at the last minute with or without notice, told the packed luncheon hall that his criticism of certain people and groups was a result of his different idea of leadership. "The totality of discrimination in the city of Detroit has generated a sickness of frustration, anger, and hatred among Negroes," he said. And the "sickness" was a result of Negro leadership that had become accustomed to "pussyfooting" with discrimination. He also ruffled his business and professional audience a bit by suggesting they be concerned with the total problem of discrimination and not just as it related to their own professions.[11]

"His (Cleage's) goals, I don't necessarily share," Remus Robinson said in the fall of 1968, at his desk in his white doctor's smock. "Progress in a community is made by those who make extreme demands," and also set back by such people, he said. "Demands," he said, in understatement, "ought to be framed in the area of reason, and I am not necessarily referring to Cleage." He added, "Our philosophy of the board of education is not based on someone's evaluation. A citizen has a right to protest and be heard and to demonstrate. When it comes to individual cases of administrative structure, for me to disagree with him (Cleage) would be stupid." Dr. Robinson noted that in 1968 there were 4,000 black teachers out of 12,000. "When I was first on the board in 1955 there were less than 600 out of 8,000." He also noted that quality education takes time, and experience is needed to develop principals and administrators, "and we have done reasonably well."

Cleage has continued to strike sparks in his approach to

the schools. "The crisis in Detroit's inner-city schools is fast approaching the dimensions of a forest fire," said the *Michigan Chronicle,* in a headline article on "Student Crises Hit Inner-city Schools."[12] Post Junior High was hung up on a controversy whether gunfire was used against student demonstrators and clubs against clergy, parents, teachers, and others. At Pershing High, whites refused to accept the democratically constituted black student government; Winterhalter school forestalled a shutdown when seventh- and eighth-graders were organized into a negotiating committee; Marcy and Stephens Elementary School parents were organized to seek ouster of white administrators.

Cleage fired off telegrams demanding black administrators for the troubled schools to Detroit school superintendent Norman Drachler — who as a former associate superintendent had also been superintendent of the religious school of Detroit's Temple Beth El. He wired Mayor Cavanagh and the police commissioner calling for an end to "storm trooper" tactics and a suspension of police officers allegedly involved in firearms and beating incidents at Post Junior High. Cleage also asked the Department of Health to inspect existing school lunchrooms in the inner city and issue its findings. Failure of the mayor or police commissioner to act, he said, "can only be construed as encouragement of police efforts to provoke America's first winter rebellion."[13]

Later in September 1968 Cleage and his Inner-city Parents' Council went after Maurice Lax, principal of the Field Elementary School, and Lax was soon moved to the Edison school in the northwest outskirts of Detroit as a result of Cleage's efforts. Lax, however, leveled a sharp blast at Cleage et al. He called Cleage's Inner-city Parents' Council, which had caused his ouster, "a self-centered and power-seeking group of malcontents." Lax also had worked with the Neighborhood Education Center project, involving six inner-city schools. The Cleage parents' group charged that Lax was moved from an earlier post to Field because of "his inability to work with inner-city parents and children" and asked "that he be transferred completely out of the black community."[14] In his own defense, Lax elaborated further in a full statement in the *Chronicle* aimed at clarifying his views and repeated his charges:

Unfortunately the irresponsible efforts of a self-centered and power-seeking group of malcontents have negated my work of a quarter of a century. I have always been personally, professionally, and financially involved in the support of all programs which are designed toward the achievement of equal recognition, both socially and educationally, for all minority groups—regardless of their origin or creed. This group of dissidents under the aegis of Mrs. (Katherine) Kelley and the Rev. Cleage has succeeded in removing me from the NEC project. Teachers, children, and the immediate community were not consulted in this situation.[15]

The author of the original headline piece in the *Chronicle* on the Lax-Cleage tête-à-tête, C. C. Douglas, commented in his own "People, Places, and Situations":

George Atkins, president of the Hutchins Junior School PTA, says that those reports that Maurice Lax was pressured out of his inner-city principalship primarily by Rev. Albert Cleage's Inner-city Parents' Council are not quite right. Atkins contends that, despite Lax's statement that "most of the community" wanted him to stay, parents' groups from at least three schools—Goldberg, Hutchins, and Field—sought Lax's removal.[16]

Cleage in his *Michigan Chronicle* column made his own response to Dr. Lax's statement: "Stupid racism is not confined to white politicians. A white so-called educator, a white principal who has been kicked out of a black inner-city school, blasted the Inner-city Parents' Council for demanding his removal. He felt that the fact that he had been in the black inner city for all of his professional career entitled him to continue to miseducate black children. Check all of the black schools he has served and you will find a dismal record of failure—his failure. He has failed to raise the achievement level of black children.

"In every school in which he has taught, black children are two, three, and four grades below grade level. This was reason enough to move Dr. Maurice Lax out of the black community. He failed. Why should black children be crippled by his continued presence in a black school? Why can't white teachers, principals, and administrators understand that we don't want them in our inner-city black schools? They cannot motivate and teach our black children. They are symbols of the very white power we are struggling to force out of our black communities."

Crediting the "sensitivity" of Superintendent Norman Drachler "to the realities of the situation," Cleage said a city-wide boycott was averted. Continuing his personal attack on Lax, in the 1968 election year in his column that had started off with a discussion of George Wallace, Cleage said: "Dr. Maurice Lax is much like George Wallace. Neither recognizes the fact that he is sitting on a volcano. Out of their ignorance they posture and make foolish statements which evidence no capacity to touch base with reality."[17]

By the end of 1968 Cleage was caught up with what he called the emerging big school issue of 1969, the community school. This issue received national attention in the strike of New York teachers when they defended teacher seniority and other rights in experimental neighborhood-controlled school programs such as Ocean Hill-Brownsville in Brooklyn, which used personnel not approved by the United Federation of Teachers. Cleage no longer talked of intregration of schools and re-mapping boundaries as he had in 1962, when even then "integration" with him was couched in latent black nationalist militancy which sought new gains for blacks.

Why he is disenchanted with even using the word integration in regard to schools now is evident in his column dealing with community schools: "I have been pointing out the failure of the Detroit schools for more than ten years. The schools have systematically failed to educate black children. All of these facts explain the growing na-

tionwide demand for 'community control of schools.'"[18]
He outlined his recommendation:

> In Detroit it would seem that we ought to keep one
> school district, one tax base, and our present central
> board of education responsible for the general ad-
> ministration of the entire system. In addition to this
> central board, we ought to have local governing boards
> for each high school constellation. The election of
> these local boards could follow the basic pattern set
> by the Ocean Hill-Brownsville experiment, with
> seven parents elected from seven areas. The seven
> elected parents would then choose five community
> leaders for inclusion on the board. Four teachers and
> two principals would also be selected by their col-
> leagues in the constellation to serve on the board.[19]

High on the agenda of the Detroit Board of Education in
1969 was an examination of ways to decentralize the
schools with "promise" of some action.

Cleage has come full cycle in regard to school millage.
Back in 1963, he was cast as a "madman" and a member
of the "lunatic" fringe for opposing an increase of school
millage for Detroit. Cleage's reason for opposing a millage
vote then was his profound dislike of Superintendent
Samuel Brownell and what Cleage considered a system
which protected and developed white schools at the ex-
pense of inner-city schools. The full wrath of the Negro
Chronicle in 1962 was poured on Cleage and others for
opposing a millage increase:

> In voting on the millage porposal, we must decide
> whether we will follow in the paths of destruction and
> chaos of Negro and white extremists . . . or take the
> sunlit path toward a brighter tomorrow for our young
> people.
> By voting against the millage, we are automatically
> casting our lot with the lunatic fringe. . . .
> We cannot afford to sacrifice the future of our
> young by following the foolish counsel of the rad-
> ical elements in our midst. . . .

The philosophy of . . . progress is one of positive and constructive action. Those who advocate anything to the contrary constitute a minority of radicals who are our misguided madmen. Let us not heed their counsel on the millage or any other issue.[20]

In 1968 a millage increase (which lost) would have gone to helping build a new Northwestern High, Cleage's alma mater. Cleage anticipated a possible white backlash in the vote and the defeat of the measure because "white folks are very much disturbed about the dollars and cents cost of the new Northwestern High School." The new 9.2 million-dollar school approved finally for construction bids by the board of education in 1968 will have an extra 26,000 feet of space for a performing arts center, which school officials predict will be "the best in the state." The school is one of the most expensive to be built in Michigan. "This seems strange to white people who can remember that just a few years ago Dr. Samuel Brownell could boast that the new McGraw school (in the inner city) was the cheapest school ever built in terms of cost per foot. This kind of white racism will be reflected in a large white vote against school millage."

Cleage's turnabout in support of millage in 1968 in contrast to his 1963 negative position came, he said, because of his confidence in Drachler, "who is at least trying to bring the Detroit school system out of the Middle Ages." Also, "Today's situation makes it important for black people to support school millage. In a very few years, the entire city, including the school system, will be under black control."[21]

The year 1969 found Cleage in the thick of the boiling pot of school controversies. Two articles on the front page of the *Michigan Chronicle*, March 29, 1969, were headlined: "Cleage Column Garbage, Claims Ass't Principal" and "Miller Jr. Teacher Rips the Rev. Cleage." In the first case, Cleage had charged the assistant principal who was involved in a scuffle at the Miller Junior High School as unfit, and suggested he be replaced by a "sympathetic, intelligent, black educator." The second article, a front-page letter, came from a Miller Junior High teacher who invited Cleage to leave his "luxurious abode" and visit her class any day unannounced to see that it wasn't rat-infested and also to ascertain the great number of black-orientated studies. "Mr. Cleage, as usual, spreads vitrolic condemnation based upon half-truths, surmises, piecemeal information, and downright lies concerning his descriptions of the conditions at Miller Junior High School," she said.

In his sermon the following Sunday, with his crowds beginning to pick up a little again (with daishikis, about a dozen, more in evidence than previous recent Sundays), he alluded to plans to sue him for slander. "But they can sue me for all I got, which is nothing, and I will not apologize. They may be serious enough to do so, but it's stupidity. . . . We're going to run the schools the way we want them run." He supported a bill by James Del Rio in the state legislature to split up control of the Detroit school system into districts, and denounced positions of both Detroit dailies—the one opposing naming of the McMichael Junior High as Malcolm X Junior High and Northwestern as Malcolm X High School—"Who are they to tell us they don't know enough about Malcolm X yet to name a school for him? We know enough about him, and that is the name of the school now whether the board passes it or not" (white board members rejected the name; two of three blacks, one of them Perdue, voted for it). The other paper, he denounced for putting "protection" and "security" as the number-one school problem in Detroit's troubled schools, which included a stabbing in the Butzel Junior High. "Education of black children is the number-one problem!" shouted Pastor Cleage in his pulpit. "We are in black America!" The congregation burst into applause.

CHAPTER 6

Neorealism vs. Hope

It was nearly 1:00 A.M. on Thanksgiving morning 1968 in Cleage's sky-rise apartment, after nearly four hours of talk, that I got around to the question Cleage has to answer in every panel and every interview: Just what does he see for the long-range future of race relations in the United States? Is there a possibility of hope, or is the outlook wholly nihilistic?

Cleage had mentioned in his sermon the previous Thanksgiving Sunday, in between thanking God for discontent and denouncing what he considers the outmoded integrationist NAACP leadership, that in New York where he had been the week before on radio and TV shows reporters "were always asking about violence and always wanted someone to repudiate Rap Brown. They were almost a-beggin' on their face" — this brought an "Amen." "They (reporters) always end up asking if Eldridge Cleaver is hurting your cause. He's not hurting my cause, but hurting their cause. They'd felt better, yeah . . . if the Black Panthers quit. They (whites) are afraid but do not know what to do. They say it for you, 'ain't that right?' and you know it's not right."

My interest in posing the question was to determine (1) to what extent hope or some condition of brotherly love on a jointly participating basis could be correlated with his present themes, and (2) to what extent his mind has changed or developed on this question.

I had noticed an evolution in his response to the question over the past year, going from a near-nihilistic viewpoint (largely because he'd ignore the attempts to pin him down in eschatology) with a "there's some room for optimism" attitude, but "in reality you can't expect anything good with human nature (read 'white man')." From such very vague responses on earlier occasions he seemed now to move toward a greater optimism, and if not optimism, a greater precision.

I cited for Cleage two instances where there seemed to be some evolution or contrast in this area of "hope" in his utterances before groups. One was at Madonna College, Livonia, before a classroom of Felician nuns and novices and several outsiders, among them myself. Moderator was Mrs. Ed Davis, wife of the first black Chrysler-Plymouth dealer in Detroit. She made Cleage a little ill at ease in the classroom by calling him Toddy, his nickname since he was a toddler (they dated way back, in college). Fellow-panelist was the Rev. James Chambers, tall, distinguished black member of the Detroit Housing Commission and pastor of the integrated St. John's Presbyterian Church that recently relocated from a dilapidated building into new half-million-dollar quarters in the Lafayette Park, part of the landscape under Cleage's twelfth-story apartment. (Chambers has since quit the ministry and become a minority affairs officer director for Parke Davis.)

"I am an incurable optimist. Unfortunately Cleage doesn't disturb me, " said Mrs. Davis, the former girlfriend.

"I am pessimistic only in the framework of white liberal thought," said Cleage. "I don't expect a solution in that. I am optimistic of what blacks are going to do. . . . You feel dejected because you like to tell us what to do." This was a direct reference to a member of the audience, Frank Kowal, head of a grinding firm that hires blacks and who himself, he said, had been involved in civil rights demonstrations in the South. Angrily, Kowal stood up and told Cleage before the nuns that Cleage had shattered all the hopes of liberals and to "speak five minutes, so we can go home."

Said Cleage, "If the liberals feel let down, it means they are mixed up in their own minds. . . . When you get to the point of accepting us, then we can be optimistic together, and talk together. Then there can be diplomatic relations. Consider a child smothered with love. White people think we are children. That is why they say, 'Child' — be as you are, work in terms of reality. The only pessimism I have is in our relationship to white folk."

Earlier that evening Cleage had said the eyeball to eyeball type of relationship between blacks and whites is "discouraging for many blacks and whites," which introduces a note of empathy into his remarks. Empathy — suffering with and for another — is a twin of hope. But he added in his usual exasperation, "We will not change. White people apparently will not change. So there is no course, it seems, but violence."

Said one nun, "I could accept Cleage's belief if he didn't rule out the impossible; if he does, then we are meeting in vain." Chambers, strong on integration, finally exploded as Mrs. Davis turned to him and said, "I know we can't compete with a celebrity like Rev. Cleage, but would you ask us a question too?" Said Chambers, "I totally disavow the separatism of my colleague as impractical, impossible, and unworkable. To say no change is possible is to disavow all the basis of education, and that one can change. Remember 1954 (school-desegregation ruling) reversed 1896 (separate-but-equal ruling). It (the 1954 ruling) gave us a sanction in which we can build," continued Chambers. "When you say, give us our black community, what is it? When you have Twelfth Street, what do you have? I conceive of myself as a man. And I always have pride and conceive of myself as an individual. We need to elevate ourselves into being a man . . . why not take our differences and make them positive? I disavow building a black ghetto to have dignity."

Cleage made some remark that "Twelfth Street is all that we have" to explain why he wants to build a Black Power community there; then trying to restrain himself, he said, "I know what you want to hear, and Rev. Chambers is more gifted in saying what you (white folk) want to hear." There were some rumblings from the lecture-room audience of "unfair." Continued Cleage, "You applaud at the most naïve statement . . . you want to believe it. Blacks shout on Sunday, and I (also) hope in some way in what you are doing. I don't criticize (your interracial discussions). God bless you."

Following the interruption by Mr. Kowal, the only other male—besides Cleage's bodyguard—in the audience, Cleage said, "If you came just to feel good, I would preach salvation. Most white liberals, not you (with irony in his voice), work for Negroes, but participate in segregation. Democrats are liberal but don't give jobs; there are liberal white churches, but there is no powerful black in any church, for they are structured to keep blacks in place. . . . I am not here to make you feel good. For 400 years you have made me feel bad . . . nothing tangible is being done in the United States . . . no force, church, or otherwise, is realistically trying to change. . . . Twelfth Street is important to me . . . we are going to control it, just as whites control their communities."

MRS. DAVIS: This gap is frightening.

CHAMBERS: I do agree we need to speak from a position of power, but do we do it to look like a threat, or do it to look like we are willing to cooperate? The genius of the Negro community is not extremism. I don't think the black community is going to commit suicide. I believe in Black Power based on unity for all. Here (in Cleage) is an inverted racism, that my pride is not based on myself and my dignity as a person but on our situation. . . . We must speak from solidarity. Much of what Cleage says holds water; but the trouble with Cleage, Stokely, and other militants is they threaten the daylights out of every white man and woman, so we cannot communicate, and this therefore creates a gap.

A bit disturbed that her meeting was more lively than she had bargained for, Mrs. Davis said finally, "I know why we got hot and bothered tonight. Sister Danatha (the school's president), you forgot to pray!"

I chatted with jolly, elderly Sister Danatha, C.S.S.F., afterward. She said she had prayed on Monday night, during an earlier program. "I thought my prayer was strong enough for the rest of the nights," she laughed. On Cleage and Chambers, "I love both of them." Many of the young nuns had difficulty with Cleage's remarks, despite a certain openness on his part, evident in his empathy, in his failure explicitly to write off the future, and in the fact that his pessimism was only relative and not final.

The only black sister present commented to me afterward, "I like Cleage. He says something. There is a magnitude, essentially something. Cleage is the more terrifying man (than Chambers) but it is sometimes necessary to say what he (Cleage) says."

Cleage's language turned more precisely to underscoring hope in an interchange with city officials from around the nation at a panel on "Working with Militant Minorities." This was at the 54th Annual Conference of the International City Managers' Association in the Statler Hilton in Detroit on October 21, 1968. The significant part of that meeting to one who has been making a point of trying to understand Cleage, without getting hung up on reporting just his rhetoric of revolution in fragments, is the change of language concerning hope.

Here's how the dialogue went, as a white city manager finally got around to asking "the question":

GIFFORD MILLER *(city manager, Monrovia, California):* We are on the path of two separate societies—personally, I feel this is wrong. Rev. Cleage, how do we get back a fully integrated society?

CLEAGE: We were never on this path—never on the path of integration. The closest integration we had was in slave days; everybody slept together. Black militant separation is a separation which the white man created. If the black man can go back to the old situation of exploitation, we will never go forward.

MILLER: We should go on to a united society—if we go the way you go, we go the way of a separate society. . . .

CLEAGE: You speak in ideal terms, but we should speak in real terms. All we do is in separation. We can use separate, Black Power, or let exploitation continue. We have to go through a period of development of power if we are ever to move beyond the period of separation. *(He continued talking — of Irish, Polish, Italian power blocks that accomplished aims of immigrant groups in the past.)* The Poles are still separate in Hamtramck (Detroit inner-city Polish area). Today whites do not want integration. Whites must make integration possible. With Wallace (George, who caused a disturbance with his campaigning in Detroit) it (integration) seems off at least 100 years. Blacks must utilize the separate existence for their benefit.

QUESTION: So you say it is necessary, separation?

CLEAGE: With white man as he is today, it is the only possible step.

RICHARD SEXTON *(Dundin, Florida):* You're the first intelligent (militant) I've heard; if whites heard you, there would be more understanding.

CLEAGE *(after praising a summer Project Hope program of the Archdiocese of Detroit that set up forums, TV programs, and house-discussion groups to make suburbanites conscious of their own role in creating racism and a divided society):* It is my judgment that it would be helpful if more whites could hear, but most whites are incapable of comprehending what black militants talk about. The idea of separation is only a realistic appraisal of what exists today.

In this dialogue with city managers and other city government officials, Cleage underscored optimism in his thinking and a willingness to say integration is possible (though not presently achievable). Besides demonstrating empathy and an openness, as he did at Madonna College, Cleage was now saying, as far as I could tell for the first time, that "integration seems at least 100 years off" — white men have been mean to blacks for over 400 years, and integration may be possible in 100 years? This is not the view of a separatist nihilist, but of a man who tolerates, if not espouses, hope along with all of mankind.

So, I asked Cleage in the late-hour discussion in his apartment if the more precise terminology concerning hope in his public appearances meant anything.

"There's been a little development," he said, hesitating,

not quite knowing how to put it. "They (whites) want a timetable. At this stage, there is a utilization of separatism. White folk put more emphasis on the future (integration). If there is to be integration or what you call it (by this method of separatism), I feel there will always be tension, but not necessarily fight."

"Has your thinking changed in this area?" I said again.

"I am not a great deal more optimistic," he said; "the struggle is as intense. . . ."

"Are you more open (in the area of hope)?" I asked again.

"If black people really get a new self-image, white people have to act differently. So therefore, there is either (1) an increased fear or (2) increased effort to deal realistically. I cannot say in any certainty, which way . . ."

"You were not saying it this way a year ago?"

"Possibly," he said, leaning forward, his hands on his knees, deep in thought. "Right after the rebellion, I might say white people would not do a thing, and there is still a preponderance of such. But at the same time, there is a possibility some whites are moving in another direction. But to blacks, if they sit around and wait, they would be back in slavery."

"Do you see yourself changing?" I asked, still persisting in seeking his full explication of "hope."

"I don't know . . . integration is so far off. I don't see a difference myself, but the emphasis might be a difference in the way of stating it. I still see whites and blacks involved in power struggles. The nature of it can shift and not need the crudity of it. It can take on a slight sophistication (rather than rebellion). It can be different, but also can degenerate, in an illusion of power, like in New York (the Ocean Hill—Brownsville community-controlled school battle with the teachers' union), and chaos. Yet the community didn't burn down Harlem. . . . Whites have developed methods of dealing with the new black image. They move within a calculated framework. There are efforts to contain belligerence; therefore they have to offer something. Before, nothing was offered. Now a little is offered. Much depends if the black militant can develop some sophistication concerning whites (by forcing them to respond to the new power of blacks by confused infighting and indecision of their own). Wallace was a dinosaur come out of the woods; he hurt the white racist who is trying to be more sophisticated."

Cleage is talking as are other leaders (Ron Karenga, Leroi Jones, and others) about unity of blacks. Though he has seen attempts at structured, federated unity of black groups fall apart, he nevertheless is now declaring "there is a growing sense of unity" despite differences, which is significant, for what "can be" can also be "hoped."

In Cleage's philosophy of the moment add to "openness," "empathy," a growing sense of "sophistication," and "unity." It all adds up to hope—whether you color hope white, thinking white people can change; or black, thinking Black Power will achieve a new creative and constructive power that results in equalization of opportunity; or a bright color for hope, growing out of rebellion; or a loyalist, traditionalist blue, a favorite color of Cleage's—he drives a blue Chevy Biscayne and one of his favorite pictures, a Copuletti painting, has mostly blue sky and people tripping off into a horizon of hope.

Cleage is essentially a realist—a word, if he had his way, he would likely use to replace "militant." "Black realism would be a term we could use," he said. "Get a realistic evaluation, then work within a framework of reality, rather than in a dream world. Dreaming is great, but you can't do much in programming with it."

In an earlier discussion I asked Cleage if he were advocating a sort of secular mysticism of "ascensus" through his talk of a progression of blacks through (1) black consciousness, (2) black pride and rediscovery of the black past, (3) unity of blacks, (4) self-determination for blacks. "The Eastern religions progress to nothingness and seek to escape from the problems of life. This is quite different. We progress in pragmatic terms to complete realism. If we do not use the term black nationalism, then we would use the term black realism. Martin Luther King's 'I Have a Dream' is beautiful, but it is nonrealistic. There must be realism in facing problems as they are—not as they will be or were."

Ron Karenga, head of US, a coalition of blacks in Los Angeles, praises Cleage for his ability to use the things at hand. "He is one of the best community organizers on the scene," Karenga told me at the annual meeting of the National Committee of Black Churchmen in St. Louis. "Cleage uses the church, and the special power it has, to do the job." Karenga's thesis is that "reality does not exist where you want it to, but where it is" – precisely Cleage's own philosophy.

This realism has permitted Cleage to use many methods, and to espouse viewpoints and techniques which change with the times. On the one hand, despite his feelings about Dr. King at the time of King's death, Cleage back in 1963 was a director of the "Walk to Freedom" with Dr. King in Detroit on Sunday, June 23, 1963. On a later occasion, as times changed, Cleage's Federation of Self-Determination, of which he was chairman, took a less popular approach and used the "People's Tribunal" approach, distasteful to many because of its association with Bertrand Russell, Jean-Paul Sartre, and others who conducted a "people's tribunal" in Sweden to get across their indictment of America's war policies. On August 30, 1968 Cleage's "kangaroo court," as a newspaper called it (thus bringing up the nasty images of Fidel Castro's summary trials), found four persons guilty in absentia of "coldly assassinating" three Detroit blacks at the Algiers Motel annex during the previous month's rebellion (the incident on which John Hershey based his *The Algiers Motel Incident*). The mock trial was held in Cleage's church before a packed sanctuary of more than 1,000, with another 400 listening to proceedings over a loudspeaker in an adjoining room. "If we can't have justice in Detroit, we can't live in Detroit," Cleage said at the trial. "Some of you may think we are playing. When a people decide they want to be free, there ain't nobody can make them slaves no more."[1]

Cleage's espousal of realism is consistent to a large degree with new considerations in the hierarchies of the churches. The World Council of Churches and various denominations, such as the United Church of Christ, have scored "systematic violence" and recognized times when structural violence might be on occasion penetrated by physical violence. The World Council of Churches' World Conference on Church and Society said in 1966:

> As Christians, we are committed to working for the transformation of society. In the past, we have usually done this through quiet efforts at social renewal, working in and through the established institutions according to their rules. Today, a significant number of those who are dedicated to the service of Christ and their neighbor, assume a more radical or revolutionary position. They do not deny the value of tradition, nor of social order, but they are searching for a new strategy by which to bring about basic changes in society without too much delay. It is possible that the tension between these two positions will have an important place in the life of the Christian community for some time to come. At the present moment, it is important for us to recognize that this radical position has a solid foundation in Christian tradition and should have its rightful place in the life of the church and in the ongoing discussion of social responsibility.[2]

Said the Board for World Ministries of the UCC in a manifesto released in 1967 jointly with the UCC Council for Christian Action: "Believers in a prophetic religious faith must discern the will of the God of justice who is himself active in the very midst of the revolutions of the disinherited."[3]

Such things as Cleage's mock tribunal get a boost from the reasoning of Richard Shaull, former Latin American missionary and now professor of ecumenics at Princeton Theological Seminary. Shaull wrote:

> Those of us who function in terms of political realism might well take a new look at the role played by moral outrage in the initial stages of a revolutionary struggle. Was it not an important factor in the early development of the civil rights movement as well as in the opposition to the Vietnam War? Perhaps nothing short of such emotional reaction is capable of

breaking the stagnation and stability of our middle-class complacency and getting us moving.[4]

And a symposium on realism in the August 5, 1968 issue of *Christianity and Crisis* sounded like Cleage talking, particularly the comments of Roger Shinn, dean of instruction and professor of ethics at Union Theological Seminary. Shinn mentioned "a few qualities" of Christian realism that he found important. He said:

Realism understands power, especially economic and political but also intellectual and spiritual power. It takes seriously Marx's critique of utopian socialism. When it hears rosy-cheeked coeds talking about guerrilla warfare and sabotage with no notion of what it actually means to destroy another person or who actually has the weapons of destruction, it asks for a cleansing of rhetoric by reality. . . . Realism appreciates the importance of technical issues. It knows that passion without technique cannot build a bridge, an economy, or a social system. It does not despise passion, but it asks passion to go to school with fact. . . . Similarly realism appreciates the political arts.[5]

It might seem Cleage would part ways with Shinn when the latter says finally, "Realism looks at human nature and refuses to divide the world between the good guys and the bad guys." Cleage, of course, stresses the gap in society. But does the dichotomy mean that all who are on one side (blacks) are saints, and all who are on the other (whites) are sinners? What he does is move the pointer of accusation to another group, for are not whites big sinners when they think rather that only blacks are the sinners and criminals? Cleage in reality is saying in good Christian tradition that all men are sinners—and he is going to talk about the white sinners. But his whole concept of organizing for power and working through corporateness, over against depending on gifted individual leaders as blacks did with their pastors and others in the past, recognizes the inadequacies of man—his weaknesses, or sin, if you will, of blacks as well as whites.

It is important to understand Cleage's theological training. In the 30's when he was in seminary at Oberlin, neo-orthodoxy was the *ordre du jour*. Neoorthodoxy was a rediscovery of the old orthodoxy that believed every man was a sinner, and God an omnipotent judge, a *deus abscondus*, a hidden God, who directed man's affairs but was not wholly approachable by man. Karl Barth placed a special emphasis on drawing the faith from the scriptures, and Cleage shows a decided dependence on scripture. Except for the fundamentalists, Cleage is probably the most scriptural preacher in Detroit in the mainline denominations. He never quotes poetry, or literature, or anecdotes from a homiletic collection. He quotes from the Bible and life, in that order.

Cleage was exposed to American neoorthodoxy in Reinhold Niebuhr, a former Detroit pastor who served on a mayor's committee to study race with Cleage's mentor, Donald C. Marsh, Wayne State University sociology professor. He has met with Niebuhr on several occasions. He said, "I read Niebuhr for a time, especially as an antidote to the social gospel. Horace White (pastor at the Plymouth Congregational Church who influenced Cleage) was essentially social gospel, which had little connection with reality. It was too utopian, full of action, but not much realism."

Cleage confesses a continued affinity to neoorthodoxy. "I paid a lot of attention to this, and still think it valid, especially where it talks existentially about where people are." Niebuhr, once a starry-eyed youth, learned his realism as Cleage did in observing oppression in Detroit. Niebuhr's congregation for thirteen years was the Bethel Evangelical Church, a workingman's congregation where he learned firsthand the ends to which industrialists would go to keep the laborer down and out. Niebuhr paid less attention to the omnipotence of God and the Bible than Barth, and dwelled primarily on the sinfulness of man, especially in association in a society. To him original sin was real, in the natural makeup of man, who as an individual could be moral but as a society was inevitably impersonal and immoral. Thus his most famous book, *Moral Man and Im-*

moral Society. Like Cleage, Niebuhr in his heyday was noted for his gloomy outlook on society which he believed more likely to be changed by organized power than by the direct hand of an interfering deity or any of his few saints on earth.

"This is a kind of realism necessary for a revolutionary struggle," said Cleage. "We've got to make sure the definitions of human nature and society are both sound. If they are not sound, then your whole revolution gets off the track. This was the problem of Dr. King. He was not realistic. You can hope for change, but it must be predicated on reality, not what we dream of. It must be based on people — and their nature — rather than dreams. White liberals ought to all go back and read Niebuhr because they react when you say all whites are part of immoral society."

Cleage is also influenced by existential writings, although this emphasis per se developed in American theology after his own seminary days. Cleage liked particularly Jean-Paul Sartre's *No Exit,* a tense drama of three persons trapped in a Louis XIV drawing room, incapable of escaping and creating their own little hells. "This creating hell for each other in *No Exit,*" said Cleage, "is terribly true, though people wish to think something else. It's like an elevator — all get stuck, and they become more and more frightened. The alarm is sounded, and God, the great elevator operator, comes and lets people out. This is absurd, but this is what preachers say. In fact, nobody is really outside to straighten out the situation if people themselves do not do something."

Cleage is aware of some influence from Lutheran Rudolf Bultmann and his demythologizing attempts to bring the three-story-universe terminology of the Bible and medieval Christian faith into modern terms. He also cites Baptist Walter Rauschenbusch, popular theologian in the 20's. "Rauschenbusch emphasized the Old Testament prophets. He related religion to social problems that exist." In psychology, Cleage is influenced by Freud's "dynamic concept of the human mind in terms of subconscious struggle." However, he says he feels more drawn to Freud's disciples, who emphasized the motivating "con-

cept of power" over against Freud's emphasis on sex. "It's
not sex, but a will to power that motivates the subconscious and gives all a desire for power. Much of human
nature is concealed and is beneath water, like an iceberg."
Cleage warned about trying to formulate philosophies of
realism too precisely. "The whole thing can run off and
build a new factory of its own, and it is then no longer
realism."

His daughter Pearl, nineteen, a budding playwright,
pegs her father as a realist. "Some people think he is pessimistic; they don't look at the real situation. They are used
to make-believe. He is very hopeful. He is trying to work
within the framework as things are. He believes in politics,
voting, running a clothing factory, gas station. A whole lot
don't agree with him."

Pearl, a charming person, is light, wears a black-and-
white striped dress, and a tossed coiffure, unlike her sister
Kris's "Afro." "It's a personal choice that I don't have an
Afro," Pearl said. "It takes something to happen in your
mind." She doesn't like to be confused as white, which
invariably happens, and she is going with a black boy-
friend at Howard where she's a drama major. He's a "mi-
crobiology major, a black militant, yeah. A little bit quiet;
he does not go around and make speeches."

There must be hope of attainment to keep anyone going. Cleage says, "You have to believe that there is something you can do about conditions even if it is nothing
more constructive than throwing bricks and Molotov
cocktails."[6] He has a realism more profound than that
of empiricist philosophy or that of hopeless neoorthodoxy,
and more idealism in his realism than Hegel's — or Marx's —
long-suffering dialectic looking toward an ideal society.
Cleage preaches an evolving realism that includes attain-
able goals. There is room for a hope of substance within
his realism. There is little room for a sweeping, inclusive,
rhetorical hope. But which is the greater hope?

CHAPTER 7

Threshold of Fear

The Rev. Albert Cleage has a number of reasons to be afraid.

Other black leaders in the limelight have been dropped summarily by gunfire. First, Malcolm X, Cleage's idol, by blacks on February 18, 1965, while giving a speech in New York, and then Martin Luther King, Jr. by a white gunman. In Detroit, in the summer of 1968, Fred Lyles, chairman of the United Tenants for Collective Action (UTCA), was critically wounded and paralyzed by a .30 caliber bullet from a sniper across the street as Lyles stood in the second-floor window. The assassination of the two Kennedys hardly lessened the fear of one who stood in so controversial a spotlight and whose enemies are legion.

Besides the enemies there is the lunatic fringe who can sneak up on you and suddenly plunge a knife or letter opener into you, as happened to Dr. King during an autographing book session in New York in 1958. "Cleage gets his share of hate letters, some of them threatening," said Oscar Hand, who collects many of these letters mailed to the church address. He went up to Cleage's study and got a fistful of them for me one night. "There are a lot of cranks like those who shot Robert Kennedy and Dr. King," said Oscar. "I pray to God that he takes care of him."

About a quarter of the letters include religious tracts aimed at "converting" Cleage, with strong racial overtones. One of the printed religious items sought to prove from the Bible that blacks are the cursed people on the earth. Two letters were from disgruntled members of a mainline Methodist church in Detroit who said that their church was now in the red because of the blacks around it and in it. Another was from an Episcopalian who condemned all blacks because of a black youth who sat in the balcony one Sunday and used a pellet gun on the members in the front row. About half of the letters were clippings from the *Detroit News,* which gives extra space to crime stories and identifies the alleged criminals by color—most of them black since crime is heaviest in the inner-city ghetto areas. The policy, which was also followed by the now defunct English edition of the Polish American newspaper during the nine-month newspaper strike, has been roundly condemned by various civil rights spokesmen. A blue-ribbon ad hoc group signing an ad in the *Detroit Tribune,* an occasional publication initiated by the Rev. Hubert Locke, head of religious activities at Wayne State University and former administrative assistant to the Detroit police commissioner, condemned the practice of racism in crime reporting and also ran the ad eventually in the *News,* which continued to defend the practice as part of its crusade against crime.

Samples from letters to Cleage: "White police in Detroit should stay out of black neighborhoods. Let the animals fight and kill one another—why bother with them? The nigger will always find something to gripe about." Another: "You black bastard, I hope you get all that is coming to you, nigger. Stay on Linwood where you belong, not with good white folks. Damn blackbird." Another: "With the nationwide revealing that 75 percent of our crime is currently committed by your black race, where in hell do you Negroes get the idea that it is capable to rule?" (from a church tither who once made the "mistake," she said, of letting some of her contributions go to King's group). Another, written on a sympathy card: "Too bad Billy Graham couldn't have talked to you when he was here. Do you ever read the Bible? God preaches love and not hate. Unless you and some of your Rap Browns—Dick Gregorys change, your cause will go back 400 years. There are 20 million blacks, 180 million whites. You are fighting a losing battle. Your head may be off sooner than you think."

Cleage's own incendiary words, as they appear to many, stand, some believe, as an invitation to violence. Rational men are moved to emotion over him; for example, Dr. Elliot Luby, associate director of the Lafayette Clinic, Detroit, who with the aid of a federal grant after the 1967 rebellion studied the "psychology of the Detroit riot." Dr. Luby sought to explain the rebellion in terms of psychological disorders among blacks: "The civil disorder was a symptom of a disordered community; that is, a sick community." The position so incensed Cleage he urged boycotts of Luby's appearances. Luby struck back at Cleage. In a WJR radio interview he argued that the news media should steer away from "extremists, both left and right." He identified Cleage as one such extremist who did not represent the black community. Luby insisted there was "an intensity of fear in both camps. Both white and black people in this city today are terrified of each other. We've heard enough from the angry, violent, extremist people."[1]

Whites continued to be extraordinarily hostile after the rebellion, itching for a chance to shoot a "nigger." Overheard from one white man who lives in Detroit, "If one of those damn niggers dare step across the line (into my neighborhood), I'll shoot him." Such bravado was translated into action in white suburbia when Isaac Jones, first black graduate of Oakland University, out in the country, near Rochester, Michigan, stopped for gas in 1965 and the attendant came out, returned for his gun, and blasted the young social worker to death.

Gun-carrying by whites became a mark of honor. Even a state legislator boasted of having his gun at all times. In the first two months of 1968 Detroit granted 2,511 permits for hand guns; in the first two months of 1967, the number was only 1,288. The number of registered hand guns in Detroit jumped from 4,876 in 1965 to 13,145 in the first eight months of 1968. Warren in January 1968 issued 400 permits, five times more than the same month a year previously. Troy issued 160 a month compared to 20 a month a year earlier. Allen Park went from 5 permits a week to 75 a week. Who wouldn't be scared, especially if one were an angry black spokesman who got angrier and angrier each day as the sense of hostility increased? And suburban bumper stickers said: "You loot, we shoot" and "Warning to Black Power—This Area Protected by Michigan Citizens Militia." At least one leading department store chain carried full-page spreads on where to buy lawn lights, locks, and other special equipment to protect the home. One suburban newspaper declared: "Snipers will travel residential streets sniping on small children. . . . Innocent Negroes will join innocent whites as casualties."

Cleage was invited to be the lead-off speaker of a Sunday Evening Fellowship forum program in the all-white First Baptist Church in white Royal Oak, to the north of Detroit. A church writer on a suburban newspaper found it unbelievable, in a conversation, that a church would be bold enough to face the difficult issues of society head-on. "All the other churches invite the usual PTA speakers!" With some dissent, it had been decided that the actual leaders of the black community, including the leader of the moderates, the Rev. Roy Allen (who at that time had found an unexploded gasoline bomb attached to his door), and the militant, Albert Cleage, would be invited to meet directly with white suburbia in a church program. It was still in the aftermath of the rebellion—though as late as April 1968—in the heat of white-black tension, and during the climax of Cleage's own struggle within the Federation of Self-Determination (see chapter 12). For balance, the mayor of Royal Oak was also scheduled, but he nearly backed out for fear of questions from civil rights workers who live in Royal Oak; and hostile to the whole idea, he agreed to come only if the questions were written. In the fourth session of the Sunday evening series, Royal Oak's most conservative councilman (a woman) gamely came— "I never run from an issue"—after three councilmen had turned down the invitation, to appear with the quiet-mannered but strongly militant Frank Ditto from the *East Side Voice of an Independent Detroit*. Cleage, the biggest fish in the series, was offered $100. Usually in this program the main speakers were given $25 or a high of $50. The forum was regarded as a course on social action; an ecumenical course was also scheduled at the same time. The ecumenical speaker was paid a token $15 for his goodwill.

The whole day of the first of the Sunday evening programs in this black-white confrontation series was a particularly uncomfortable one for the church. Here was to be Cleage, the nasty militant, scheduled in the evening, with the ecumenical course for the same evening dealing with Christian Science, which also did little to appeal to the Bible-study crowd in the church. Moreover, it was youth Sunday; and in the morning, for the first time, a folk music program by visiting Methodist seminarians and their judgments on the Vietnam War and the race scene had the church's conservatives hopping mad. "It wouldn't have been so bad, but all this in one day," said a gentle old-timer. Before the four-week series was over, despite the balance achieved through scheduling the moderate, bland mayor and the conservative commissioner, a dissenting group had been formed which held meetings secretly at first and then in the open. The pastor, who himself had favored more moderate programs, resigned in the fall. The Sunday Evening Fellowship chairman resigned over procedural problems and as a result of efforts in the church to renege on program plans for the next year already approved in the minutes of the church's board of education.

But on the first night of the controversial series the church was packed in anticipation of the coming of the Rev. Albert Cleage, a testimony to the interest of suburbia in him and also to the concern of many in suburbia to pursue issues and understanding instead of buying firearms. A number of plainclothesmen were in the audience, although only one identified himself. No disturbance was anticipated. Present also were some members of Cleage's church and several other blacks.

Just two hours before the meeting, the church and SEF chairman both received separate telegrams from Pastor Cleage, which said: "Phone calls from your area indicate that my appearance in Royal Oak this evening would precipitate racial conflict and disturbances which I do not wish to cause despite the lateness of the hour. I therefore believe that you should make other arrangements for this evening's program. I have tried to reach you (SEF chairman) by phone but find that your phone is unlisted."

Attempts to reach Cleage failed, and the SEF committee at the First Baptist Church, Royal Oak, was in a dither. Too late to cancel the meeting, what does one do? In the audience that had now gathered were officials of the Metropolitan Detroit Council of Churches, including its new head, Robert Kincheloe, priests, and various human relations officials. One suggestion was to put a number of these men on an impromptu panel. The other suggestion, which prevailed, was to read some of Pastor Cleage's columns from the *Michigan Chronicle* and one of his sermons; since the people had come to hear Cleage, it was maintained, they should hear him anyway, in absentia. The several members of Cleage's own church who showed up declined to take part in the readings, as did some white churchmen. However, a number, including Dr. Kincheloe, who did not agree with Cleage, graciously agreed to take part in reading his columns. Cleage later said he had had four or five calls of undetermined origin; he said he did not actually fear for his life, but did not want to be a source of a possible conflict, in light of the calls. "If it is announced that I will come, a number will come; and in a sense, there is a security problem. Most of them who live out there are not crackpots, but are fairly sensible. One lady who called said her husband wouldn't let her go, but she did not identify herself as a church member. It wasn't the kind of thing you consider as dangerous. But it could be another one of those Lobsinger (Donald) operations (extreme right groups) that does not kill anybody but creates confusion. After four or five calls, I figured it was serious, and wondered if it was important enough to do."

Perhaps utmost in Cleage's mind was the fresh memory of the assassination of Dr. King on April 4, 1968 and also of Dr. King's last visit to Detroit in March just before the assassination. King had been the featured speaker at the suburban Grosse Pointe High School in what he termed afterward "one of the best organized protests" in his career. The rally, mainly youthful supporters and their teachers from the ritzy suburb, cheered King on, while minutes apart through nearly the whole rally protesters, from elderly housewives to young white truck drivers, stood to denounce King. The evening began lively enough as 200 precision pickets of the extremist Breakthrough group of Lobsinger's and its youthful college-age brigade, Counterthrust, shouted in step outside the school, "King has to go," with a barrage of anti-King slogans: "King's Klan Meets Tonight," "Martin Lucifer King," "Traitor," "Carrier of Red Plague." A near riot ensued as an equal number of youthful supporters of King who couldn't get into the jammed school pelted the pickets with snowballs. Police had the whole street parallel to the school barracaded. Porch lights burned up and down the streets in the $50,000 to $100,000 homes. That afternoon the school at the "discretion" of the city fathers had been insured for one million dollars.

Inside Grosse Pointe High, Dr. King was introduced by the Rt. Rev. Richard S. Emrich, Episcopal bishop of Michigan and a Grosse Pointer, who said he was an admirer of King's but had questions for him concerning the value of big demonstrations in Washington that paralyzed the city, and concerning King's preoccupation with opposing the war in Vietnam. Presiding was Harry Meserve, minister of the Grosse Pointe Unitarian Church, and editor of a national psychology journal.

The packed auditorium included a wide smattering of nuns, priests, Protestant clergy, and some distinguished Grosse Pointers, such as former Michigan governor G. Mennen Williams. The bulk of the 2,800 were Grosse Pointe High School and other white students who came with the enthusiasm of a football homecoming game.

The carefully planted hecklers throughout the speech of Dr. King rose to holler "traitor" and other epithets. One, who identified himself as a naval technician, in civilian clothes, was invited forward by King. Police had the young man remove his coat before he shouted out his views as King sat down.

"I don't want to hear him, I came to hear King," complained pretty Peggy Colvy, 17, a Grosse Pointe senior, who typified the voice of the groaning crowd in the auditorium-gym. The young man spoke for only about 30 seconds, enough to declare himself a patriot and to denounce King as a traitor.

King returned to the platform, saying he wanted "our boys back too," and declared "the unjust war is tearing up the whole world." Then he proceeded to answer Bishop Emrich. "I appreciate Bishop Emrich's questions, but the two issues cannot be divided. It is absurd for me to work for integrating schools and not be concerned with a world to integrate. I cannot segregate my moral conscience. The war in Vietnam hurts civil rights more than my stand against the war. There is a time when we must take a position that is not safe or politic or popular."

King, when he wasn't being interrupted by hecklers, was interrupted by thundering applause, as wild as any after a touchdown or spectacular basket. The youths needed no cheerleaders.

Rightist leader Don Lobsinger, of Breakthrough and Counterthrust, who was arrested six weeks earlier for interrupting a program on open housing at Ford auditorium (a false bomb was also found on the premises), merely staged a walkout from one corner up front and down the center aisle with one of his aides. He could not have been heard, if he had tried to speak, for the thundering boos and shouts by the youthful crowd. Lobsinger, who normally tries to speak, was apparently avoiding risk of another arrest. He had just been convicted on a year-old charge of breaking up a St. Patrick's Day parade. Once out of the auditorium, demonstrators could not get back in through the doors latched from the inside.

As I followed the protesters to identify them and to keep up with the police side of the rally, I found myself next to a main floor exit of the gym near the rear. Suddenly there was a muffled boom, not quite a bomb, but an explosion. I rushed through the exit right away. Smoke poured from the boys' restroom. Inside, pieces of porcelain had been chipped from one of the toilets by what was thought to be a cherry bomb or firecracker. Plainclothesmen swooped in like an army and sealed off the area. Two boys who were seen laughing when they came out seconds before the explosion in the empty room were taken to police headquarters.

Dr. King in his message that night said, "There are two Americas. One is beautiful whose children grow up in the sunlight of opportunity, and there is another America which instead of wall-to-wall carpeting has wall-to-wall rats and roaches in substandard housing. America is still a racist country and racism stands at the center. The logic of racism is genocide." He said at least Hitler was honest. "Once he (Hitler) accepted something inferior about the Jews, then he paved the way for genocide. If one is not good enough to live next door, to have jobs, to marry his daughter, if this is so, then he says, he is not fit to live."

On occasion, people, including racists, recognized Dr. King easily in Detroit; and I remember once walking with him from the Statler Hotel across the street to Grand Circus Park, and a taxicab came right at him but missed him by a hairbreadth, giving us both quite a scare. He said something, which I don't recall, but his eyes followed the cab intently.

This is the climate which has given Albert Cleage, or at least his followers, reason for concern for his safety. There is always fear from within. Dramatizing this to Cleage was the brutal beating of Ed Vaughn, one of Cleage's closest aides, by a fifteen-year-old tough. A tape of an interview with the young man who did the beating, which was not reported to the police, reveals he resented the comparatively mild programs of Vaughn and Cleage as over against buying arms, and the failure of Cleage to make an accounting of his projects to the umbrella Federation of Self-Determination. Cleage actually had no special reason to reveal his expenditures to the larger groups (see chapter 12). The youth, it is also likely, was disgruntled at being dropped from helping in the organizing efforts of the Citywide Citizens' Action Committee (CCAC)—the youth was making about $40 a week.

Cleage's churchmen and followers no doubt are impressed by the necessary but near melodramatic efforts of some of the leading militants who come to Detroit with a small arsenal and army. I remember going one night to an inner-city church that had been turned over to followers of Stokely Carmichael for a rally. I was told by a staffer of the church that whites could get in, which I doubted, but I went anyway. A huge crowd was funneled up the stairs to one of the doors in the array of doors. I figured, as I have done on other occasions, the key places to stand so I would be moved in by the current of the crowd. I was conspicuous in the middle of this Stokely crowd at Redeemer Presbyterian Church, the only white amid the tiger skins and African spears. Really the people were very friendly and for the most part, it seemed by the conversation, they were sophisticated schoolteachers. Once inside the door, where each person was being searched for weapons before he could enter the church, I was stopped, as I expected, and told to go out the other door. "Why?" I asked. "I was told I could get in." Answer: "Man, you are the wrong color." At the side entrance to the church two of Stokely's militia with M-1 rifles stood, scanning carefully a stretch of open windows of apartments in a high-rise business building. Stokely arrived, his car right next to the door, and dashed in. A duck pacing a formation high in the sky would not have been harder to hit.

Cleage's own personal body guard, Beverly Williamson, a young very black black, with a pleasant manner, is unarmed, according to answers I got from him and members in the Shrine's security committee, which has a subcommittee of five guards who are also sometimes called in to accompany Cleage to rallies. Possibly several blacks who showed up at the First Baptist Church, Royal Oak, for Cleage's scheduled but suddenly canceled appearance were members of this committee. One that evening said he was leaving when he found that Cleage was not coming. The general security committee, which has a dozen active members but which has about forty others it can call on, is also concerned with the "security" of the church, which has had considerable vandalism damage and now has steel grates over the windows and a massive metal door, kept locked during the week. You don't enter that door unless Beverly Williamson, trim, six-foot, muscular fellow, convicted of larceny of property from an auto in 1966 and put on probation, lets you in.

Williamson sits up front during each church service, to Cleage's right beneath the rostrum. Usually in a plain black daishiki that could almost pass as a short-length choir robe, he stares into the faces of the congregation, ready to warn and to shield Cleage if trouble develops. There would be little reason for him to be armed, for any assassin could possibly be handled by usher members of the security committee if he moved forward or sought an escape. Several other strongly built fellows in daishikis are in the front pews and have other jobs such as taping the service.

A good reason for being unarmed is the event of other turmoil and emergency measures that might be clamped on the city. In the 1967 Mardi Gras, as maverick Irishman McIntyre calls it, police with drawn guns came into the church at 4:00 P.M., five hours before any curfew, and ordered out several ladies and Cleage's cousin, Dave Cleage, as they were setting up food distribution services. The church members cleared out, Dave Cleage recalls, as the police closed down the church and plans for relief measures; the police also demanded an explanation for the cars out front. All were accounted for except a new red Buick. Police came back, Dave Cleage said, with a crowbar and smashed open the new car, but found nothing. Obviously a man bearing arms in Cleage's church who might be seen by a policeman or another bearing arms could cause a shoot-out, or an accusation of armed assault.

In his book *The Black Messiah* Cleage seems aware of if not preoccupied at times with the possibility of assassination. In that book he says:

> —Some of us, if need be, must die. Anytime we forget that we must be willing to die, the Nation is through. Because anybody can oppress us if we're afraid to die.[2]
> —Now Rap Brown is doing a tremendous thing. I think we have to keep him alive just as long as we can.[3]

—We had a meeting the other night, and Brother Dowdell warned, "You know, Rev. Cleage can't live forever." I'm very conscious of that. We must start getting young men ready now.[4]

—They'll try to stop you, just like they did Jesus.[5]

—(Black) people . . . killed Jesus. Not the white gentiles, but his own black people.[6]

—If he (Jesus) had to die, he was willing to die. . . . He preached revolution and black nationalism all the way to Jerusalem.[7]

—We'll do everything possible to keep you alive because you have to carry on the Nation when we're gone. And everything we are doing is for you. We don't want to give you nightmares, but you can't live like a plantation child because we have seen the Promised Land.[8]

—This too-young-to-die worry that bothers a lot of us, we have got to put out of our minds because we follow a Black Messiah who was willing to die.[9]

On Palm Sunday, March 30, 1969, the whole city was electrified over a shoot-out the night before when one policeman was killed and another badly wounded. Police reports had it that they were fired on by a group of armed blacks outside the New Bethel Baptist Church of the Rev. Cecil Franklin, up the street from Cleage's church on Linwood, near midnight. The wounded officer summoned aid and fire was "returned," police reports said, to blacks in the church. Pews were riddled with multiple bullet marks, and four were wounded in the church. A national meeting of the Republic of New Africa had been held there, and Milton Henry, who makes a point to never stay around after a meeting, had just left by car. In his Palm Sunday sermon, Cleage said he expected the true facts would show police provocation. Some 142 persons were taken to police headquarters, most of them released by the next morning; some whom the police wanted to retain, released by black Recorder's Court Judge George W. Crockett in a 6:00 A.M. session Palm Sunday. Crockett was criticized by most whites, from newspaper editorials and the governor, William Milliken, who supported an investigation, on down; as the air eventually cleared a bit in emotion — if not in facts — Crockett was supported by the state bar association and prestigious Max Fisher, head of the New Detroit Committee, in a bold, courageous endorsement; blacks, and some whites, supported Crockett; whites by and large were anti-Crockett; and Detroit had a polarization between whites and blacks more pronounced than perhaps ever before in the city history. Crockett also cited Wayne County Prosecutor William Cahalan for contempt when Cahalan ordered the arrest of a man released by Crockett.

Cleage, in his sermon, on that Palm Sunday of tension, moved from the mention of the incident, asking prayers for all "our brothers," to citing the continued conditions of slavery as it was in Moses' and Jesus' time. "Palm Sunday might better be called confrontation Sunday. The most holy thing to do is confrontation. The Romans stood around the top edge of the temple court and the people practiced only ritual and talked themselves into saying 'how good it is,'" he said. "When they get together, there's nothing to do but to shoot them up, just as the Romans were ready to 'shoot up' the black Jews. The things that really make for peace were hidden, as the scriptures say. Jerusalem was like a Mardi Gras, all a-shouting and eating hot dogs. The disciples tried to take ritual and talk and turn it into *now* and a program. You know how hard it is to talk to people who don't know what you are talking about. They call you a troublemaker. The disciples just couldn't turn it into a triumphal entry. Here was a little country preacher with disciples hollering and people laughing and joining in the fun. Jesus came for confrontation and wasn't about to call it off. He was like a clown at a Mardi Gras, trying to make a serious speech. There was no triumphal entry. That's Palm Sunday. They laughed." And then Pastor Cleage said, as forces began to persuade the authorities that Jesus was serious, it took only a week to kill him.

Cleage is at his best in style — and at his peak in controversy — when he deals with the subject of an assassination in the events of the day. He remains forthrightly honest, refusing to sing the praises of those martyred if he has not sung their praises in life. Martin Luther King and Robert F. Kennedy were criticized by Cleage right after their deaths, in his sermons and columns. He would have it the same in life as in death, and in death as in life.

I was on hand, on another tense Palm Sunday, and as at other times the only white man in his congregation, when he gave his much publicized sermon on Dr. King—the Palm Sunday of 1968, the day before the funeral. The versions in printed form vary from the more spirited and angry sermon as it was actually given. Cleage speaks from an outline, and tapes each message. He either edits these himself or writes them up anew for printed media—he insists he does his own editing. "He was murdered by a white man," Cleage said of King. In the actual sermon, he added with emphasis, "I ask you to remember that he was murdered by a white man!" This exclamation, not in the book, brought applause.

Other differences between the sermon as delivered and the edited tape version: "Even as you sit in your home scared, aren't you glad that somebody did something about it?" Here he was referring to the wave of rebellions across the United States following King's assassination. Detroit was in a preventative siege and National Guard troops were in evidence outside the church on the sunny spring day. His actual sermon had "we" in place of "you." Says McIntyre, whom Cleage finds amusing, "During the Mardi Gras, they say he sat there at his mother's house with a shotgun over his knees. He is not endowed with a great deal of physical courage." But, really, isn't that more sensible than certain death parading up and down the street with a shotgun during the rebellion?

The past tense is used in the edited version, but Cleage's own use of the present has a sharper ring. The sermon: "Those who break windows are disciples of Dr. King." The book: "Those who broke windows . . ." The sermon: "Black people should recognize he (King) made a contribution." The book: "Dr. King made a genuine contribution." The sermon: "I hope to God some leader" will come out of the black people; the book leaves out the exciting exclamation, and has Cleage pleading for a "leadership."

Another version of the sermon on King's assassination, perhaps not meant to be a version of it but a rewrite, appeared in Cleage's *Michigan Chronicle* column, which he also reprinted with a picture of him with Dr. King. It is more erudite and more reserved. Cleage regards the pulpit, column, and book as "different art forms."

In his sermon on Dr. King—the liveliest version, as it was given amid applause in his own church—Cleage outlined his own philosophy of leadership, a new definition of nonviolence, and a rationale for a form of violence. On leadership: "Sometimes the best leadership is to go off and sit down, and wait till they get through. When they are through, let's see if the white folk have learned, and maybe we will then have a little program, if . . . ."

He talked of people and black nationalism as though they were synonymous. "People want a program. 'Let's march,' they say. Sometimes programs just come up. I trust black people, not black leadership. I hope to God some leader—a leadership out of black people—will take us in the next thirteen years as far as in the past thirteen years. We are a people and a nation set apart. White people can't use his death to make us forget it. We are one people. Let's understand that and build."

On nonviolence: "We are in a material society. You hit a man hard when you tear up his property . . . it's not by accident. . . . If you tear up his property, you are hurting him where he lives. Somebody had to do something. We had to retaliate. We had to let white folk know we don't like it. We say you can't go around and kill black folk. Somebody had to say it. So don't go around and apologize. America is different now because forty cities are in flames."

Cleage described blacks who looted right in the face of police, and in one case, pushed aside two policemen to enter a store window. "The looter wasn't even armed," said Cleage amid applause. "This is exactly what King taught. That is nonviolent protest. The looter is telling them, 'I got to be free, and if you don't like it, do something about it.' Dr. King turned out some strange disciples!"

And further: "Not a thing was won in Albany, Greenwood, or Birmingham in 1963. These were not a victory.

But we were changed. Dr. King in a unique way made possible the confrontation. This is his contribution. Thirteen years after Montgomery, he was killed at the bottom, not the peak of his career. A Black Nation now exists, and he had a part in creating it. He created the confrontation which Malcolm could interpret. We needed both of them." Applause continued for statements such as Cleage's denunciation of white murderers and men he called Toms— Wyatt Walker, Roy Wilkins, and Sammy Davis ("Sammy looked so pious on TV")—and his statement that "if Dr. King's death proves anything, it proves nonviolence will not work in a violent society. He believed in the goodness of white folk and America. There he lies dead. There is no sense making it fancy. He is dead."

Reluctantly, because he said it was "ostentatious," Cleage called on his congregation to join with other blacks to wear black armbands in memory of Dr. King. "We owe a profound tribute to Dr. King, though few of us agreed with his program. But we pay tribute to him because he was a black leader."

In a black unity rally called by Cleage's Citywide Citizens' Action Committee, Saturday, April 20, 1968, at Cobo Hall, he told 2,500 persons:

> I spoke in '63 with Martin Luther King. In '63 we had them hanging from the chandeliers, and all the big white folks up here on the platform. We don't have them hanging from the chandeliers tonight, and we don't have any big white folks on the platform, either. I think I like it better this way. . . . I thought we'd gotten over this integration thing. Then someone killed King and now a lot of folks want to integrate again. I don't understand how they do it. . . . This integration thing is not going to work. If you're waiting for the white man to love you, to reach down and help you, drop dead. As long as you believe in integration, there is no place for you but on your knees. . . . Integration, that was the real question, the real thing at that funeral. It wasn't violence or nonviolence. It was integration or separation. As long as we believe

in integration we are helpless. If we don't believe in anything all black, we are waiting for integration.[10]

When Robert Kennedy was assassinated, Cleage took a position incredible to many—including the readers of the *Chronicle* who protested much in an avalanche of letters, five to one against his position. The new editor of the *Chronicle,* Russell Jackson, told me he was disturbed over Cleage's column on Kennedy, but that he would nevertheless continue to print his columns. Whether one agrees with Cleage or not, the RFK column was excellent rhetoric and had an important message: "I do not pretend to understand the mass hysteria which swept America last week in wake of the senseless assassination of Senator Robert Kennedy in Los Angeles," wrote Cleage. "I cannot even understand why he was killed. He wasn't important enough to kill. He didn't really stand for anything. His record as attorney general was most unimpressive. . . ."

He called the funeral train trip from New York to Washington "a social occasion—an extended cocktail party," and "for most of the mourners, the services at Arlington cemetery were conducted in a kind of rosy glow.

> Perhaps the most important question growing out of the entire national mass hysteria was simply why did black people get caught up in it? Why did black people stand in line for hours to walk by the casket? Why did black people wait for hours to watch white celebrities go into the service at St. Patrick's Cathedral in New York? Why did black people line the tracks from New York to Washington?
>
> He was young, but not as young as Emmet Till, and certainly not as young as the children murdered in the church in Birmingham. More black people cried for Bobby than cried for Emmett Till and for the black children slain in Birmingham. More black people mourned for Bobby than mourned for Medgar Evers, Malcolm X, and Martin Luther King. . . .
>
> More than 50 million black people were killed in the slave trade, millions were killed during slavery, and millions were killed by the Klan during Reconstruc-

tion days. Black people were killed nightly by police brutality in every urban center. America murders thousands of innocent nonwhite people in Vietnam every day. Why, then, did black people participate in the national hysteria following Bobby Kennedy's murder?

Sad as it may be to many of us, the masses of black people still identify with the white oppressor. When they hurt we hurt. Like Brother Malcolm said, the slave comes in and sees his master sick, and asks, "Is we sick, master?"

We do not yet identify "the enemy." I could cry for a thousand years about the violence in America and I would never have the time to shed a tear for Bobby Kennedy because I would be too busy crying for my suffering black brothers and sisters.[11]

Cleage also sheds no tears over what must be certain fears for his own safety. He avoids talking about it, and dislikes mention of his own security churchmen at the Shrine. He did say, "I do not have any fear, but recognize a possibility (of assassination). When you get crackpot letters — how crackpot does one have to be before he shoots? Anyone can shoot anybody. We try to see no one comes into the building. . . . Some members ask at board meetings how we can minimize some crackpot person doing something stupid." Beverly Williamson, who received $2,600 in 1968, but is not included in the budget for 1969 as such (there is still $3,000 allowed for security as in the 1968 budget) is "just security—full-time security." As an added measure, Cleage's window has been grated up to make a throwing of a bomb from the outside difficult. Members point to what is believed to be a bullet hole in the heavy door downstairs.

Concerning the security group: "They are elected by the executive committee of the church, on basis of (1) loyalty and (2) ability to be of some assistance. . . . But if we talk about security, then it is ineffective. The best security is invisible." Detroit Police Commissioner Johannes Spreen says, "Concerning Rev. Albert Cleage, our records fail to disclose that he has ever complained of being threatened or of requesting police attention."

Somehow, one night in New York, in a cab, the question came up about Cleage's safety. He never rides the intricate noisy New York subways on the grounds that he is a seldom visitor in New York and it is too confusing to figure them out, an underscoring in some ways of a certain conservatism in his makeup.

I mentioned that a talk column in the *Detroit Free Press* had mentioned a price on his head of $100,000. Others have guessed in print that there must be $5,000 reward on his head.

I joked, saying that for a much lesser fee somebody could be found to pop either one of us off. Especially a minister, such as he, who reports regularly to regular places at a set time. Cleage remained silent.

Milton Henry put it this way, "Beverly is necessary. After all, Malcolm, look at what happened to him. We do all we can to protect him (Cleage) – he is valuable to the movement; although he is not a separatist, he is very valuable. . . . He used to live on Calvert, and a person could lie on a roof and look right into his house." Cleage has just moved back to a house within three miles of the church, a parsonage in a duplex, as the Shrine budget wore a bit thin and Detroit passed a second quiet summer. He says, "I never did like it (the sky-rise), but I stayed the term of the lease" (one year).

At another time, as I looked out over Detroit from Cleage's then high, secluded apartment, with its locked door, unlisted number, and a doorman standing watch below over an electronically sealed door, I realized that one of Cleage's most profound joys at that time was the knowledge that he could sleep without fear at night in his skyscraper fortress.

CHAPTER 8

Black God, Black Gospel

"If God created man in his own image, what must God look like? I know if you close your eyes, you see a white God. But if God created man in his own image, then we must look at man to see what God looks like. There are black men, there are yellow men, there are red men, and there are a few – a mighty few – white men in the world. If God created man in his own image, then God must be some combination of this black, red, yellow, and white. In no other way could God have created man in his own image."

Cleage goes on to argue, in a style that is a display of satire and humor, his theory of a God best described in nonwhite categories. In his book *The Black Messiah* (also published in Italian and French) he says:

So if we think of God as a person (and we are taught in the Christian religion to think of God as a person, as a personality capable of love, capable of concern, capable of purpose and of action) then God must be a combination of black, yellow, and red with just a little touch of white, and we must think of God as a black God. So all those prayers you've been sending up to a white God have been wasted.[1]

For Cleage any personifications of God himself should be black. Whether a Michelangelo painting that envisions God as an old man, or the configurations of God in the Bible, or the burning bush (at night?), or Jacob wrestling with an angel (with a natural hair style?), or the baptism of Jesus (why a white dove?), each could be reframed or read in some perspective of blackness.

Before considering Cleage's thinking about blackness and the Bible it is perhaps wise to probe what he means by blackness. Were Jesus and the Bible characters as black as the smooth, midnight-mahogany skin of the Zulu or were Jesus and other Semites of his time merely dark-skinned, or tanned, or just "nonwhite"?

Cleage, when asked about his own light skin, admits that there is hardly anyone with a pure racial background, that all, in fact, have some mixture. He said one night, "I speak of 'black' as 'black' – all people of Africa are touched with the Negroid central strain, and are mixed with black Negroid. So when they left Egypt, the Israelites roamed the desert and mixed with the descendants of the Hamites, the black of Cush (Ethiopians) and Midianites (Arabians), who were blacker than the Egyptians."

I pushed the question as to whether black meant black or more inclusively, nonwhite. Is Nasser of Egypt black? I asked. "Nasser," Cleage said, is "mixed with Negroid, and he is more black than Adam Clayton Powell. The Semitic mixed with Negroid, I'd call black. Most Arabs are mixed and have black features, hair – the whole thing. If there are any Negroid characteristics, one is therefore black."

I suppose his thinking can be understood through the analogy of merely mixing colors. Take black and white, not to mention other colors. If you mix white and black, you get gray. The blackness is certainly there in the gray – if you go shades lighter, you will always have a tint, a gray, but never white again. If you go darker you go black. To the extent that races are mixed, the dominant factor in culture if not in genetics, especially in a developing revival of black as beautiful, will be black. Blackness is not lost. "We are all colors. We are mixed up with everything under the sun, but we are all black. Do you know why? Because white people made us like that."[2]

Cleage's mystique and style of generalization also cause him to talk in terms of total blackness ("Israel was pure black," he says), much as the Indian is regarded generally as a red man, whether he is red or not; to speak in general terms of blackness at all to fit an era of history or a people is to speak of blackness as black. To Cleage black is always more than nonwhite.

"All through the Old Testament every people Israel touched was black," said Cleage in an interview in Cleveland. The Jews were black, Cleage said, because "historically you can't find any justification for anything else. Abraham came out of Ur, Moses married an Egyptian — and the Egyptians were black."[3]

Cleage dropped into the pressroom of the Gateway Hotel in St. Louis at the second annual meeting of the National Committee of Black Churchmen and outlined anew his case for Bible blackness. "Abraham married Hagar (an Egyptian), and begat Ishmael, the father of the Ishmaelites.[4]

"Not only did they venture into Egypt — there were friendly relations with Egypt (cf. Genesis 12: 10 ff.). Abraham because of a famine went to Egypt. Once there he was fearful that he would be killed by the Egyptians who are eyeing his wife. He pawns her off as his sister. Pharaoh's special interest in her perhaps as a concubine leads God to send plagues 'because of Sarai, Abram's wife' (Gen. 12: 17).

"Later in bondage, there was intermarriage — you know how this could be, following such a friendly state, it would naturally lead to intermarriage.

"Moses had a black wife who had black children," Cleage said. Fleeing into Midian, Moses took Zipporah as wife. Some Jewish writers in Alexandria speculated that Moses before going to Midian handled Egyptian armies successfully against the much darker Ethiopians, and took an Ethiopian wife. "If Moses could marry and have black children, then others could also. It is a historical fact, that Israel at that time were black Jews all over Africa."

Today there are the Falasha Jews from Abyssinia who regard themselves as

> the true representatives of the house of Judah. This branch of the house of Israel (according to one tradition — another ascribes them as descendants of the Hamites, the name meaning "hot" or "black") is

from Solomon, the son of David, and Sheba, queen of
Ethiopia (2 Chronicles 21: 8). From Menelek the
first (Solomon's son) to Menelek the great, to Haile
Selassie I, are 613 kings in an unbroken strain.
Ethiopia is the true home of the Falasha Jews,
indisputably.[5]

Cleage says much about the blackness of the Egyptian
and refers to studies of the dental school at the University of Michigan concerning Negroid features of early
mummies. Lerone Bennett, Jr., in his *Before the Mayflower*, gives an impressive catalog of discoveries in
Egypt and elsewhere in Africa that tend to underscore
the blackness in the progression of the children of Israel.
He cites finds in the Sudan and Nile Valley which

> prove that peoples of a Negro type were influential
> contributors to that cradle of civilization – Egypt.
> Discoveries at excavations near Khartoum in the
> Sudan and at El Badari on the Nile indicate that Stone
> Age Negroes laid the foundation for much of the
> civilization of the Nile Valley and manufactured
> pottery before pottery was made in the world's
> earliest known city.[6]

Also Bennett notes that Henri Lhote, a French explorer,
found rock paintings in the Sahara which suggest to some
writers such as Basil Davidson that "peoples of a Negro
type were painting men and women with a beautiful and
sensitive realism before 3000 B.C." And:

> – Scholars who examined some 800 skulls of the
> predynastic Egyptians found that at least one third
> of them were definitely Negroid.[7]
> – Herodotus, the Greek historian, visited the
> country some 500 years before Bethlehem. The
> Egyptians, he said, were "black and curly-haired."[8]
> – [The Egyptians] painted themselves in three
> colors: black, reddish-brown, yellow. The color white
> was available to them, but they used it to portray blue-
> eyed, white-skinned foreigners.[9]
> – Ra Neshesi and several other pharaohs have been

identified as Negroes by eminent scholars. So has Queen Nefartari.[10]

— There was prolonged and intimate contact between the dark-skinned Egyptians and the dark-skinned Ethiopians. For fifty centuries or more, they fought, traded and intermarried.[11]

Says Cleage, "Abraham and all got black as they went into Palestine via Egypt. Even Pharaoh was black. They didn't stay apart, but intermarried as Abraham did." I asked Cleage if he went back farther than Abraham to say what color Noah was, for instance. "When you talk of Noah, all you do is to go back to mythology, and the starting of the world," he said. Cleage preaches on Moses and the Exodus, and seeking and winning of the Promised Land more than any other topics, probably says more about Moses than many rabbis. There is a direct parallel with modern bondage of the black, he believes.

In a sermon, September 15, 1968, he said, "I meditated this week on the sojourn of Israel in the desert. Their oppression was like ours. They were filled with hatred, for they desired the power of their oppressors. Moses had difficulty to move people from bondage. It was difficult, for at each step they had to go through steps — steps of organization and education.

"Moses was fashioning a faith. He had his moments of betrayal and faithlessness. Even as they moved out of Egypt, there was great doubt about it all. 'Wouldn't it be better if we stayed?' they said. They were afraid and they had real dangers. The Red Sea and Pharaoh were certainly dangers. They did not have the power of Pharaoh. There was some sense in their wanting to go back; that is, if they really wanted to be a slave. People who fight for freedom don't come together at one time and say this is it, but rather struggle each step. . . . They marched in the wilderness for forty years — they got slavery marked on their heads. 'Take them out and march them,' Moses was told to do. It seemed a harsh thing to do; they had come a long ways. Seems God could have worked out something easier than this."

For Cleage, "the Old Testament is the best Black Power document. Stokely, etc., none come close to it. The Old Testament tells of a group of people who can engage in battle and believe God holds the sun still. If Black Power (advocates) say that today, they get locked up. But in the Bible, they hold up the arms and the slaughter continues. The Old Testament is profoundly significant. It is a religious document without parallel."

Cleage leads into the theme of action and revolution from the analogy of the young fighters in Moses' and Joshua's day to his own day. It is not a philosophy of violence, as such, despite his phraseology, but a philosophy of realism again, where the confrontations are gradual and increase in proportion to the degree of continuance of oppression. In this gradualism as a method of realism, the young have a lot of learning to do, including successful expression of hostility. "The Jews stole and looted in Egypt before they left; but they were afraid, and so they were taken out in the wilderness. . . . How do you teach one to fight? The first time a youngster wanders off the block he will get hand-whipped. You don't learn how to fight, unless you fight. You can't even argue unless you learn by doing. . . . They were in the wilderness, not because they were chicken but because they were out to learn – to learn discipline. Most of the young had learned after a while to fight, and the older ones died. Joshua became a general, but this wasn't where he started as a fighter. The Jews respected their enemies. Sensible people don't have a pitched battle at the outset, unless they try other means."

Cleage's emphasis on the blackness of the Jews gets some raised eyebrows from the Jewish community. I asked Rabbi Arthur J. Lelyveld, of the Fairmount Temple, Cleveland, who was himself severely beaten by white racists during a voter registration drive in the South, what he thought of Cleage's thesis of Jewish blackness. "There are references in the Bible one can cite," he said, "such as Amos 9: 7: 'Are ye not as children of the Ethiopians unto me, O children of Israel? saith the Lord'; and Miriam was cursed and became a leper for criticizing Moses for marrying a Cushite (Numbers 12: 1–16); and in the Song of Songs (1: 5), we find, 'I am black but comely, O ye daughters of Jerusalem.' " Concludes Rabbi Lelyveld: "I am willing to say black is beautiful, but the Bible is generally color-blind." (Rabbi Marc Tanenbaum says also the Bible is color-blind, but "Moses could have been black, and most likely dark with Semitic features.") Concerning the Amos reference, Rabbi Lelyveld said, "Amos was looking for a distinct people to cite from various regions — he also mentioned other regions: 'Have not I brought up Israel out of the land of Egypt? and the Philistines from Caphtor, and the Syrians from Kir' (Amos 9: 7)? God is God of all mankind: he does not mean only black, as he mentions the Ethiopians along with others. Cleage's view doesn't disturb me, but there is not much support for it in history. The passages I pointed out would lose their point if they had their inception in a total black community."

When Rabbi Lelyveld's view was presented to Cleage — that the Bible was not selective in regard to black, but mentions various localities and shows no real color consciousness or preference, he said, "He's right. The children of Israel wandered through Cush and elsewhere. And there was much less consciousness (of color), and so really there was not much to prevent mixture." So, with much less sense of color, the Israelites could intermarry quite extensively with the blacker Africans, even central Africans. "When color consciousness developed," says Cleage, "is when whites went back in the Middle Ages and whitewashed scripture."

Cleage has stayed generally out of the "black anti-Semitism" debate developing mostly after the black-Jewish confrontation in the Ocean Hill-Brownsville school district in Brooklyn. His view is that the tension between blacks and Jews is largely the work of white racists trying to pit the two against each other. However, he has warned: "Black people are going to control the black community. If Jews stand in the way of this Black Revolution, they are going to have every reason to denounce anti-Semitism. If Jews support the Black Revolution, there will be no anti-Semitism!"[12]

For Cleage, whose Jesus is black, a rebel, and a nation-builder, the blackness of Jesus is understood in the same sense as the blackness of Old Testament personalities. And it does not do black militant Cleage too much injustice to read "nonwhite" when he says "black" in reference to Bible people. Note here his attention to nonwhite as he discusses the blackness of Jesus:

> For nearly 500 years the illusion that Jesus was white dominated the world only because white Europeans dominated the world. Now, with the emergence of the nationalist movements of the world's colored majority, the historic truth is finally beginning to emerge – that Jesus was the nonwhite leader of a nonwhite people struggling for national liberation against the rule of a white nation, Rome. The intermingling of the races in Africa and the Mediterranean area is an established fact. The nation Israel was a mixture of Chaldeans, Egyptians, Midianites, Ethiopians, Cushites, Babylonians, and other dark people, all of whom were already mixed with the black people of central Africa. That white Americans continue to insist upon a white Christ in the face of all historical evidence to the contrary and despite the hundreds of shrines to Black Madonnas all over the world, is the crowning demonstration of their white supremacist conviction that all things good and valuable must be white.[13]

It's something to see when the blunt-speaking, generally bland-faced, straightforward Cleage with a certain reputation, if not charisma, stands up before a white group and says that Jesus is black. Cleage does not get hung up on the "black is beautiful" bit – he takes it for granted; Jesus is just black, which must hit many of his white audience in the subconscious pretty hard ("Jesus is a nigger?!").

The Bible blackness of Jesus hit like a bombshell at the U.S. Conference on Church and Society, despite the liberal character of the crowd. The white audience at the Statler ballroom in Detroit, in October 1967, a bit hung up them-

selves in seeking a rationale for violence, especially in
face of systemic and institutional violence and injustice,
was right with Cleage when he described a violent but just
God who "made the sun stand still as the Israelites completed destroying their enemies." But then he was suddenly out with it—Jesus was a black nationalist. "We
preach the same way Jesus preached to the black people of
Israel," whom he again described as descendants of
Abraham "who was a deep tan to start with" and whose
followers roamed all over Africa for years. "Jesus did not
preach universal brotherhood. Jesus told one lady who
asked for help, 'I don't have time for gentiles!' " He rapped
integration as an easy way for whites, and Martin Luther
King for detracting from the real power struggle. "Jesus as
black may be a horrible thought for you," he said, "but
it is a beautiful thought for us. Jesus and his disciples as
black binds us together."

The blackness of Jesus is not a real stumbling block
when you get down to it. "So what if God and Jesus are
black? Who cares?" So says the Rev. Edgar Flood, former
assistant to Cleage at the Shrine. The face of Christ on a
statue of Jesus at the Sacred Heart seminary up the street
from Cleage, was painted black but nobody said much
about it and it is still black, at a busy inner-city inter-
section. Even Polish Catholics in Detroit, often anti-black
along with other immigrant European populations who
find themselves in competition with blacks from the South
for assembly-line and other jobs in auto plants, are con-
ditioned to a Black Madonna. Polish churches hold forth
the black ancient flat icon painting of Mary attributed to
Luke as their most sacred relic. I remember in southern
Poland kneeling (why *stand* conspicuously in the middle
of other kneelers?) before that Black Madonna, with trum-
pets sounding, at the 4:00 P.M. presentation of the gold-
gilded icon of the famous Black Madonna (once pierced
and nearly destroyed by Gustavus Adolphus' Swedish
invaders, who because of the miraculous picture, so
tradition goes, were finally driven off). She's as black as
can be, and there around me at the castle-like shrine on
Jasna Gora, the "Blue Hill," in isolated Czestochowa, amid

some of the most conservative Poles in the world (Stefan Cardinal Wyszynski's fierce traditionalists), all white, people were kneeling to a Black Madonna.

If Cleage's Black Madonna is not so terribly radical as an isolated idea, neither is his strong dependency on Samuel George Frederick Brandon's concept of Jesus as a Zealot. Brandon's book, in its British version, is on Cleage's shelf in his drab church study and he refers to it immediately when asked about books that influenced him. Brandon's *Jesus and the Zealots* (originally published by Manchester University Press where Brandon teaches, and now reissued by Scribner's) is, of course, an updating of sorts of the younger Albert Schweitzer (*The Quest of the Historical Jesus*) at the turn of the century and the work of Ferdinand Christian Baur, Bernhard Weiss, Theodor Zahn, Oscar Holtzmann, Joseph Klausner, Ernest Renan, and others who in some form or other painted Jesus as a rebel and political figure caught in the web of his own rebellion. The views of Jesus as a Zealot are not new, though modern attempts to peg him strictly as a Zealot got hung up in the efforts of the more speculative Dead Sea Scrolls commentators, John Allegro and A. Powell Davies, and others, to make Jesus out as a captive of the Essenes, with some help from the sophisticated writing of Edmund Wilson. Without forcing Jesus into an Essene mold, he is clearly a rebel to anyone who reads the Gospels with any seriousness. A master's thesis which I once did on Schweitzer et al, to explore how their criticism related to the social imperatives of the Gospel of Luke, made a point of the way in which Jesus carefully and deliberately paved the way for his crucifixion through no uncertain challenges to civic and religious authority.

Cleage's emphasis on group action and group salvation is not new. Down through the Christian era great men, some of them heretics, some saints, from Pelagius and Augustine on, talked of the collectivity of man, of cities of man, and of God and a perfect people. Any concept of Christian history takes into account a final eschaton which is more than a judgment of individual merit, which is also a new state, a utopia of some sort, here or out there.

It may be that Cleage's special contribution will be his genius for bringing together some of these never-ending themes, which heresy trials, wars, and reformation have never stamped out—the nonwhite or non-Western qualities of Jesus, his zealous rebel and political spirit, his relevance in a historical context, and the grouping of individuals into various categories—a church, a movement, a belligerent force, or a body politic (Calvin and Geneva), experiencing redemption as a people in a covenant sense like the early Hebrews.

Cleage has involved himself in a new "black theology." Theologians have not really yet discovered black theology, and there are to date no titans of philosophy of religion or theology in this area. But black theology seems bound to be at the least a fad, and at the most a nucleus for a new system of thought, a new realism, a new existential historicism, concerned not so much with establishing theological and philosophical categories of thought as with reevaluating and rediscovering historical "presents" and processes.

Cleage takes a strong historical approach to the scriptures and excises the works of Paul, who Cleage believes had a passion for saving only gentiles (white Greeks and Romans) while keeping the Old Testament, unlike the great exciser Marcion, who kept only the Gospels. Cleage, however, with all of his emphasis on the Bible, can do without even the heart of the New Testament, the Gospels, especially when it comes to doctrinal formulations. He ascribes a late origin to the first-written of the Gospels, Mark, saying Mark "was written at least 70 years after Jesus was dead. During that time, many things happened to the teachings of Jesus. Other Gospels were written, some as much as 130 years after Jesus died." His historicism here is more figurative than exact, for Mark is usually placed from about A.D. 52 to shortly before Peter's martyrdom in A.D. 64. But Cleage's point is the same whether Mark was written one year or 70 years after Jesus.

You know how hard it is for you to remember things that happened last year. If I ask you today about some-

thing your wife said last Christmas, you would have
a hard time remembering. Seventy years after Jesus
died, they were trying to remember the things he said
and did. A hundred and thirty years later they were
still trying to remember. This means that little in the
Gospel stories is accurate in a historical sense. The
Gospels reflect the importance which people attached
to the life of Jesus.[14]

Paul, in Cleage's terms, "was one of the biggest Uncle
Toms in history." Cleage describes Paul as so proud of his
Roman citizenship that he made up a whole new religion.[15]
To newsmen at the 1968 National Committee of Black
Churchmen meeting in St. Louis, Cleage said:

Jesus was concerned primarily with salvation of a
nation and its growth. This is much different than salvation by the blood of the Lamb. This is Paul, who
tried to make a religion acceptable to white gentiles
by salvation through faith. There are two religions in
the Bible, the religion of Jesus and the religion of the
apostle Paul. When blacks were brought to this country, they were given the religion of Paul. The basic
mission of the black church is to rediscover the religion of Jesus. . . . to build a Black Nation, rather
than to shout on Sunday. [Countering Pauline mysticism and transformation in an eschatology of resurrection, Cleage says:] Let's get something started and
expand it as we go along. But first we have to believe
that something can be done. We must have some ex-
pectation of success. Like Jesus, we must believe that
"the kingdom is at hand." Even in his day, Jesus was
saying that conditions are such that things must
change. In this kind of crisis situation we have power
enough to direct the way things will change. "The
kingdom is at hand; the Black Nation is coming into
being."[16]

Paul had never seen Jesus in the flesh, Cleage says in
his discussion of Paul in *The Black Messiah*, but "his
interpretation dominated the early church . . . he was a

great organizer" and he "wrote letters and they (Peter, James, and so on) wrote nothing" to speak of. He discounts Paul's own little event, "his little experience" on the road to Damascus, as any hot day's vision. Cleage points out quite rightly that the flare-up in Jerusalem between Peter and Paul was over Paul's insistence on a wider church, an integrated one, if you will.

> Paul was taking the religion of a Black Nation to white people who had no background in religion. But to make it acceptable to them he had to change it. . . . He distorted the Black Messiah to make him fit their primitive conceptions. To understand what paganism did to Jesus, compare the Gospel of Mark with the Gospel of John. That is because the Gospel of John has taken on the pagan, heathen philosophy of the gentiles and tried to weave it into the life of Jesus. . . . The historic Jesus is completely lost. Paul's distortion of Jesus could even be taken into Europe where there were nothing but heathens, pagans, and barbarians who lived in caves and ate raw meat. They accepted violence as a way of life. These were the white barbaric European gentiles who now dominate the world. The apostle Paul kept trying to change the religion of Jesus to meet their needs.[17]

As Albert Schweitzer, who felt Paul got too involved in mystical and Hellenic thought-forms (see the new reissue of Schweitzer's *The Mysticism of Paul the Apostle,* Seabury Press, 1968), Cleage takes a position that parallels Schweitzer's declaration that Jesus was but caught up and thrown on the wheel of fate by his own actions. In reminiscence of Schweitzer, Cleage says: "When Jesus turned his face steadfastly toward Jerusalem, it took a long time because he didn't go straight to Jerusalem. He just started out in that general direction. He stopped, he talked, he preached, he organized, he did all he could all the way to Jerusalem and there was a growing tension all the time."[18] Schweitzer presented what he called Jesus' *interimethik,* or "interim ethics," which he believed explains the impracticability of many of the passive, idyllic statements of

the Sermon on the Mount, because the end of the world
was thought to be at hand. Says Cleage: "If you read the
Gospel you will feel this growing tension. Jesus himself
became erratic and made statements that he normally
wouldn't have made. He began to talk about coming back
on 'clouds of glory.' He's a revolutionary; he's building
a movement. He's trying to free black people, the nation
Israel."[19]

Among various strands of influence, Cleage's black
theology, it seems, embraces ten important aspects, all of
which differentiate it from the normal, mainline denominational church down the street, although most of these
points by themselves or in combination are not strange to
the scholar, exegete, or theologian. In combination, in the
milieu of a changing society marked with forms of expressed and unexpressed violence, and in a society of total
new awareness mixed with hope of achieving, Cleage's
ten radical formulations spell a new dynamism within an
old vocabulary and a historic faith.

The main categories of Cleage's black theology:

1. *A chosen people.*
   We are God's chosen people. . . . The Black Nation,
   Israel, was chosen by God. Out of the whole world God
   chose Israel to covenant with, to say, "You will be my
   people and I will be your God." What else does a man
   need for dignity? . . . If we could just remember that
   we are God's chosen people, that we have a covenant
   with God, then we would know that God will not for-
   sake us. Even in the midst of violence and oppression,
   we should know that we are God's chosen people.[20]

Rabbi Tanenbaum believes all peoples have a chosen
task in God's divine "orchestra," although the Jews have
3,000 years of history of chosenness in God's scheme of
things. "Every historical people has a particular genius as
though by divine design"—the Greeks, a genius for philosophy; the Romans, for law; the Jews, a talent for religion and morality; blacks, for a peoplehood and an identity of beauty to be worked out in the context of history.

Joseph Washington, Jr. in his *The Politics of God* gives a special significance to the idea of chosenness. When people think blacks are not aware of their chosenness, Washington, who is dean of the chapel and associate professor of religion at Albion (Michigan) College, counters that this only highlights their chosenness. The Puritans knew they were chosen because they chose themselves, he says. But God's true suffering people whom he delivers let God direct them, even in a certain unawareness. In a suffering role, God works through them for the benefit of all mankind. Washington says: "If the Negro is the 'suffering servant,' God has called him not to make group differences irrelevant but to make them enriching for all mankind. So many white liberals have made this mistake, such as Will D. Campbell (in the magazine *Katallagete*) who proclaims as the objective the irrelevance of differences, so antibiblical and negative."[21]

The Rev. Dr. James H. Cone, a 30-year-old black, bearded Ph.D. and new assistant professor of systematic theology at Union Seminary, New York, is suspicious of any concept of "redemptive suffering," conscious or unconscious. "Any concept of suffering of black people by white to be saved, I reject," says Dr. Cone, whose *Black Theology and Black Power* (Seabury Press, 1969) is one of the first real efforts in formalizing black theology. He believes Cleage is unnecessarily too literal on the blackness of Jesus, a concept that he has no difficulty in accepting, however. Dr. Cone says, "Certainly Cleage is right in emphasizing Christ as nonwhite, but the blackness of Christ is a theological concept. As I see it, Christianity is primarily a religion for and of the oppressed. The resurrection of Christ means his concern for the oppressed is not limited to the oppression in the house of Israel, but all oppressed people become people of God." So Christ is identified with the Vietnamese, for instance. "If I were in Vietnam, I would regard him as identified with the Viet Cong [not South Vietnam]. South Vietnam happens to be attached to an imperialistic nation like ours. When I think of South Vietnam, I think of its relation to the United States. Viet Cong as a symbol best explains the manifestation of Christ." Dr. Cone equates

"Black Power" and "black theology." "Black Power is even in its radical expression a manifestation of the Christian faith, and in America it is the only possible manifestation of it" because "Christianity is the religion of the oppressed and the coming of Christ means liberation. Black Power is the most liberating force right now."

2. *The non-personalistic Jesus.* As a rebel seeking to overthrow a "nation" and a mentality, Jesus now, in Cleage's thinking, is hardly a mere nice guy out there receiving prayer cards and bets like a bookie, bestowing the best favors on one who comes up with the right number. Jesus launched a "movement" and can be understood only as part of that movement. "Jesus spent his life trying to resurrect a nation and he pitted himself and his movement against enemies who were deadly serious about destroying him."[22] In his Christmas Sunday sermon, December 1968, he quoted Isaiah 9:3, and said Christ came not as a "personal savior" but to multiply the Nation and to rejoice as in harvest.

3. *Non-Hellenic faith.* With Catholic theologian Leslie Dewart, Cleage would take the concepts of church tradition, put them in an ashcan, and start anew with reconceptualizing God. Dewart puts God beyond thought categories of the past; for to predicate any of his attributes is to predicate existence, and to say God exists implies that he is a being and therefore less than an omnipotent or omniscient God. Dewart begins with reality, the human conditions, the philosophy of change as an essence more important than essences themselves. Cleage fits in well here, for his absolutes are literary and grounded in history rather than classical philosophy, in the records of man rather than the speculations of man.

4. *Contraindividualism.* Scoring pie-in-the-sky preachers who promise salvation out there and nothing here, Cleage sees no real value in preaching individual salvation. The "release and heavenly help" was enough to sustain whites for another week. The church moves now to

build a world here and should go back to essential teachings of Jesus. "You can go up and down the aisle and holler, and save all, or none." And from his book:

> The Resurrection Faith, as preached by the early evangelists, took on a definite form in no way related to the teachings of Jesus. [Cleage scores the belief that] he died for us while we were yet sinners and we are saved by grace, [and] we, too, will rise after death to join him in heaven . . . a better land up yonder. This is not the religion of Jesus. This is not the religion of Israel. In it, the concept of the Nation is destroyed. This is a corruption of the religion of Jesus by the apostle Paul for the white gentiles.[23]

And in his 1968 Christmas sermon: "What good will your waltzing around and flying around in heaven do, when all your friends are still in hell down here?"

5. *Doctrinal agnosticism.* I asked Cleage about several traditional points of doctrine, beginning with the resurrection, for he says much about the resurrection of a nation. He had said in his book, "Jesus undertook the resurrection of the Nation," which "had come into being at Pentecost."[24] Concerning "individual resurrection," Cleage, admitting influence by Paul Tillich's emphasis on the necessity of "doubt" as part of the "Protestant principle"— that doubt is not only essential but a part of truth itself— said, "I wouldn't argue it (individual resurrection), but as far as I am concerned, it is not an important matter. I don't deny it—but there is no need to emphasize it. It would be pleasant to be resurrected, but I don't worry about it. Personally, it is of no concern. I do what I can here. . . . I preach funerals, but the sermon is very short. I comfort people with the belief in the resurrection. I don't disbelieve it. But there is enough reward and punishment here." On the virgin birth: "It is equally unimportant. If you are concerned with it, you end up with a theology of no importance. The significance of Jesus has nothing to do with the virgin birth. The virgin birth grows out of the fact that his life was significant enough and mystical—

therefore, the virgin birth was added or deduced. Mark, the earliest Gospel, makes no mention of it."

6. *Rejection of reconciliation.* Perhaps the key trumpet note, so to speak, of theology of the last decade has been an emphasis on reconciliation. There are many books on this theme; magazines are named "Reconciliation" and there is even one called reconciliation in Greek — *Katallegete* ("be reconciled"). Reconciliation to Cleage is tied too much to the idealistic reconciliation of individual man to God for the achievement of heaven. Cleage's creative realism is for the emergence of a Nation, reconciled at the outset with God by his acceptance of them, but not yet victorious or emergent in the process of the real world. He puts reconciliation, the favorite term of white liberals as it refers to man-and-man reconciling, on the garbage heap of theological terms over the centuries.

7. *Theology of violence sustained.* While not advocating violence, Cleage recognizes that it might be a natural part of the process. "We're in the middle of a Black Revolution in America, but we haven't come to the plain of Moab (people immediately east of the Dead Sea conquered by the Israelites claiming the Promised Land). We're not even about to enter into the Promised Land," he told Howard University students in Washington, D.C., as he mixed words of caution about revolution: "Sometimes, when you get involved in a revolution, the revolution becomes an end in itself. And then you begin to lose the people." The real purpose, he said, should be "building a kind of unity, to build a people."[25] More explicitly in his column:

There is violence associated with revolution because a revolution means rapid change. And those who have power usually fight against any change which lessens their power. As black people we have entered upon a revolution rather than the evolution or gradual change which white folks would like us to accept. We want to move fast enough to be able to see that we are moving.[26]

8. *A new theodicy.* The rationale of a just God is maintained not in the redemptive suffering of a Christ as such, nor in the redemptive suffering of a people willed to do so, or ordered to do so because of their chosenness. But meaningful suffering comes out of a dialectic between groupings of mankind, out of humanity, out of the creative role of a people, chained by circumstances, rising on their own, through organizing, as Jesus did, and possibly doing so through revolution. The justification of God is in the dialectic of history, not a developing philosophical dialecticism centered in class versus new class, in thesis versus new antithesis – in the plain innate sinfulness of man, in the perpetual conflict of society versus society, the blacks and the third world versus the affluent, oppressing, white-power structure of the big nations, in a realism and neoorthodoxy more concerned with the present than with an ideal society programmed in philosophy.

9. *Situation ethics.* When the rationale for the present is the conditions of the present, situation ethics or the new morality, or whatever name is given to the ethics of acting on the immediate situation in light of a love principle, exist. Cleage, however, says little about any love principle except as it applies within the group. His whole philosophy is predicated on an existential analysis of the present conditions of a people of which he is part, drawing political concepts and know-how from the past, with some use of religious terms in a movement geared to achievement of group status and power. Concepts of love, morality, brotherly love, are as irrelevant to him as the concepts of theology and philosophical categories. He doesn't speak of morality, except in sociological analysis as he describes the fallacies of the morality of the whites today or the fallacies of the church-going moralists, who he says slept with blacks in plantation days. Perhaps he is more concerned with what Wright calls "ethical religion" as over against moral religion, which is always tied to a culture.[27]

10. *A non-church ecclesiology.* There are similarities between Cleage's thinking and the non-church movement

of the Japanese, which has reacted against "Westernization" of the church and emphasized the Christian relationship directly to the Bible through Bible study. Cleage pays little attention to keeping up or modernizing the interior of his church building. His is a people of God, a non-building concept of the church. Unlike the Japanese non-church movement, he keeps a semblance of a traditional congregation in a place of worship. Church to him is a place for identity, in association with one another, for inspiration, by linking with the great biblical traditions that can be reinterpreted in particular terms to the black oppressed. The church for him is a point of correlation of action groups, strategy planning, and setting of new goals. "The church is the soul of the Nation." He says the little "wheels" or organizations whirling within the Nation, all stem "from one common faith and commitment. We buy property, train leadership, build for our great-great-great-grandchildren. And our unity, our commitment, our dedication to the Black Nation are all symbolized in the sacrament of Holy Communion. . . . The broken bread is the symbol that we are willing as individuals to sacrifice ourselves for the Nation. The wine is the symbol that we're willing to shed our blood for the Nation."

Rumblings of a new black theology are found in the pledge of the National Committee of Black Churchmen (formerly "Negro" Churchmen) to develop a "new style of mission" as requested in the NCNC board of directors meeting April 5, 1968. The NCBC said the four areas of the new style to consider are (1) the renewal of the church in terms of its liturgy, theology, and "understanding of its mission" in life; (2) "the development of the black church, not only as a religious fellowship, but as a community organization" to combat the "estrangement, resignation, and powerlessness in the political, cultural, and economic life of the black community"; (3) the "projection of a new quality of church life" that would make use of the "cultural heritage which is rooted in the peculiar experience of black people in the United States and the faith that has sustained them for over two centuries on these shores"; (4) "the contribution of the black church, out of its experience of suffering and the yearning for freedom, of that quality of faith, hope, and love which can activate, empower, renew, and unite the whole church of Christ."

In October 1968 the NCBC theological commission was ready with its first report which was given to its members but not released to the press. Cleage had even misplaced his copy. The report in its prologue pays special tribute to the influence of Cleage: "From the beginning, the theological program of the Church of the Black Madonna in Detroit has been a constant challenge to the NCBC members – especially that congregation's view of the relevancy of the New Testament and the color of the historical Christ." The report said its members asked seriously "whether or not a theology of violence were possible and how it should be articulated."

In various papers submitted to the committee, members differed on such questions as the inevitability of violence and its necessity as a means of change, the role of blackness in the Bible – is it a useful tool or does it pervert the true universality of Christianity?

For the most part, the 18-page NCBC paper on black theology concluded, its members were not willing to mix traditional theological concepts with Black Power and to confuse the two areas.

The Rev. Gayraud S. Wilmore, chairman of the Division of Church and Race, Board of National Missions, United Presbyterian Church, who wrote the summary paper, said, "These scholars see the peculiarities and integrities of 'the black experience' as matters of sociological rather than theophanic or even theonomous significance. This does not mean that they are not held to be important. It simply means that the secularization of the church is positively construed and regarded to be so far advanced by these writers (in the study) that they see no good reason to value some residual spirituality or devotionalism in the black community."

Wilmore noted there is "great interest in, but some uncertainty about, the unique and distinctive qualities of black religion and churchmanship." Yet while still pondering for a sense of direction the writers have a continued "suspicion" that "something is stirring in parts of the black church. There is a kind of 'black theology' aborning."

But, he says further, "Even if, as with most of the writers in this project, there is talk of the 'gospel of blackness' or 'soul theology,' no radical changes from what may be thought as mainline Reformation theology and ethics are suggested in these papers. . . .

"None of the respondents go as far, for example, as Albert Cleage, in a radical redefinition of the Christian faith. With few exceptions they reach back for a purer version of 'the faith once delivered to the apostles,' but corrupted by the culture religion of both blacks and whites."

CHAPTER 9

Strife at the Shrine

"I'll hang this microphone over your fat head. . . ."

The Rev. Albert Cleage wasn't through talking. Each attempt of two trustees, one of them chairman, of the church and society committee of the Metropolitan Detroit Association of Congregational Churches, to limit his remarks or to put words into his mouth, in the drama five years ago, stepped up Cleage's fervor until, in exasperation, he suggested he might just melt the microphone around somebody's head.

"I can raise my voice as loud as you," said the chairman. But he never really did. His voice was confident.

According to the tape of that hearing on June 8, 1964 at the Bushnell Congregational Church, the meeting opened with prayer, an appeal to God for a healing of the factions. "Bless us as we search for truth and ways to carry on together . . . and give us wisdom. . . ."

The chairman, pastor of a 1,200-member eastside white suburban church, announced that the gathering was a "special meeting of the church and society committee" of which he was chairman, and "authorized by the board of trustees of the Metropolitan Association." His job as chairman of the church and society committee was one of the portfolios he held as a member of the trustee board.

The purpose was, he said, "to explore the question of associational aid to the Central Church. . . . As a preliminary step, the church and ministry committee was to meet with Cleage to discuss a couple of items. . . . Al, are you out there? There you are."

Voice of Cleage: "You want me to sit in any special place?"

The approved agenda was to deal with two memoranda, one dated May 5; the second, May 25, 1964. The memoranda were issued in the name of the two trustees (one is now in Florida). The first was a listing of times Cleage had mentioned hate — some paragraphs with ellipses, and single sentences. The second included a six-point indictment of his views on Black Power, and of his dissatisfaction with integration — points which today have won a favorable hearing in many high church circles.

The first memo began: "A group of members of the Central Congregational Church, including deacons, trustees, charter members, and members of the executive committee, on April 29, 1964 requested the two trustees to present to the board of trustees of the association their plea for review of and action on the problems faced by their church.

"This is not a new problem. The problem of the Rev. Albert B. Cleage, Jr., and of his ministry at Central Congregational Church of Detroit, has come to this board's attention a number of times. Each time the problem has come up there has been general agreement that Mr. Cleage ought to mend his ways; but we have consistently said, 'We can't interfere with the operation of a local church.' How long can we continue as a board to avoid our total responsibility in this matter? We have obligations to our other churches as well as to Central Church. Can we continue to ask our churches to give mission money to support the 'gospel' Mr. Cleage preaches? We do not think we can. His 'gospel' is rapidly becoming one that is based on hate and the threat of violence."

The second memo charged: "He takes, we believe, at least six positions which should be considered seriously and urgently by all who call themselves Christian: (1) nonviolence has failed; (2) the federal government is anti-Negro; (3) racial conflict is inescapable and interminable; (4) integration is not the goal; (5) black nationalism, not Christianity, is the vehicle for achievement; (6) black-white cooperation is rejected."

The charges in this second memo came as an analysis of an article, "The Next Step," by Cleage, which appeared in three issues of *The Illustrated News* in November and December 1963 and was reprinted in the *News* of May 4, 1964. "We assume this article and the fact it was reprinted would seem to emphasize this is a true and forthright statement of Mr. Cleage's views and convictions."

At the start of the excitement-charged hearing Thomas Williams, one of an estimated thirty supporters of Cleage who had tagged along, rose and asked that a letter of those "not opposed to Rev. Cleage" be included also in the minutes.

CHAIRMAN: This was supposed to be a narrow agenda . . . (*some rumbling from the floor*) . . . go ahead . . . but there is no guarantee I will have it put on the agenda.

MR. WILLIAMS (*proceeding to read the non-agenda letter from Cleage loyalists from Central Church*): We have examined the May 5 and 25 memoranda of . . . and we are sure the association has no right (in this matter). If these (twenty complaining) members are troubled by doctrine, they have every right to take it to a church meeting. No one has brought such charges at the Central Church. (*The letter said the charges were arbitrary and contrary to the Congregational spirit.*) If this meeting grows out of doctrinal charges, then it is a different thing, but the committee was to decide if he is teaching black nationalism — he is, no question about it. The real question is, Is it a Christian doctrine? He has maintained that it is Christian. If they say it is not Christian, it is to prejudge in advance. Rather than a hearing in which he is prejudged, we would do better to hold a meeting to understand black nationalism. Perhaps the two trustees' fitness might also be questioned.

We request that the trustees seek the guidance of the association on this and that any future inquiry into the teachings of Rev. Cleage be organized and framed in such a way as to make clear there is no suggestion that Rev. Cleage is on trial or is presumed to be teaching anything but Christianity in his doctrine of "black nationalism."

CHAIRMAN: We designed this as a creative exploration, not prejudging. There are no charges. Mr. Cleage is not being tried. (*He then proceeds to question Cleage.*) Are there factual errors in the memoranda?

CLEAGE: Before we get to that, there are other questions, for my satisfaction. I have not received any notice of this meeting. I received a copy of the memoranda but no notice. . . . You say the purpose is for me to make a statement on black nationalism.

CHAIRMAN: Focus on (1) factuality of the statements in the memoranda and (2) Is Cleage proclaiming for the lack of a better term, black nationalism?

CLEAGE: I am not clear on some little items. Then I would be glad to make a statement. . . . (*voice rising*) I'd like names of the members of Central Church complaining. (*It was pointed out that the memoranda were personal documents from the two trustees "and supposed to be basic information." Cleage continued protesting.*)

CHAIRMAN: Al, we think the memo speaks for itself.

CLEAGE (*very loud, and fast*): You got no business asking my views. Who are the members (complaining from Central) or are there members? Did you and . . . think it up? We don't know if there are members, or you made it up.

(*The chairman, softly, told of protecting the identity of the complaining members.*)

CLEAGE: From my point of view . . . why lie in public and seek to judge me, you, in the name of twenty black members of the church?

CHAIRMAN: Where did we libel you . . . or (if not) shut up.

CLEAGE: Who are they?

CHAIRMAN: We're not here to represent Central Church.

CLEAGE: You got a whole package (of lies). Twenty from Central—you and . . . say it. They requested you to review. You speak for them and not say who . . .

CHAIRMAN: I want to remind you . . .

CLEAGE: You purport . . . you are not authorized to meet with members of Central Church. You have no authority.

VOICE: You are wrong to say that the committee (from

the church) has no right to talk to us. Dissident groups in any church may make an appeal to the credentials committee.

CLEAGE: This is not a credentials committee, but the two making charges.

VOICE: True, it's issued over their names.

CLEAGE: I have already been judged.

(*There was continued quick banter between the chairman and Cleage, and it was at this point that the chairman said he could also raise his voice just as loud.*)

VOICE (*away from mike*): Is there anything not true . . .

CLEAGE: Yeah, there is . . . (*The chairman spoke, and Cleage got out only a couple of words.*) It says . . . (*Cleage was interrupted again, and now he spoke directly to his inquisitor and threatened to blend him with the mike. He went on to accuse the two of being a court, and was interrupted by objections.*)

CLEAGE: It is a court. I preach something . . .(you) don't like. And let me tell you, I don't like what they're preaching. Why are they eavesdropping—there must be some reason.

CHAIRMAN: They were asking for a hearing.

CLEAGE: Who are they?

CHAIRMAN: Are you implying . . .

CLEAGE: How would he (chairman) know members? It's an impossibility.

(*They got hung up on whether the quotations from Cleage were from sermons in the church. Most, apparently, came from his* Illustrated News *weekly.*)

CLEAGE (*now much quieter, and in response to the charge that his new black militancy wasn't Christian*): I seek to make Christians out of all, and if I can make Christians out of you tonight, OK. The association has no authority whatsoever. Our constitution which covers completely all doesn't admit the right of this association, its board of trustees, or any committee in this association to judge actions of Central Church or actions of its minister or the preaching of its minister from the pulpit of Central Church.

VOICE: *The Illustrated News* too?

CLEAGE: We hold Central Church as completely autonomous and this is recognized in the Congregational association and in the new constitution of the Metropolitan Association of the United Church of Christ, which does not give (the two trustees), acting as individuals, any right to trespass upon the autonomy of Central Church.

The chairman kept pressing Cleage, wanting to know, "Do you stand behind the quotations—are they in error?"

The same two Association trustees also said in their memos: "By giving financial support to Central Church, the Detroit Association is supporting a political party, Freedom Now (Cleage in the 'hearing' refuted this, for he had treated Freedom Now, an all-black party, as any group, he said, charging them the usual fee, although he had now become chairman). We believe the Congregational public would not appreciate the fact that they are supporting hate propaganda. He is preaching hate."

The two trustees in their memos to the association had recommended: "It is time for this association to withdraw all financial support from Central Church, assume the responsibility of the mortgage if need be, and hope that such action would enable and encourage Central Church to alter her collision course and assume again her rightful role among the Christian churches of Detroit."

At the hearing, as the chairman pressed for a yes or no, Cleage, who sounded more and more like a Black Luther, said, "I'll go through the quotations."

CHAIRMAN: We are trying to ascertain . . .

CLEAGE: You have all you can ascertain in these two pieces of paper. Both of you (the two trustees) have a lack of understanding. It is idiotic for me to say yes or no—you don't know enough about the Negro to ask . . . (*noise*) . . . if you will just be quiet, this may take four or five sessions, but I will try to bring you into the 20th century. You can take something out of context and say "therefore Cleage teaches hate." Any sophomore in college could come up with a better set of facts and better sophomoric conclusions.

(*The exchange continued between the chairman and Cleage, with the chairman questioning if Cleage could deal with factuality.*)

CLEAGE: Your obsession with facts—I believe you can read and copy, I don't think we need to waste our time as to whether you can copy.

Cleage proceeded to go item by item. The memo cited his remarks that Martin Luther King, Jr. was a failure, and he retorted that this was an established fact, that there was no enduring change in society as a result of Selma, Greenwood, and other cities; after the rights workers had gone, white men settled down to a new terror, "castrating Negroes with broken glass on the streets." As to being asked in the memo to mend his ways Cleage said, "You speak this way to little children, and this is the way whites speak to Negroes."

To the charge that he appeared on the same platform with people such as Malcolm X,[1] Cleage said, "Yes, and you'll note in reports that I gave a Christian invocation and I did it as a Christian clergyman, and you ought to have Malcolm out to your churches. He's better than the stuff they get. He would come. I would say hurry up and get him here, he could do you so much good."

Accused of supporting Freedom Now politics, Cleage said, "I give them as much support as you give Goldwater."

The memo cited statements of hate, and a comment from a Central parishioner, "How can you take communion after hearing hate?" But, said Cleage, "I say how can you take communion after nothing, an empty sermon?" He said references that he preached hate of whites were distorted. "White men bore me, I don't hate them. I never preach hate. They bore me to tears." Asked if he hated all white men, Cleage said, "They are all part of the same system. You hate me, though I love you. You wish I hated you, it'd be easier for you. I feel sorry for you."[2]

Cleage was "acquitted," as members of the church and ministry committee voted four to one not to request the board of trustees of the Congregational Association of

Detroit to review Cleage's ministry at Central or to decide whether or not "he preaches hate."[3]

Cleage went to work the following Sunday to nip in the bud the effort to oust him. Congregational bylaws permitted the pastor to chair meetings. Cleage put his childhood buddy Oscar Hand in charge of the nominating committee. In a closed meeting, all posts on the 12-man trustee-deacon board were declared vacant. "I have reason to believe several members of the deacon-trustee board were among those who went to the association rather than request a church meeting to air our differences," he said afterward.[4]

Jerry E. Webb, a postal employee and real estate salesman, was one of the six discharged. Webb told me that on paper it looked like a Congregational church, but in reality it was like a union or a corporation which is really run by its top man and his aides. "Oscar would screen all his selections as nominating chairman with Cleage, so in a sense all were handpicked by Cleage."

Webb became one of the "Good Shepherds," a group of about thirty dissidents who left the church about this time and continued to meet in homes for nearly two years before disbanding and joining First Church or Plymouth Church in the inner city. According to Webb, nine members of the twelve-member deacon-trustee board joined that group, "which means Cleage had only three of the twelve on his side." Cleage questions this figure; he said "maybe nine out of the twenty members of the executive committee" (which includes the deacon-trustees and eight members at large).

Nobody seems to know how the group got the name of Good Shepherds. They became disenchanted with Cleage at different intervals, some as far back as the days of the inception of Central Church, others not until he preached his black nationalist series in the spring of 1964 after Easter. Webb stayed longer than most until all hope of others wresting control away from Cleage seemed futile.

Mrs. Malzetta Doyle was with Cleage's loyal followers when he broke off from St. Mark's and took a group to the Crosman school. She sat in an immaculate living room, accented with Japanese motif, with chairs covered with plastic protectors before a stone fireplace. "He seemed to be a good speaker and all. I never got suspicious of him at all until one board meeting at the parish house, I remember. We were talking about buying a building at Hamilton and Chicago (which was eventually bought by Catholic Charities). That's when I became disillusioned with him. The deacons were discussing the care of the building. He got up, red as fire, and said if he couldn't hire and fire, he would have no part of it. I couldn't understand his being so cross." She was chairman for a project group, Area #5, in the church. "He wanted to do all himself, and have all under him. But I went along with him. I had liked him and I said, 'Oh, well,' but I was surprised a minister getting that mad and flaring up at a deacons' meeting, for I liked the people and the members."

The church school nursery in the old Brewster-Pilgrim church that the congregation bought was in disarray, she said. "Another member and myself fixed it and painted it. Cleage had two keys. He was against me letting Rev. Flood (Edgar W., director of education and assistant) go in and get chairs. It was hard for me; I wanted to be friends with all."

She cited his "attack" on whites from the pulpit – "He mistreated Mrs. Jandy pretty badly." Also there were various rhubarbs over his letting groups rent the hall, when the board maintained it had the say-so on who was going to use the building.

"On one weeknight there were grade and high school kids around. After the program ended around 10:00 or 11:00 P.M., it was time for youth to go home. But he put on a record for them to dance." She recalled one lady of the church who "said it was time for the children to go home. She took off the record, but he'd put it on, back and forth, and he won. The kids stood around to see what would be done. He always had his way. Kids liked him at that time, I don't know why, probably because he let them have their way."

Several other Good Shepherd members and former members of Central noted that about twenty-five left around 1961 after what they called an attempt of Pastor Cleage to railroad through a change in the bylaws that made policies of the church subject to the trustee board instead of to the congregation. "He was like a dictator," one of them said. "There was a close vote but the count was not announced, except for Cleage to say there was a tie vote, and that he would break the tie by voting. There were little things that never came out; I remember one time one of the deacons getting up and crying, saying, 'I didn't think you would do this to me,' but I don't remember what it was all about."

Cleage said he never attempted to railroad through a constitutional change, but that it was the other way around. "The efforts to change the bylaws were made by members who left—they suggested a constitutional change which was defeated. They, as I recall, wanted the executive committee to control the building. According to the constitution from the start, the pastor in between the executive committee meetings had authority over the use of the building. They tried to change the constitution but were not able." On the close vote in question, "I don't count the votes. The vote was announced—it was a tie vote," and it was his place as presiding officer to break the tie, Cleage said. Only members were allowed in the meeting, and they had an opportunity to challenge the vote if they wished, he said.

One cited a conflict between Cleage and the women's group. The women had scheduled a musical and a reception, only to find out on the day of the reception Cleage had scheduled a black nationalist meeting of some group. "We're not going to have those bushy-head people poking their heads into the fellowship hall," one of the women leaders told him. And the women finally canceled their reception. They got hold of the trustees and "a heated argument followed. They asked him who rented it to the group, and he looked funny. They told him, 'This is our church, and our women.' " The feud with the women continued, a source said, and "he banned the women from making their announcements from the pulpit. He used to go to King Solomon Baptist Temple when Malcolm X was around and told them, if they wanted to be black, to join Cleage's church. After this, they poured in and disrupted the church."

Most of the Good Shepherds with whom I talked kept referring to a sermon in which Cleage denounced Mrs. Edward Jandy, the last white woman in the church, who, as mentioned earlier, had been the only member from the fleeing white congregation of the old Brewster-Pilgrim church to stay behind when Cleage's offshoot congregation from St. Mark's, the new Central congregation, bought the church.

Mrs. Jandy had her heart in integration, and doubtless meant well, but Cleage's philosophy had moved into an exclusive black orbit and the sight of a white woman with a long tradition going back to the white roots of the previous congregation bugged him particularly. She had long been a leader and was exercising that prerogative, as well as speaking up, and she had a habit of saying what was on her heart. When I interviewed her and her husband in suburban Washington, D.C., where they are retired, she didn't talk about the sermon that everybody else referred to, except in passing, and I didn't pay much attention to it until I returned from Washington and talked with other members of the Good Shepherds.

I made a point to run down a tape of that pivotal sermon which drove the last of the whites from the congregation. The tape was a bit muddled, but these statements came out, and many of the audience applauded (including Louis Cleage, the M.D. brother, a source said).

In that pivotal sermon Pastor Cleage had said, with Mrs. Jandy in the audience: "If you can't stand it, get up and get out. Right here in our church we have a white woman who a long time ago belonged to this church, before we came. She was a liberal white, so she joined anyway. She loved the church, it was so warm and so spiritual. She couldn't stand it. It's a white man's world, and he made it. Stand up and be counted. She couldn't take it or stand it. If you can't stand it, get up and get out. An old white woman, she's going to sort out members of the church and tell them what they are supposed to believe.

All Negroes who believe in Freedom Now is crazy as far as she is concerned. You know it's true, the white man has created the oppression, and we are the oppressed. The old white woman calls the Negroes to tell them what to do. It's a symbol of what is happening in the world, a strange notion, that any white folk can tell Negroes what to do."

I asked Cleage about the Good Shepherds and that controversial sermon about the "old white woman." "They visited other churches, but could not find one they liked, so they met in homes. It is a good thing to look around and decide what to do. Their argument at Central was they couldn't understand the new black feeling. But when they left they couldn't find anything else, but were too proud to come back. There is no hard feeling." Asked if he would invite them back: "I never invited them out. It'd be nice if they came back – if they accept the concept of the Black Nation." On the "old white woman" references: "I don't remember preaching this, but I do not deny it if one finds it to be so. She was not just disliking it, for it is legitimate to change and seek change. But she was carrying on. If she was an old black woman, I would treat her the same. Either you face this kind of thing, or any idiot can destroy the whole thing. She was no big addition. The fact that she was white we were willing to overlook, but if she used it as a weapon, that is another thing. It is better then to go out into the suburbs. There was no name mentioned, and I was not just talking about her." Concerning the procedure of singling out one person: "I wouldn't hesitate to do it again. Her action made it necessary. She called people seven days a week. I would not hesitate to call a person by name in the pulpit, if necessary, and I would do the same with an old black woman if she's tearing up the church. I don't remember the actual reference. I am not trying to deny it, and it is very possible I did it, and if I did, at the time I thought it justified."

Mrs. Jandy and Cleage share one viewpoint – she was a symbol, but they had a difference on what kind of symbol. To Cleage she was the symbol of lingering white liberalism which in the name of goodness continues inadvertently as part of the subtle, hard-to-get-at disease of oppression. To Mrs. Jandy herself, she was a symbol of at least some white interest in integration, though her earlier congregation and friends had fled away, selling all, including the church, to Cleage and Central. "I rejected our people running, and I felt we ought to integrate. We liked Cleage—he was scholarly, good-speaking intellectual (he had been a sociological student of Dr. Jandy at Wayne State, although Jandy himself in the interview in their home could find little enthusiasm for Cleage). We enjoyed Cleage and the choir immensely. Then all of a sudden, he became abusive of Negro members and called them Toms. He was always asking money for some cause, and he could always get money out of people. All of a sudden the Black Muslims started up; it disturbed us concerning the kids and what they were learning. I called Cleage about it— then he was delving in it himself. I wanted him to curb it. He pretended not to know about it. The crisis began to come as he raved and raved as though unbalanced."

The Rev. Edgar W. Flood, whom Mrs. Jandy thought a "peach of a man," and who was described as getting a particularly raw deal at Central Church, was found for an interview at the new out-in-the-countryside complex of civic buildings for Oakland County near Pontiac. Flood was Cleage's last director of education. He is now director of Protective Service Program (delinquency prevention) for Oakland County. While at Central, where he was on the denominational payroll, part-time, he was also coordinator of welfare service for Royal Oak Township (a black ghetto strip at the edge of Detroit, separated by several suburbs from its namesake, white Royal Oak).

Flood, former classmate of Cleage at Oberlin Graduate School of Theology, is a short, alert, sophisticated sort of black J. Edgar Hoover. You wait a half-hour past your appointment while he cleans up his telephone calls with his clients; then he sits back, as the winter sun begins to set behind his first-floor office in the juvenile court wing, ready to chat about Cleage and his differences with him.

"I respect him as an individual and still think he has a lot to offer," said Flood. However, Flood made it clear that he questioned Cleage's basic premises. "He is sophisticated and can bring together some points of view to defend his deviant philosophy. Maybe Christ was black, who cares?"

On the squabbles in the church, Mr. Flood said, "We found ourselves differing openly. We differed in board meetings concerning the responsibility of operating the church school. I said the superintendent has the responsibility and must be given a latitude to function."

Did Mr. Flood have difficulty in getting keys to the church school rooms? "This is true, but trite and small. The bigger factor is the conceptual idea. Cleage recognized I did not agree with the methods he used. Cleage is like many administrators. All who do not agree totally with me, I will eliminate, they say. People like Cleage — it's a part of their pathology — have to burn themselves out, and many people get hurt.

"Many in our society would give persons like him money if they could count on separation of whites and Negroes."

Flood mentioned Wallace, and I asked if he regarded Wallace and Cleage as in the same boat. "From a pathological point of view, I'd put them in the same boat — a form of hate is a part of their total movement. Hitler was aimed at the Jews, Wallace at the Negro, and Cleage at the whites.

"You look at Hitler, you look at George Wallace, there are people who will follow anybody and who look to them as savior. Here are people who are frustrated, and a man speaking out on their behalf. Hitler got strong enough to control. Cleage never did. Cleage's inflammatory material must constantly come forth, otherwise there is no Cleage. But the rabble rousers who fill a church, can also tire easily and fall out."

With their differences on integration versus separatism insoluble, Flood said he was fired by Cleage in a letter. Cleage maintains today that Flood was employed by the church though funds came from the denomination and the church had a right to bounce him out. Says Cleage, "There was no real dissension. He was all right. He doesn't agree with the kind of theology I like. He worked with the Sunday school primarily. It was not so much disagreeing, but he was not doing what I wanted done with the Sunday school. I wanted the Sunday school to reflect the theology of the church. This is difficult, and demands curriculum revision and this is asking too much, like bricks without straw."

"The last time I saw him," said Mr. Flood, "was at the Friendship Baptist Church two years ago, and he was preaching there basically the same kind of negative deviant material he has grown on. He is like Wallace; if there is no segregated environment, there would be no Wallace, and there would be no Cleage. I had dropped by his church to pick up some material some time before that meeting at the Friendship Church, and had run into Dave Cleage who welcomed me as I went out. Cleage told me, 'Dave said you were at the church and we were happy to have you back.' There is no animosity between us."

CHAPTER 10

The Rebel Committeeman

The four clergymen sat behind a table before reporters in New York mapping out a new coalition that they hoped would create a tidal wave of private funds for investment in the inner-city ghetto projects. Wisely, perhaps, leaders of the Operation Connection experiment gave themselves only eight months to produce or call it quits. It took Albert Cleage only two months to see that it wasn't going to work, and within two months he resigned.

In the star-studded lineup for the announcement of Operation Connection, Cleage seemed almost out of place. He sat among men, long-time leaders in their faiths, who were scholars and mediators. He was the only pastor of a local parish, but nevertheless the chosen clergy representative of black nationalism.

Cleage leaned forward. The presiding bishop of the Episcopal Church, the Rt. Rev. John E. Hines, sat slightly behind him with a sort of pondering frown wrinkling his brow. At opposite ends of the table flanking Cleage and Hines were Rabbi Marc Tanenbaum, director of Interreligious Affairs of the American Jewish Committee, and Rabbi Abraham Heschel, of the Jewish Theological Seminary, New York, both listening attentively.

Cleage emphasized the current separation of blacks and whites and maintained that separate building of power was the only way for blacks to gain dignity and strength. Only with their own power, he said, could blacks face up to the "corruption of the white community" and "white power." He said blacks wanted to control their own communities. Positively, that meant to white people they could dump their guns and go back to barbecuing.

Twenty Protestant denominations plus Jewish groups and the Roman Catholic Church backed the new coalition. Bishop Hines, the cochairman of the project with Cleage, said $90,000 was on hand at the outset, which would be a step toward a goal of 10 million dollars. The bishop said the anticipated funds would go toward building black economic and political power in five cities, among them Detroit. He pledged an attempt to mobilize the sizable resources of white affluence, including Episcopalian, for the creation of power. He said he concurred with Cleage's basic philosophy that the real problem was the "powerlessness" of blacks. Cleage added that if Operation Connection fails, the churches and synagogues in America could close up shop. He insisted that none of the money should have any strings attached, that blacks could use the money as they wished for programs to build up their communities. He said this could include using the funds for support of efforts to elect black candidates, a concession he could not secure in funds offered from a local civic committee in Detroit (see chapter 12).

Bishop Hines, in a prepared statement, said, "We believe that the current social, racial, economic, and political divisions in this country are not inevitable. The poor themselves must design, conduct, and control strategies which will lift them to power from their present condition of powerlessness." Rabbi Heschel said, "It is time to indicate that the so-called white backlash does not represent the best of the white community." Tanenbaum was squarely behind the indigenous control factor. He said of Operation Connection, "You have here a coalition of religious leaders who are joining together in a program that a black militant has outlined." He said the project was an effort to get away from "the classic pattern of making programs" to hand down to the black communities.

The membership of the executive committee indicates the prestigious backing of the project and the wide national religious sentiment behind Cleage. That committee included Dr. Arthur S. Flemming, president of the National Council of Churches, the Most Rev. John F. Dearden, archbishop of Detroit and president of the National Conference of Catholic Bishops, various Protestant bishops, and others. Heschel and the Most Rev. John J. Wright, bishop of Pittsburgh, now in Rome, served as vice-chairmen.

On May 17, Cleage submitted his resignation as co-chairman of the Operation Connection (the resignation was not announced until nearly six weeks later). Cleage said he still accepted the goals of Operation Connection in seeking to tap white funds, but he thought the whole process proved to be too slow. Cleage said he would continue to work with the one-year-old Interreligious Federation for Community Organization, of which he was a board member. The Rt. Rev. Paul Moore, suffragan bishop of Washington, D.C., and a longtime civil rights activist, on leave to be director of Operation Connection, accepted Cleage's pullout with regret, and said Operation Connection would not seek to open any programs of its own but would work with IFCO.

IFCO was to become the solid thrust of the denominations as hinted in the remarks of its executive director, the Rev. Lucius Walker, Jr., in regard to Cleage's Operation Connection resignation. "IFCO has as one of its purposes," he said, "consultation and evaluation in connection with community organizations. Operation Connection has as one of its purposes to put white leadership in the know, about where they ought to be providing moral and financial support for urban crisis programs." Without declaring any organic relationship between the two, Walker indicated they would nevertheless cooperate "where our activities can complement each other."[1]

Overlooking inferences that Cleage was being difficult and playing the part of Peck's bad boy and a spoiler of grand plans, Rabbi Tanenbaum praised Cleage's resignation as positive and constructive when I asked him about it some months later in New York. "He just didn't feel there was sufficient response from the white denominations and his resignation made this more evident, and as a result it made IFCO more effective. It's not a change in his basic position. He wanted this from the beginning. He is very positive. I remember one meeting (at IFCO) when there was a question of our funding a suburban white action group in Philadelphia." Pastor Cleage, he said, "was surprised at the small amount of the budget ($20,000), but if it was something useful, he was for it (white or black)."

Why specifically did Cleage quit Operation Connection? Rabbi Tanenbaum said, "(1) There was a genuine concern which he had about the established institution, if it was going to continue to behave in traditional style, long on rhetoric and short on meeting real needs, or if it was going to have an authentic concern for the black community – Cleage was asking them to 'put up or shut up'; (2) a part of his decision grew out of the internal situation in Detroit – I think it was necessary for him to spend more time there and to get out of Operation Connection and not be regarded as compromising with the white paternalistic establishment; (3) there was a vagueness in the purpose of Operation Connection, and there was no dollar or time schedule commitment to give confidence it was ready to do something. Since then there has been a self-examination and a development of style. Cleage compelled us in making his decision to center on IFCO, and his resignation served to sharpen our purpose and to create greater sensitivity. Cleage's dramatic personality and his decision to quit early in the game precipitated the (necessary) crisis. There now also emerged a unique phenomenon in IFCO – black militant leaders meet with white Christian denominational and Jewish and Roman Catholic leadership to try to identify areas of need and to respond creatively."

Cleage said Operation Connection was rendered next to useless because "I don't think that the major religious bodies, Protestant, Catholic, or Jewish, are ready to undertake that kind of urban involvement (10 million dollar goal set for Operation Connection). They are almost incapacitated by the suggestion that that kind of money is necessary, which would involve a redirection of denominational funds."[2] He also noted that it was probably too much to expect on a practical basis for denominational leaders "with vested interests in certain operations" to reroute their budgets in a short time.

Cleage's own failure to effect an across-the-board federation of blacks in Detroit was weighing on his mind at this time; but he denied that the Detroit situation, where he was under fire for association with whites on occasion, such as in the Operation Connection, was a factor in his quitting Operation Connection. The latter was a largely white thing, despite the presence of black Catholic bishop Harold Perry, auxiliary of New Orleans, and several members of black Protestant denominations on the board.

To Cleage, IFCO was a different matter. The federation was to fund his work in Detroit with $85,000 (out of the IFCO funding of 37 projects in 1968 at $781,600). Two thirds or more of the faces around the conference table at any IFCO meeting are black, and IFCO was headed by Walker, a very black black. The IFCO symbol is a combination of geometric shapes blending finally into a black overlapping circle. In its own promotion literature, the organization says, "The IFCO symbol combines the colors green (life, hope, fertility, and growth) and black (dignity, strength, and beauty) into the intertwining triangles (the tripartite churches and faith), the interlocking diamond (the preciousness of all life), and the encircling unity of the circles (the interdependence of all life and all people) — ending with a black circle embracing all that it has touched, yet having emerged an autonomous entity."

In justification of his continued efforts to work with the mixed, "integrated" IFCO, Cleage said separate power could still be developed for blacks even in association with whites. He said his own views have never been geared to a "popularity contest" in the black community. "My only insistence is that the white community recognize the principle of self-determination. My leadership emphasizes economic, cultural, and political development, and control of the schools. There may be other militants with a non-programmatic approach, but I don't offer leadership to them. I'm trying to structure the transfer of power to the black community."

In the IFCO quarterly board meetings on the eighth floor of the National Council of Churches headquarters on Riverside Drive, New York, Cleage is a devoted and diligent worker whose suggestions are constructive. He sits near the head of the table presided over by the recent IFCO president, Rabbi Tanenbaum. He speaks only when necessary, but usually is able to carry the day for the project he is interested in, or to defeat measures he dislikes.

When Lucius Walker finished outlining a new procedure for IFCO that "would begin a process of general persuasion" with the twenty-two denominational members of IFCO and with the NCC to "accept responsibility" and to give "a higher place for community organization," Cleage merely said, "I second it—that we accept the language as you have it," and the ball was rolling. He later pointed out that the archdiocese in Detroit had promised one million dollars of its annual Archdiocesan Development Fund, normally for church construction, to community and other nontraditional programs.

Sitting with hands folded at the head of the table next to Tanenbaum, Cleage joined in a discussion on a key question, as posed by board member Douglas Still of Evanston, "Should IFCO be limited and narrow in style like the Industrial Areas Foundation (Saul Alinsky's Chicago-based community protest organization) or heterogeneous in style? Or should IFCO claim to be the exclusive means of funding community organizations for the church?"

Operation Connection inevitably became the enabling body for IFCO. "Operation Connection did some useful things, such as opening lines to the foundations," said Tanenbaum. Renny Freeman, former director of the Detroit West Central Organization (an Alinsky-related group, now largely defunct), whose appointment to the IFCO staff was revealed at that meeting but not announced, pointed out that Operation Connection enabled Bishop Moore and others to talk to Henry Ford and Max Fisher (chairman of the New Detroit Committee), and helped dialogue at a crucial time. As a result, the Inner City Business Improvement Forum, an indigenous effort to fund a hospital employing blacks, new banks, and supermarkets, received funding from the New Detroit Committee.

Cleage put on the brakes briefly. He said, "the basic reality is that as an independent operation it (Operation

Connection) had a destructive potential in the black community and could very easily become paternalistic, but as it is supportive to IFCO, using its skills, as long as it realizes its existence depends on IFCO, then it has a function." Rabbi Tanenbaum: "It might be said that 'Dr.' Cleage helped us to understand this early in the game."

Lucius Walker pointed out to the IFCO board members, "If IFCO could be solely fund-raising, we could be happy. But there is a question of responsibility. We have to exercise sanctions, and we must have a clause to enable us to withdraw support on a project. We need some controls, but how far, is the question."

The Rev. Douglas Still, a United Presbyterian, executive secretary of social welfare of the Church Federation of Chicago, talked in terms of assuring "accountability," since the group had some special concern about the use of some of its funds in Ohio. Accountability meant some control and responsibility in shaping the total local program, he said. "I agree," said Cleage. "Organizing to meet needs will eventually call for setting up training and organizing, if they accept accountability." Cleage was not worried about imposing certain national controls through a doctrine of accountability. "As I look over this board, it looks black to me; and if the board is largely black, there is not the same fear. I don't see any escape from control if we accept accountability in funds. If the administration of a project breaks down, we go in and do a contract ourselves. Really, there is a vacuum (with Alinsky out of the picture). We can act coy, but either IFCO is going to take over the field of community organization, or somebody else."

Lou Walker: "This is all right if it is presented well and doesn't sound threatening, but a lot will regard it as threatening, even if it sounds nice."

Freeman: "It has been clear a long while that the Alinsky method is not acceptable." This was made clear in the July 1968 meeting of IFCO which heard Ron Karenga, chairman of the Los Angeles US organization say concerning Alinsky, "If you are going to organize the black, you have to talk black. If you are organizing the Mexican-

American, you have to talk Mexican-American." Cleage said he concurred with Karenga on this 100 percent.[3] "The interest of Alinsky had always been in the organization itself," continued Freeman. "We bring flexibility and responsibility to the community directly. We don't pose the threat the IAF does."

At the suggestion by another board member that money alloted to an organization which suddenly becomes involved in internal problems be put in escrow, Cleage said, "If money is put into escrow until blacks agree, that sounds like an old-time white liberal position."

The debate continued until Cleage said, "Do we want a resolution asking the staff to set up accountability for funding, or do we just want to talk about it?"

Walker questioned "if we are informed enough now" and suggested the matter could be tabled for a future meeting or the staff could be instructed to prepare a memo. Cleage put a motion that "the staff prepare a memo and consult such authorities as necessary and report back at the next meeting." He later expanded the motion: "I move that the staff draft a memo covering accountability and funding and additional information concerning IFCO moving into organizing and training" and that the memo treat "accountability of funding and the implications, with member bodies as part of the preparation of the memo."

Cleage's other key national work within a structured church or interchurch setting is with the National Committee of Black Churchmen. He was due to conduct a morning workshop on "Black Churchmen and Economic Development in the Black Community" at the 1968 convention of NCBC in St. Louis. He did not show up until 4:00 P.M., due largely, he said, to difficulty in plane connections in Los Angeles where he had been speaking the night before. "I'm always late," he said, with a laugh. He has forgotten to show up for seminars on occasion—twice this happened at his own alma mater, Wayne State. "He's not absentminded," insists his daughter Pearl, "but runs late sometimes. He'll run the same amount of lateness every Sunday—11:15 A.M. is the starting time, but he always gets there at 11:17" and it's usually 11:30 before the service starts. I remember the first day of a two-day meeting of IFCO in New York; Cleage was just about on the button, but it was forty minutes before the meeting actually got underway. Rabbi Tanenbaum apologized to the predominantly black board for starting "according to Jewish time." The next day Cleage made it a point to be forty minutes late.

Cleage writes down his appointments, but this is not always foolproof. I remember his saying he had to be in St. Petersburg, Florida to address 1,000 demonstrators in a march on city hall in support of 211 sanitation workers ousted in a dispute over an increase in wages. The appointment was a week ahead on a Saturday, he said, consulting his date book, but it was happening the next day.

When Cleage breezed in for the NCBC meeting in St. Louis, too late to conduct any workshop, he was immediately taken under wing by convention officials who saw to his comfort. At the registration desk he was asked if he was part of the convention. "I guess so," he said. "I've been hanging around enough." He played an advisory and consultative role at the meeting and kept a number of TV and radio commitments. That night he was to take part in an unprogrammed sit-in. I was summoned from bed about 2:30 A.M. at the Gateway Hotel, convention headquarters, by the NCBC press agent. When press agents call me at 2:00 A.M. I presume they are drunk and when this one said a half-dozen people were conducting a sit-in at that impossible hour in the morning, I assumed they were all drunk. When the Rev. Henry Parker, information officer for the NCC Delta ministry in Greenville, Mississippi called and said, "You'd better get on down here," then I moved a little faster.

NCBC delegates in the sit-in—now some 50 of them—had gathered to protest an incident involving black clergy members of the convention who were allegedly called "boy" by an elderly cashier in the hotel cafeteria. The woman refused to apologize. Other incidents were cited by the conventioneers. Money for payment to the hotel was put in escrow, and by dawn all of the delegates had checked out and gathered at Trinity Episcopal Church, three miles away. Hotel management eventually flew in from Milwaukee, with assurances to meet a series of demands, including sensitivity training of future employees. During the middle-of-the-night sit-in, Cleage merely sat along with the other delegates on the floor, and leaned, exhausted, against the Delta Air Lines counter. He huddled only briefly with the convention's officers, letting the sit-in be their thing.

Although he has organized and supported pickets against the A & P, Sears, Roebuck & Co., and other firms in Detroit, Cleage's penchant is for community organizing and economic development, with blacks seeking control of institutions and not merely demanding a fair shake. The Poor People's midwest section of a national 1968 march in Detroit taxed his thinking in this area. However, he was to find some value in it, despite his repudiation of King and King's methods. "Some black militants say that the march is a waste of time," he wrote in his *Chronicle* column.[4] " 'We're tired of marchin',' they say. 'It never got us anything before and it ain't going to get us anything now.' But despite a philosophical rejection of marching, most black militants are supporting the march because either consciously or unconsciously they realize that the Poor People's March will create a framework within which meaningful struggle can take place. The Poor People's March is significant for white liberals because it creates an opportunity for them to try to take over the Black Revolution. It is significant for us because it creates the opportunity for us to see the forces of counterrevolution at work on a national scale and to understand the need for us to fight together to destroy the common oppression."[6]

Back in 1963, after an NAACP march in Kennedy Square, Detroit, in support of demonstrations in the South, Cleage called for a larger march. He expanded on the idea in a testimonial banquet in his honor at Cobo Hall, and joined with the Rev. Cecil C. Franklin (father of singer Aretha Franklin) in setting up the march. Several of the old-time mainline black leaders aligned themselves against Cleage and Franklin at this time in opposition to the march. In June 1963, Cleage cooperated as a director of the independent Detroit Council for Human Relations in sponsoring a "walk to freedom" with Dr. King down the main thoroughfare, Woodward, to Cobo Hall arena where Cleage gave a talk on schools (others spoke on jobs and housing) prior to Dr. King's own speech. More than 100,000 joined the march, with a great sea of people unable to get into the Cobo arena, which seats 14,000.

By fall of 1963 Cleage was in charge of the DCHR's efforts to launch a Northern Christian Leadership Conference similar to that of Dr. King's. Cleage announced on September 19 that a conference to which northern black leaders were invited would be held at Cobo Hall. The meeting eventually had token attendance. Before the meeting "basic philosophical conflicts between factions of the Detroit Council for Human Rights were brought to light with the resignation of the fiery and controversial Rev. Albert B. Cleage, Jr. from the DCHR board of directors," the *Michigan Chronicle* reported.[6] Cleage had played an important part in the organizing of the DCHR, having named it and having registered the name.

The breaking point came when national leaders of the emerging black Freedom Now party—Conard Lynn, war protester and former U.S. Communist party member, drummed out of the party for being too radical in 1937, and William Worthy, of Boston, correspondent for the weekly *Baltimore Afro-American*, whose passport was seized after a Red China visit and whose conviction of illegal reentry into the United States from Cuba was reversed by the United States Fifth Circuit Court of Appeals in 1964—were invited to the Northern Leadership exploratory conference by Cleage, who was chairman of the DCHR subcommittee charged with setting up the conference.

Franklin would have nothing to do with the Freedom Now party. "The DCHR wants freedom now, but not through the Freedom Now party," said Franklin. "I am not in disagreement with the goals and aspirations of the Freedom Now party, the Black Muslims, or any other independent black group. Rather, I am not in agreement with the means to obtain these goals of political power, economic security, and human dignity for all people." Denouncing the "communist" influence of some Freedom Now speakers, Franklin said the DCHR does not court the attendance of Communists or the left-wing element, and that the board members must be alerted concerning possible infiltration. Franklin also underscored "the doctrine of nonviolence" as "the only sane means" by which black men could hope to achieve their goals. Franklin's own influence was eventually diminished when he was cited by the government for failure to file income tax returns on $76,868 from 1959 to 1962. Franklin pleaded "no contest."

Cleage said that he could not accept any arbitrary limitations set by Franklin on the DCHR, and also that black leaders needed to be cognizant "that Negroes everywhere are questioning the practicality of a philosophy of nonviolence which precludes the possibility of self-defense."

In the same issue of the *Chronicle* reporting Cleage's resignation from the DCHR the troubles of Franklin with other black leaders besides Cleage were noted. A. L. Merritt, an older, distinguished man, president of the Baptist Ministerial Alliance, ignored a request by Franklin to promote the Northern Negro Leadership Conference at a meeting of the Alliance. Said the *Chronicle*:

> During a brief interchange between the two clergymen, the Rev. Mr. Franklin angrily went after the Rev. Mr. Merritt, but he was restrained by several other ministers. When questioned about this, the Rev. Mr. Franklin said, "I temporarily lost my temper, but I will not be discouraged by his (Merritt's) opposition to me and his unchristian attitude. I can't understand it. Here we are trying to sponsor a conference for Negro leaders to give greater impetus to the civil rights movement, and we can't get cooperation to the extent of making an announcement."[7]

Cleage proceeded to set up a rival rally at the King Solomon Baptist Church in contrast to the DCHR rally he had originally set up with Franklin. The new rally featured Malcolm X, who had not reached the apex of his popularity. Cleage and Malcolm X each spoke about forty-five minutes.

Concerning Cleage's split with the Franklin-dominated DCHR, John H. Burns, a businessman member of the DCHR board, said he regretted Cleage's resignation. "I didn't always agree with him, but I never lost respect for him. I felt that there could be an area of disagreement and we could still fight together. In regard to the Freedom Now party, I don't think this is the right direction for the Negro to take in order to achieve his ends."

Replying to a statement by Cleage in Cleage's *Illustrated News* that DCHR had already outlived its "very limited usefulness," Burns said, "Rev. Cleage is entitled to his personal opinion, but there are too many Negroes who have not become personally involved in the struggle. We can't have too many organizations making an honest attempt to get freedom for the Negro."[8]

CHAPTER 11

The Candidate

Nearly 20,000 persons waited eagerly for Senator Eugene McCarthy, July 27, 1968 in Tiger Stadium, Detroit. The guest of honor was delayed by other commitments and huddles downtown. Filling the bill were professional comedians; a guitarist; a state senator; the money men behind McCarthy in Michigan, among them William Clay Ford, Ford Motor Co. vice-president and owner of the Detroit Lions; former Detroit Lions star Dick "Night Train" Lane; and the Rev. Albert Cleage.

Cleage, in his earthy, simple, direct clear rhetoric, hardly played second fiddle even to a candidate for the presidency. I suppose one has to say Gene McCarthy was the hero at his own rally but up until 10:00 P.M. when McCarthy arrived, the man of the hour was Albert Cleage; and it may be fair to say that Cleage, speaking at a fresher moment in the rally probably sustained more cheers than McCarthy. Most of the McCarthy hoopla accompanied the arrival of the senator but his matter-of-fact, somewhat dry, and not the most coherent speech, typed out days before, did not compare with Cleage's fresh rapport with the audience.

The performance of Cleage at this rally, his acceptance later as a vice-chairman of the New Democrats in Michigan, his bucking of the Humphrey-aligned black ministers' conferences in Detroit, his own rising role in national life in contrast to his somewhat also-ran image in Detroit indicate Cleage may make a bid as a senatorial or vice-presidential candidate on some third party New Democrat-Black Coalition in the future, especially if the Nixon

174

administration and Nixon's all-white cabinet fail to involve and satisfy black militants working for black self-determination. *Chronicle* columnist C. C. Douglas noted that Cleage's vice-chairmanship of the New Democrats "may be an indication that he has gotten the OK to seek political office sometime in the future."[1]

At the big stadium rally for McCarthy, Cleage was introduced by Michigan state senator Roger Craig, of Dearborn, as "an extremely controversial, but extremely verbal and extremely talented member of the black community." Cleage immediately caught the mood of the crowd: "This is something of a first in the nation for a black militant to speak on the platform of the next president of the United States. Tonight represents a turning point in this campaign. It begins to take on the support of blacks largely ignored by other candidates.

"There is no black community united for Mr. Humphrey. The black establishment is much like the white. They go along with the one in control. Up until recently, there was no candidate. If Mr. Humphrey was nominated, we would still have no candidate. What Humphrey says about all you 'colored' is warmed over Roosevelt New Deal policies."

The crowd was in fact 99 percent white—a preponderance of youth of all ages, some beards, and entire families, with children sleeping on the knees of their parents.

That Cleage was putting himself out on another limb by his endorsement of McCarthy, who really didn't have a ghost of a chance to win the nomination, was evidenced by refusal of U.S. Representative John Conyers (D., Mich.), perhaps Detroit's most politically powerful black, to support McCarthy. And Cleage's fellow black ministers were quick to do him in following Cleage's getting on the ill-fated McCarthy bandwagon.

The Rev. Louis Johnson, an independent and often militant black whose parish is in a half-million-dollar new building in the urban renewal medical center and whose congregation is jointly aligned with National (black) and American Baptist conventions, and the Rev. Roy Allen, also a Baptist and a consistent moderate and rival of Cleage for funds, announced their endorsement of Humphrey and said they spoke for fifty-five of "Detroit's most prominent ministers." They cited Humphrey's "record of solid achievement on behalf of all minorities." Johnson added that he found it "particularly unfortunate" that Albert Cleage, who he said represented only "himself as a spokesman for the black community and for black militancy," saw fit to endorse McCarthy. He argued that although McCarthy was "well intentioned" Humphrey had the record in politics to back up his promises. "His record in the area of human rights is an open book," these ministers said, and "he was a champion of civil rights when it was unpopular to be so." They cited Humphrey's battle in 1948 for a liberal platform at the Democratic convention and his Senate leadership in helping to get the civil rights bill of 1964 passed.[2]

Attorney Milton R. Henry, first vice-president of the separatist Republic of New Africa, formerly active in Cleage's church and now a Muslim, also saw fit to rebuke Cleage concerning McCarthy in a joint statement with the Republic's chief Detroit officer, Lavis Simmons. The statement said:

> While the Republic cannot be completely disinterested in what occurs in U.S. politics, the Republic has received no indication from any major presidential candidate that he would be interested, if elected, in negotiating the claims of the Republic to reparations—that is, money payment for slavery and damage suffered by black people—or to sovereignty over all the subjugated areas in America where black people live.[3]

Cleage in his speech at the stadium referred to the advance text of the senator's remarks and Cleage's own trip to Washington to consult with McCarthy arranged by Ford and Wayne State professor Otto Feinstein, a campaign manager for McCarthy. In that text the senator had declared himself foursquare for black power and the creation of black dignity and responsibility: "It is time to do more than talk if we are to be truly a party of the people. It is time for a new administration to address itself to the condition of powerlessness. Black people are poor because they are powerless."

Said Cleage in his speech, "Black people have changed. We do not want Congress to pass new legislation. We have changed. We are concerned with power. We are powerless people and our suffering is a result of our powerlessness. We wish to escape. Our determination is to take the black ghetto and make it a beautiful community for black people. Black people want political, economic control in the black community, and schools, and it is time a presidential candidate understood what we want intelligently and reasonably.

"Black people have not been concerned about the campaign. Only the establishment has been concerned, but from tonight forward when he makes the statement (on Black Power and self-determination), the campaign takes a new turn. For a candidate understands and has the intelligence to understand not only the war (in Vietnam) but also Black Power. Black Power is not a threat, but a solution and answer. You don't have to be threatened by Black Power. He (McCarthy) will bring peace to the city as well as to the world. Black people will find dignity in control of the black community."

Cleage qualified his endorsement a bit in his conclusion: "Candidates have been speaking about black people. I hope he will speak to black people in urban America. If he does this in clear terms, we will support his candidacy in such a way people will be forced to accept his nomination in Chicago. We hope we have a candidate in Senator McCarthy to give us a reason to participate in . . ."

Nearly every one of these statements of Cleage's was interrupted with loud applause. Craig returned to the podium and said, "What do you do for an encore after that, except to adjourn?" Former state Democratic Party chairman Zolton Ferency remarked as Cleage and his black aide, Beverly Williamson, strode off the field, "Following Rev. Cleage is sort of like coming on after Sammy Davis, Jr." McCarthy, when he eventually appeared, was more vague than his text, but did "promise power to farmers, young people, to black people of this country."

Later I asked Cleage about the rally and how he liked being compared to Sammy Davis, Jr., whom Cleage has criticized on occasion for being too naïve and pious. "In the sense he (Ferency) used the remark it was OK. It's a show-business phrase, if you are following somebody. I have nothing against Sammy Davis. He's changed recently, and is more militant." Cleage said he saw McCarthy in Washington on July 17, eleven days before the Detroit McCarthy rally, when he received an advance copy of the speech. "I think he is clear. I know enough about the other candidates."

Why was Cleage selected among others to represent the black community? Besides the fact that he was probably one of the very few willing to stick his neck out for McCarthy in the black community, Cleage said "the Michigan committee wanted a new position on the urban crisis rather than the warmed over New Dealism. The black establishment is tied to the machine, and that is Humphrey, and they would hesitate to come out against the machine candidate, so it would be difficult to get a black of the establishment to be with McCarthy." NAACP head for Michigan, Albert Wheeler, a dermatology professor at the University of Michigan, was on the platform but did not speak.

Cleage showed up again at a Cobo Hall rally for McCarthy on August 15, 1968 although McCarthy was not present. This crowd was notably small, about 4,000, due perhaps to the in absentia quality of the rally. Cleage, however, flanked by two bodyguards, received a standing ovation in the middle of his speech and at the end. "Senator McCarthy is desirable for black people," Cleage said. "He understands what black people are trying to do. I don't have a lot to say. I've made my point—I am here. And with the kind of pressure the establishment is putting on black people who would like to be for McCarthy, that's quite an accomplishment." McCarthy was at Madison Square Garden in New York City and his speech came to the Cobo Hall rally over closed-circuit TV.[4]

Cleage was playing the role of the prophet who is looking ahead beyond particulars, even in his endorsement of McCarthy. The principle was more important than McCarthy, a sure loser. The principle had the germ of new politics, and hope in the future, a view that came through in Cleage's survey of the 1968 presidential hopefuls in September 1968:

> So, very little that is going on in America today makes sense. Wallace is the voice of the new, uncomplicated America. Nixon and Humphrey have a sense of the psychological shift and are stumbling along behind Wallace, crying, "Me, too!"
>
> The inner psychological conflict has now emerged as a new external conflict which will more and more split American white people apart. We can see the polarization of the ignorant and frightened upon one hand, and the coming together of intelligent whites who must oppose this campaign of stupidity designed to leave America in flames and destruction if only because of enlightened self-interest. Eugene McCarthy sparked the polarization which will continue now without him, and will lead to the birth of a new Democratic Party out of the ashes of the LBJ-HHH fiasco.[5]

Cleage is not new to third-party politics. In October 1963 he and other black militants pooled their resources and launched the Freedom Now party in Michigan. It was a follow-up of a national effort to organize such a party after the massive civil rights demonstration in Washington under Dr. King in June 1963. At a public rally in Cleage's Central Church (Shrine of the Black Madonna) participants were asked to sign a petition to qualify the party for the 1964 election ballot. By spring the new Michigan Freedom Now party submitted petitions containing 19,892 signatures — 1,557 more than needed to put the party on the ballot. Besides Cleage, who became state chairman and eventually the Freedom Now candidate for governor, only black candidate for governor in the United States since reconstruction days, organizers included Richard Henry, president of the Group on Advanced Leadership (GOAL) through which Cleage also participated in fighting urban renewal as urban "removal" projects; Wilfred X, brother of Malcolm X and head of Detroit black Muslims; and Luke Tripp, chairman of an African Uhuru movement in Detroit. During the organizing rally, the 250 attending gave a standing ovation to Wilfred X as he outlined a geographical separation plan for blacks, which was later to evolve into the Republic of New Africa concept.[6]

The new party said it would welcome white members but would run only blacks as candidates. Democrats were in a bit of a dither over the formation of the new party for fear it would siphon off some of the liberal and radical vote that would normally go its way. Cleage pledged, "We will acquaint Negro voters with the fact that they have no hope in either the Democratic or Republican parties. I doubt that we will endorse any Negroes who are running as Democrats or as Republicans. We think it is necessary that the masses of Negroes become disillusioned with the two parties." He said a tactic of the campaign was to bring complaints to the Civil Rights Commission created in the previous year by the new Michigan Constitution.

Receiving only 4,767 votes compared to Romney's 1,764,355 and Democrat Neil Staebler's 1,381,442 votes,[7] Cleage in retrospect says "the Freedom Now party was re-evaluated. The black community was not ready for an all-black party." Asked if he would get behind another black or predominantly black third party (and they continue to emerge, such as Eldridge Cleaver's Black Panther Party for Self-Defense and the Black Revolutionary Party sparked by Phil Hutchings, national program secretary of the Student Nonviolent Coordinating Committee), Cleage said, "We are not loyal to any one tactic. Now it seems more feasible to work through the Democratic Party" and the establishing of an "all-black independent bloc which can move anywhere." Declining to say just what is the best form in today's black realism, Cleage said, "Black realism works with what is now, not what has been done. Right now a black bloc that is tightly organized and free is the most effective means in politics. But we do not let the tactics be the end in themselves."

"Plunking" has been a favorite recommendation of Cleage in guaranteeing stronger black showings in election results. Cleage called for a plunk vote in 1962 for three black congressional candidates and a black prosecutor. In 1965, he called for a plunk vote for four black candidates – "four and no more" – for city common council members, one of whom, Nicholas Hood, eventually made it out of four blacks running. The technique, by which the voter casts his ballot for black candidates only, regardless of how many are to be elected, brought condemnation from most civic and church groups. *Detroit News* columnist Doc Greene, confessing that he is annoyed anyway when clergymen get into politics in a specific way, called a plunk vote stupid. *Michigan Chronicle* columnist Nelson Jack Edwards called a plunk vote a flunk vote.[8] In 1962, the Rev. Charles H. Williams, head of the Baptist Ministers' Conference, condemned the plunk vote, and Horace Sheffield, black executive vice-president of the Trade Union Leadership Council, warned against a plunk vote in the TULC publication, *The Vanguard.* He urged "each reader, no matter what his color or station in life, to vote only for the candidate's program and principles." The Detroit Council for Political Education, a black businessmen's and professional men's group, also rapped Cleage on the 1962 plunk recommendation.

In the 1962 Wayne County and Detroit election, the Michigan Fair Campaign Practices Commission ruled Cleage's campaign for plunking as outlined in his *Illustrated News* as racist. The Commission said, "There is no question but that these appeals are racist, that they descend to a level of campaigning that has no place in the American electoral process." Cleage defended his views: "There's no prejudice in reverse, but if we're at least 10 percent of the population, we should have 43 or at least 40 congressmen (in the nation).[9] In 1965, Cleage defended his plunking recommendation with more directness and sureness:

Negroes voted for whites in the primary, but white people did not vote for Negroes. Even though white ministers say they are going to tell their congregations to help Negro candidates, it will not do any good. If a white minister does this, he will find that his position becomes untenable because his followers will not agree. Negroes do not get jobs because they are black, they don't get support in the white community because they are black, so I think we should vote for them because they are black.[10]

In 1965 Cleage took on Detroit common councilman Thomas Poindexter, conservative foe of open-housing, and they met in each other's territories for a round of debates. Cleage said blacks did not get a fair shake, and a lot of money needed to be poured into the Detroit black ghetto or it was going to explode. Poindexter maintained that Detroit blacks had it better than blacks in the South, and he said a homeowner's rights ordinance which he authored, enabling homeowners to restrict selling if they wanted to, "is a measure of political strength which has convinced Negro leadership that it is not advantageous to make demonstrations." Cleage accused the whole city administration of pursuing "a policy of disaster," failing to give the blacks any help. "Spend some money on us if you want us to be happy and contented in that black ghetto you've built for us."

Said Jo Ann Hardee, chief of the *Detroit News* city-county bureau, quoting an anonymous observer, "The real tragedy is that there was no communication on an issue in which real communication is so vital."[11] Neither of the men made it all the way through primary and election, and the homeowner's ordinance was ruled unconstitutional. Poindexter was 7th out of 60, with 101,729 votes, and thus one of the 18 nominated (but not reelected in the runoffs); Cleage was 23d in the primary, with 17,625 votes.

Detroit, as Cleage warned Poindexter, could and did explode, in rebellion, two years later at the cost of 43 lives, with 7,200 arrested, 683 structures destroyed.

An editorial writer failed to take either side of the conservative Poindexter and radical Cleage confrontation seriously, and caricatured them thus:

We bring you, ladies and gentlemen, those worthy successors to Gallagher and Shean, fresh from their smash success at the 14th District Republican Club, that celebrated biracial comedy team: Poindexter and Cleage!

It is surely a working arrangement made in heaven, this series of debates between Councilman Thomas L. Poindexter, proud father of the lily-white home-owner's ordinance, and the Rev. Albert B. Cleage, Jr., "vote black" Council candidate and self-appointed prototype of the Angry Negro.

Each plays foil to the other. What more could Mr. Poindexter ask of Mr. Cleage than to come out to white homeowner country like Dick Durant's club-house and spout gross exaggeration about police brutality as a backdrop to Poindexter's remarks to a receptive white audience about crime and riot—his bland assurance that police brutality doesn't exist?

What greater blessing can the gods bestow upon Mr. Cleage than to have the eminently white Mr. Poindexter visit a Negro church to tell Negroes that they are getting all the fruits of the war on poverty (thus reminding them why)? How better could Mr. Cleage illustrate his pitch that whites don't know, don't care, and even delight in the Negro's problems?

One needs a Black Devil to sell himself, the other a White Devil. Each obliges the other.

Neither plays the part perfectly. Poindexter's bumbling platform manner and speaking style do not present the hard, hating face of the white supremacist among those who flock to his banner. Mr. Cleage's urbane appearance and articulate speech fail to evoke the Negro stereotype on which the Poindexters ride to popularity.

But even these failings are virtues in this grim mutual-aid society. Poindexter's very blandness and low pitch say to Cleage's Negro audience: "See, even whites who don't say 'Nigger' are against us." Cleage's unmistakably middle-class ways say to Poindexter's whites: "See, even the smart ones are fanatics who want to take over everything."

We would not go so far as to say that the two gentle-men planned it this way. Each tends to get a certain kick simply from braving "the enemy" in his own lair. But neither is so obtuse, we suspect, that he doesn't know what good it is doing him.

They are entitled, no doubt, to their fun, and to whatever additional votes this road show picks up for them. But the people of Detroit, who earnestly hope for fair and sensible answers to great community problems, who seek city councilmen devoted to that end, will learn nothing from these "debates" save reasons why these two, and some like them, do not measure up to the job.[12]

In 1966, Cleage tried for two offices at once, and sued election officials so he could run for both—congressman and member of the board of education. Cleage maintained that his constitutional rights would be violated if he were not allowed to run in both races. Circuit Judge Charles Kaufman ordered Cleage's name kept on the ballot for both posts. State law required that candidates filing for two offices would have to withdraw from one or be disqualified from both. Cleage's position was that the two jobs he was seeking were not included in the prohibitions against running for two offices. Kaufman said the part-time nonpaying post was in no way incompatible with being a congressman.[13] Incumbent Charles Diggs, whom Cleage has praised in the *Illustrated News,* won handily with 21,661; Cleage had 4,470, and David Boston, 3,639. Diggs went on in November to beat his Republican opponent 60,660 to 12,393. In the school race, Cleage narrowly missed nomination and was fifth with 40,731.[14]

Cleage sat out the 1968 elections in Detroit but found satisfaction in seeing the results come out much to his liking. He had his fingers crossed as to how well or how badly his choices would do. I asked him before the August 6, 1968 primary what he expected, especially in light of the remark of the Rev. James Chambers, minister of the St. John's United Presbyterian Church, who in the ensuing months was to leave the ministry. Chambers is also a former member of the Detroit Housing Commission, the Michigan Crime Commission, and the executive committee of the Citizens' Committee for Equal Opportunity. He had told Cleage that his type of militancy was dead and would be rejected continually at the polls. Chambers, who made his statement in a confrontation at Madonna College, Livonia, was running with forty-four others for four positions of eligibility to qualify for the runoff for two Common Council positions in the November election. In the lineup were two close Cleage aides, Edward Vaughn, executive secretary of Cleage's Citywide Citizen's Action Committee, and William M. Bell, an investment counselor and president of CCAC. Said Cleage, "If Chambers shows a poor vote, it would indicate on the basis of his own definition that that kind of Tom leadership loses support. If the black slate, if we have any success at all—it indicates a move to accept black independent action." Robert Tindal, 38, newcomer to Detroit and executive secretary of the Detroit NAACP, was also in the running but not on a list of Cleage's preferred candidates distributed at the church. Cleage's preference was his own Vaughn and Bell among the large field of forty-five. "Tindal has had enough exposure and he should run well. If Chambers gets nominated, then my concept of the black community needs to be reconsidered. If Tindal does, then there is general acceptance."

The council campaign would be one test, the school board election another. Here attorney Andrew W. Perdue, CCAC attorney who had been practicing law in Detroit for 19 years, was running with four others for two spots on the Detroit board of education. Cleage also said good showings for his friend Russell S. Brown, Jr., running in the 9th district, and his brother Hugh, the printer, running in the 16th district for Congress, "would be significant." He said if the militants showed failure it would call for a reevaluation of methods and procedures—such as going back and working on black consciousness over against Black Power. An evaluation of tactics, he said, is not a reevaluation of philosophy.

Bell and Vaughn did not win, but neither did Chambers.

Vaughn was 14th in the 45-man race; Chambers, 20th. Bell was 22d. Tindal, a black satisfactory to Cleage, was second among four qualifying candidates and went on to win in the November election a seat on the Common Council. Perdue was nominated, and also won in November. Saunders, Jackie Vaughn, and Del Rio were all top vote-getters in the primary and also succeeded in being elected representatives in November.

After the election, I asked Cleage if he felt black militancy was vindicated. "The election was meaningful," he said. "The whole community supported the black candidates. And there was growing black political strength. There could be a black mayor now in Detroit."

Nobody expected Cleage to take a shot in the 1969 Detroit mayoral and council election. His past poor showings, his age, his own individual stance in a very diverse black community, not to mention his alienation from whites, were factors that would work against him. As noted before, he has strong third-party national interests, and with continued national exposure (how many politicians can boast of prime space in *Life, Newsweek, Look, The New York Times, The Reporter, Esquire, Ebony,* and many Catholic and Protestant church and sociological journals in one year?), he might take one last fling in a larger, even though it might not be too promising, arena. Says white maverick columnist McIntyre, who has an ear to blacks and whites on the street, "Cleage couldn't be elected dogcatcher. That is how much his people think of him. In last year's Mardi Gras (the 1967 rebellion in Detroit), he hid under the bed some place (Cleage preferred to let the rebellion run its course). He was more afraid than you or I."

Cleage is not all that unpopular or disliked among blacks. A poll in October 1968 by *Detroit Free Press* interviewers discovered that Cleage is one of the "best-known and most respected" black leaders. Philip Meyer of the *Free Press* Washington staff, who piloted the survey, found among twenty-four "black leaders" Cleage ranked sixth, after five political office holders (Congressman Charles Diggs, Congressman John Conyers, city councilman Nicholas

Hood, and state representatives James Del Rio and Jackie Vaughn III). "The Rev. Albert Cleage, pastor of the Shrine of the Black Madonna and a pacesetter in the drive for black unity and black economic power, is the only non-politician in the exclusive group of Negro leaders whose names are recognized by more than three fourths of the black population." The poll queried 452 blacks also as to who in the list of twenty-four they thought "is doing the most good," and the men came through in the same lineup, with considerable less voting for Del Rio, Jackie Vaughn, and Cleage than for Diggs, Conyers, and Hood.

"Cleage's high ranking on the list is significant not only because he attained it without the advantage of a public office," the *Free Press* said, "but because his positions reflect in many ways the new mood of the black community."

The newspaper poll showed also that "seventy-two percent of those interviewed called development of strong businesses and industries under Negro control 'very important.'" Cleage's "economic orientation of Black Power, with Negro-run businesses already coming into being under his direction, is right on target." But Cleage parted company with the majority of blacks, the survey showed, over integration. "There is very little desire among Detroit Negroes to abandon the traditional civil rights goal of an integrated society. Political and economic power for blacks is a means of entering the mainstream. But Cleage's vision of the Promised Land is all black."[15] Cleage's own openness, inherent in his existential realism, is generally not communicable in the popular or practical realm, such as that of a public opinion poll. The further weakness of the poll in making value judgments on the basis of popular responses was noted by *Chronicle* columnist C. C. Douglas who warned the *Free Press*:

> *Free Press* reporter, let us pick our own leaders. Huh? You might note that despite the fact George Wallace has a lot of obviously strong support among white voters, the black press does not do you the injustice of calling him "white leader," thus lumping the white man from Don Lobsinger (widely known

Detroit extreme rightist) to Edward Kennedy into the same political bag.[16]

State senator Coleman A. Young, who ranked after Cleage in the popularity poll, who also is the new Democratic national committeeman from Michigan, declined to rank future leaders and candidates for Detroit, Michigan, or national political office. He told an interviewer of the Wayne State University *South End* newspaper, "I've always been of the school that thinks conditions produce leaders."[17]

Conditions in early spring began to produce the climate for a Black United Front, a term popular after the black community got behind Recorder's Court Judge George W. Crockett, who moved on Palm Sunday 1969 to release eight suspects police wanted held. They were hauled in six hours earlier after a white policeman was shot to death and another wounded outside C. L. Franklin's New Bethel church, which had been host to the RNA. Even the generally moderate editorial page of the *Michigan Chronicle* found itself in the same boat as its controversial militant columnist, Albert Cleage. An editorial, in a rare rapping of sister white media in the Detroit area, and quick-on-the-trigger state politicians who condemned Crockett and pressed for a review of his actions and court reform, noted that Crockett acted well within the law by summoning court to release those not duly charged. To the *Chronicle*, Crockett clearly averted a major rebellion which would have developed with the continued extension of holding people from the church without charge. To moderate former Detroit Councilman William Patrick, who wrote Crockett, "I salute you as an authentic hero of these trying times," the *Chronicle* said in capital letters, "WE CONCUR."

Signs paraded, some of them declaring, "Crockett for Mayor," in one long ring of pickets, 1,000 strong around police headquarters, and in Kennedy Square.

And Cleage wrote in his column:

The Detroit police, who have apparently been eager to provoke a situation which could be used to justify an attack upon the total black community, made a number of tactical blunders in their assault upon the Rev. C. L. Franklin's New Bethel Church. . . .

In the black community, the Rev. C. L. Franklin and the New Bethel Baptist church are just about as radical as (Michigan) Bishop (Richard) Emrich and the Episcopal Cathedral. When the police charged into New Bethel Church, with guns blazing, shooting up church property and endangering the lives of innocent men, women, and children, the total black community was outraged. Police maintain they did not know women and children were in the church and also said they were fired on from the church.

Every black pastor in the city of Detroit knew that it could happen to him and his church. Suddenly he realized that "respectability" was no protection against a racist onslaught. So the Detroit police "radicalized" a whole new segment of Detroit's black community. . . .

Now, at last, Judge Crockett has brought law and order to Recorder's Court and to Detroit, and this one single fact is the most important thing that has happened in Detroit in more than a century. The white police, prosecutor, and mass communication media have done what no black leadership had been able to accomplish. They have united the 95 percent of the black community which is necessary to elect a black mayor. . . . If the election were tomorrow, certainly Judge Crockett could win hands down.[18]

CHAPTER 12

Structure of the Nation

For six months—from October 12, 1967 to April 18, 1968 —Albert Cleage was the visible, titular head of the 660,000 Detroit black community.

It was a shaky alliance from the first that formed the Federation of Self-Determination in the aftermath of the 1967 summer rebellion. Cleage, whose own Citywide Citizens Action Committee was already in action, starting as a relief effort and moving into community organizing, was called in by L. M. Quinn, editor and general manager of the *Michigan Chronicle,* who was seeking a new effective unity of blacks. Moderates pledged their support, and in a caucus agreed that Cleage be chairman. However, when the moderate leaders from the NAACP, the Urban League, the Detroit Baptist Pastors' Conference, and other groups went back to their constituencies they found their members would have nothing to do with Cleage and his militancy. These leaders then began to try to block Cleage's election as chairman.

Several dozen fledgling groups and some individuals joined as charter members to create the federation. Besides unity, there was the appeal of new money from foundations, churches, and other sources that was more readily available to a common front than to individuals and their groups. Said Milton Henry, "The minute you get a whole lot of money around, then this is the thing to belong to, and it is a measure for coming in and lending your name to it. It is also the prestigious thing to do, and people with no interest at all in the uplifting of this race will come in it. They come in like maggots around a piece of rotten meat.

We do a lot better without money, for with money you get affiliated with people not worth a damn."

The bylaws of the new federation pledged the members "to create a nonsectarian, nonpartisan, nonprofit federation devoted to improving the political, social, and economic status of black people and oppressed people; to eradicate racial prejudice; to secure the elimination of racial segregation with all of its inherent evils; to develop self-determination in all areas of community life for black people. All members are held accountable for their activities."

The bylaws were flexible enough to allow for the enmities of long standing and for differences in philosophies in meeting ghetto ills. Each organization representative was allotted ten votes; special persons coming in on an individual basis were allowed one vote each. A quorum was 40 percent of member organizations. "Individual organizations and institutions may request, on the floor of the assembly, support on programs or issues of concern to the community," and "member organizations maintain the prerogative to decline support."

While the moderates—those closer to the city establishment, the traditional UAW-CIO establishment, and the large middle-class clergy-grouping—began strategy to block Cleage, the militant radicals were uneasy but could accept Cleage as chairman. The militants who finally constituted the federation after the disaffection of the moderates were described by one of the insiders of the federation as divided in a number of emotional categories, besides the more straight-away category of playing it cool and working on economic development. There were (1) "those who felt it was impossible to rebuild, and wanted to burn down the country and out of the ruins build something; (2) those who professed revolution for the sake of revolution; (3) those emotionally disturbed who hated themselves; (4) those who constituted the religiously confused."

The extreme, geographic separatists had not fully formed their approach and rode along with the federation for a time. It was not until after the dissolution of the federation that the militant Henrys (Milton and Richard) announced their Republic of New Africa. As late as March 31, 1968, less than a month before the breakup of the federation, the Henrys were still taking part in militant programs scheduled at the Shrine of the Black Madonna, such as the national convention of the Mississippi Freedom Democratic Party where Milton Henry, Los Angeles black nationalist Ron Karenga, and others were speakers. RNA first vice-president Milton Henry could still say after leaving Cleage's umbrella, "Whatever you say about him, he is sincere," and "I'd love to see Cleage mayor—we could do a hell of a lot worse."

The initial impetus to dissolution came from the moderates, not from the radicals. This was clear at lunch with one of the leading black moderates who has for years headed the Detroit wing of one of the staid predominantly black organizations (not the NAACP). I did not tell him what I wanted to talk to him about until we were seated at a table in the Detroit press club. He nearly blew right out of the club when I told him I was interested in his views of Cleage and related matters, such as the federation. "Don't you write about Cleage. Forget about that right now. How can you . . . ? I have never read his column in the *Chronicle;* I refuse to read anything he writes." My guest himself had a rather shabby record for doing anything important except to sit with important white executives at head tables at banquets. When he had simmered down, he did reveal that he and other moderates had gone into the organizing of the federation expecting to come out top dogs or at least to hold the controlling strings. He accused Lorenzo (Renny) Freeman, then executive director of the West Central Organization (the Alinsky-orientated interracial protest group) of a "double cross." Freeman was head of the steering committee in two meetings that gave birth to the federation, and presided at the organizing session. With Freeman presiding, Cleage was elected federation chairman.

When I talked with Freeman later in New York and St. Louis, he said, "My politics are clean." Freeman's black militancy caused him to quit the WCO and to join the Interreligious Foundation for Community Organization as a staffer in New York. He recalled that first organizing meeting of the federation, "I was nominated (for chairman), but I did not accept the nomination. I am not a leader, I am an organizer." Moderates apparently thought that Freeman, as head of the WCO, which had been largely white, could be depended on to keep the moderate blacks well in mind and dump the nomination committee's choice, Cleage. "They (moderates) came to play games. This was after the rebellion, and I declined, and said we ought to consider a nominee at that point in time who was at the cutting edge of social change." There was "no bargain," Freeman said. The moderates just "played their games and assumed I played with them. They assumed at the first I was in their camp, which was a false assumption. There was no double cross—it was a bad time to organize (after the rebellion). I played it straight up. I never played it any other way."

Some of the moderates soon set up their rival group, the Detroit Council of Organizations, under the Rev. Roy Allen, black pastor of the Chapel Hill Baptist Church and president of the Detroit Baptist Pastors' Conference, although some moderates continued halfheartedly in the federation. Allen began to concern himself with setting up centers to house day-care programs, community action groups, tenant clubs—basically a small-settlement house program in storefronts, a band-aid type of program, some called it, a rehash of the traditional white approach to the inner city, according to others. Cleage and the federation were eager for economic and political projects.

The rivalry between the moderates and the militants came to a head when a Ford Foundation grant of $137,000 was made available through the New Detroit Committee, a 39-member group of predominantly upper-crust leaders, most of them white. The NDC was backed by the Metropolitan Fund, primarily a group of businessmen with considerable property themselves who were interested in civic affairs and also, as one person suggested, in private funding of social projects to keep the tax bite for urban affairs from increasing among their own holdings. Head of the Metropolitan Fund, J. L. Hudson, Jr., most prestigious Detroit department store operator in Detroit (he is to Detroit what Macy's is to New York, and Marshall Field to Chicago), also became head of NDC when it was officially launched, with the special blessing of Governor George Romney and Mayor Jerome Cavanagh. The moderates just couldn't dig that money going to the federation and its militancy. The NDC then decided to offer $100,000 each to Cleage's FSD and to Allen's DCO.

The federation made it clear through Freeman and another militant, Norvel Harrington, a student, both members of the NDC, that the federation would want complete say on the use of any money given to it. Hudson ignored the warnings of Freeman and Harrington and proceeded to announce the grant to both the federation and the DCO. The NDC had asked to receive an accounting of funds and that the funds not be used for any political purpose, among other things. The giving of the funds with strings attached angered the militants. Allen, however, was eager to accept the funds. Though he grumbled that any money should be offered to Cleage he told me later that he had no real animosity against Cleage. "We are labeled as not so militant as his group, but it depends on the definition of 'militant.' I believe in Black Power as a measure to an end, not as complete separation."

On the same evening that Hudson had offered the $100,000 to each group, more than 150 members of the Federation of Self-Determination gathered at the Detroit Fisher YMCA to decide what to do about the grant. The executive committee of the federation recommended that the grant be rejected, and subsequently it was rejected unanimously in the larger vote of the federation. The federation also voted to sever all relations with NDC. Federation militants Renny Freeman and Norvel Harrington resigned from the NDC, although Harrington was later to rejoin. Said columnist Tom McIntyre:

> In the same way in which prohibition-era gangsters were paid tribute for illegal franchises and areas by traffickers in booze, the New Detroit Committee's

young prince charming last week caused to be announced its own terms on how Cleage's and a more supine Negro rival group could qualify for a $100,000 grant each, provided out of the treasury of the extra-official consortium. No doubt about it, agreement to the terms by either Negro group would put them in the same position as the child whose weekly behavioral report card is the criterion upon which his allowance or its revocation is based. That, mind you, in the case of the Rev. "Toddy" Cleage, who had already made it clear that nothing short of secession by the Negro community from all public affairs not dominated by himself would be abided by him.[1]

At the press conference rejecting the money, Cleage said, "We feel the (New Detroit) committee has rejected the premise on which it was possible for us to work together. They either don't understand the meaning of self-determination or have rejected it as a basis for the building of a new Detroit. We'll accept white money, but not white leadership and dictation."[2]

The almost unheard-of turning down of white money by blacks surprised apparently not only Hudson but also blacks and others across the nation. Cleage reported congratulations from "Chicago, New York, California, and across the country." He wrote in his *Michigan Chronicle* column a week later:

Everywhere black brothers and sisters were glad that a black organization had finally expressed in concrete terms the meaning of the Black Revolution without the confusion of a hot summer night. The simple action of turning down money which the white folks had offered seemed to unite black folks as we have never been united before. The white folks can't understand it. Down through the years they have figured that money could buy anything. This theory has been the working basis of their black-white relationships. After all, white folks have been buying and selling black people since the days of the slave ships. Black people have changed. The messages of support from across the country are evidence of this fact.[3]

Approval of local black militants was evidenced also in the capacity congregation at the Shrine on the snowy January Sunday following the refusal to accept the money.

The rejection of the $100,000 was consistent with Cleage's writings a month earlier. Describing problems of organizing the nation, he said one of

> the hang-ups is the argument about whether or not we can accept white money. White money is almost as bad as a white girl. Let's say that you have an organization and some white folks come and say, "We are going to give you $10,000 to carry out your work." You ask "Any strings attached?" and they answer "No strings attached. We just believe in what you are doing." You persist, "How come you believe in what we are doing all of a sudden? You must be after something." They repeat, "You say you want self-determination for the black community. Here is $10,000 to help you get it." And you say, "Lay it on the table. We will debate it." Then we spend the next year debating among ourselves, "Can we cash that check? Won't it corrupt us if we take the white folks' money? How can we use the white man's money and fight him at the same time?" We debate and debate, and meanwhile that $10,000 check lies there and just about tears the whole group to pieces.[4]

The parting of the ways over the Hudson offer demonstrated that a coalition of blacks, already divided into rival camps, could to a certain extent still have their innate divisiveness confirmed by white money on the table.

At the meeting which was to be the last one of the federation, the grants that Cleage had received for his own projects, largely through church auspices, were bothering some of the militants, especially since the federation had remained nearly penniless after refusing the Hudson NDC grant. Just how poor the federation was, was revealed in the final disbursement of funds – $250 was returned to the black students' association of Wayne State University; $1,000 turned over to the now defunct *Inner City Voice*, edited by John Watson, militant student who went on to edit the controversial Wayne State *South End*, the university paper turned into a crusading black militant and new politics paper; and $2,000 went to Betty Shabazz, Malcolm X's widow.

One leading black in the community who is a confidant of both moderates and militants said he went to the final meeting of the federation at the Fisher YMCA in response to a rumor that Cleage was to give an accounting of the spending of his funds for the Citywide Citizens Action Committee, the organization formed after the rebellion to meet emergency needs and to develop community action groups. The CCAC had received $19,000 from the Interfaith Action Council (originally the Interfaith Emergency Council), an ad hoc group made up of Detroit representatives from the major denominations and the archdiocese. The Interreligious Foundation for Community Organization by this time had given $85,000 to CCAC. (The United Church of Christ gave $25,000, United Presbyterians and Episcopalians gave about $85,000, Cleage said at the annual meeting of CCAC, January 22, 1968.) An accounting suggested by Glanton Dowdell and Dan Aldridge at a previous meeting, was asked for right away at the outset of the final meeting. Freeman, one of the vice-chairmen of the federation (with Edward Brazelton, president of the Booker T. Washington Business Association), rose to say, "Why should Cleage give an accounting of his CCAC?"

The end of the federation had already been decided by a caucus of its leaders. Said Russell S. Brown, Jr., son of the general secretary of the African Methodist Episcopal Church in the U.S., head of a public relations firm, and member of the federation, "In a caucus we decided the only thing the federation was doing was creating more division among militants."

The minutes of the final meeting, which failed to show

any of the differing ideological or emotional tensions in the group, said:

> Renny Freeman reported upon several federation members suggesting that the Federation of Self-Determination close its operations. He also reported that the executive committee had considered these suggestions and agreed that the best interests of the black community can be served by having groups operate under more vigorous individual organization initiative, rather than under the federated structure, at this time.
>
> (Attorney) Kenneth Cockrel (of the North Woodward Inter-Faith Project) moved that the federation be dissolved temporarily; that the *Inner City Voice* be the recipient of all remaining funds including the $250.00 recently donated by the Association of Black Students; and that should we want to regroup at a later time, we do so.
>
> After some discussion, Kenneth Cockrel withdrew his motion.
>
> Harold Neil moved that the federation be dissolved; motion carried.
>
> Attorney Andrew Perdue was empowered to implement all of the legal steps required to dissolve the legal corporate status of the Federation of Self-Determination.

The federation's attorney, Andrew Perdue, now a member of the Detroit board of education, told me in his skyscraper, chartreuse-carpeted office, with charging bull abstracts on the wall, that "the militants, a lot of them, figured later that Cleage was not militant enough. And, when you look at it, Cleage is a moderate—he believes in programs and economic development. Others believe in guns, which is OK for them, but they should build something too. I doubt if anybody else could have held the group together." He praised Cleage's approach in seeking to build economic projects—the Black Star supermarket was already in operation, and the Shell gas station, with plans for a clothing factory, all black-operated on a cooperative basis. "This is probably the only way possible to compete with big business, to pool assets. The whole economy of many of the new emerging countries is based on co-ops. A lot of things he's been saying over 15 years, in fact, practically everything he's said has come true – if you listen to what he says and if you don't let emotion take over." The diminishing efforts of the CCAC did not bother Perdue. "Maybe it will fold up. It was an action group. You can get up and holler (on the street) but this is to no avail. CCAC was founded as a protest post-riot group. I see it evolving into something else," Perdue said in the summer of 1968.

In a way, the dissolution of the federation among the militants, after the moderates were out, is the result of a generation gap. "We have done our protesting, and want to build," said Russell Brown, Jr. The young activists and anarchists would probably have used the money marked for CCAC (from the Interfaith Action Council) and other funds to bring arms to defend people of the inner city. Dan Aldridge, head of the Detroit SNCC chapter, it was said, would have used it for informational programs to help educate people of the inner city. Ed Vaughn, executive director of CCAC, favored co-ops and business projects, as did the committee's assistant secretary Russell Brown, Jr. and financial secretary William Bell. Brown disliked putting everything into the co-op bag and Bell, a businessman, was believed to want diversification beyond co-op stores with some of the work on a profit-making basis because more people could be involved if there were profit. Cleage's belief is that profits in co-ops should be plowed back into lowering of prices for the consumer. "He feels there would be a breakdown down the road and people would squabble over money if it were profit-making (for the investors), a valid view," said Brown.

Now as Cleage looks toward channeling funds of CCAC into more precise economic projects, the direction seems in keeping with intentions of the grants. The biggest grant to CCAC, the $85,000 from IFCO for instance, was, as IFCO put it, for the "Citywide Citizens Action Committee, a group that emerged from the ashes of the 1967 rebellion.

CCAC seeks to develop comprehensive programs for urban development and home ownership, black resident ownership of businesses, improvement of ghetto schools and other services."

Cleage defined CCAC in his New Year's 1968 sermon as uniting "masses of black people, including many who have hitherto been untouched by organizational efforts, behind a program of self-determination."

The CCAC, which emerged after the 1967 rebellion, according to Ed Vaughn, head of the committee, was concerned with street rallies, mass meetings, motorcades to pass out leaflets, various meetings with neighbor gatherings to help understand what the problems are, "but we came to feel the people generally lacked any kind of power to do anything," he said. "After the death of Dr. King, we seemed to move into a new era and it was the end of the protest era. We sought to start something more positive than empty protest. For in protest we found we were asking people to do things that we ought to be doing ourselves. Instead of asking people to treat us better, we decided to start operating our own stores, for instance."

During the active year of CCAC, Cleage was also pushing the direct-action projects of the Shrine of the Black Madonna. These were largely projects of cell groups or action groups which replaced area study and social groups and were coordinated in the Inner City Organizing Committee, now called the Action Council of the Shrine of the Black Madonna. The projects included: securing names of needy children and distributing clothing, preparing lists of black candidates and working for their election, and conducting a number of socials such as "fish fries" and black musical programs in the church. Most of the action group reports for 1968 said they were just getting organized or "we weren't too active" and "we'll do more next year."

The Action Council, with chairmen of the groups, took on the bigger, community-related projects such as launching or helping to launch the Inner City Parents Council, the Inner City Student Organization, the Inner City Housing Conference, the Afro-American Committee Against

Racist Wars, the Negro Retail Employees Association, and the Black Teachers' Workshop. The Action Council brought in various speakers, among them state representative James Del Rio, Calvin Stubbs, president of the Black Trades Union Local 124, William Patrick, of the New Detroit Committee, and U.S. Congressman John Conyers. The council supported the BUD (Black Unity Day) rally at Cobo Hall in April 1968. Cleage was a speaker, and the Shrine's senior choir sang. The council put out posters and bumper stickers for the rally. It conducted the program for the starving of Biafra and put out press releases — for example, a release announcing support of the protest of black athletes Tommie Smith and John Carlos at the Olympic games.

The programs were largely church-centered at the start of 1969, when Cleage said that CCAC, which had included community membership, would be kept alive only as a standby group that could be activated in case of another rebellion or emergency, in keeping with its origin. When CCAC was organized in the summer of 1967, according to former police commissioner aide Hubert Locke, it was considered "to be the city's largest grassroots organization, and it has become Cleage's chief power base."[5]

With the evolution of the program of CCAC into more specific projects having a direct tie-in with the church, Cleage's own philosophy of developing co-ops exclusively could be applied more directly. Certainly, with the officers of the CCAC holding different economic views, particularly Bell and Brown in favor of economic diversity, Dowdell wrapped up in more protest and organizing work, and Vaughn a bit of a capitalist with his book shop, Cleage's vision of nonprofit co-ops seemed more on track without the hamstringing of the committee.

Cleage presented an itemized accounting of CCAC at the committee's annual meeting in the church. He distributed a detailed auditor's report prepared by Detroit accountant Loy A. Cohen at a cost of $2,132. Cleage had drawn no salary at all in connection with CCAC, although Dowdell received $8,207.03 for community organizing, and executive director Edward Vaughn, $10,153.88. An educational consultant received $3,230.64 in connection with the education protests and black teachers' workshop and related projects. Cleage's brother Henry received $250, which Cleage explained was only a drop in the bucket for the long hours of legal work that Henry performed.

Cleage's salary comes from the church. It was $11,000 in 1968. With annuity ($1,513.00), car allowance ($1,040.-00), plus hospitalization, electricity, gas, telephone, and $4,081 rent allowance, his salary would be $17,395.27, not counting lecture honoraria. The working budget for 1969 has a base salary of $9,360 and a trimming of rent allowance to $3,000. Cleage is planning to move to less expensive quarters. In all, the Shrine salary will be down to $14,920, with fringe items included. This cutback apparently allows for frequent lecture tours to promote his book *The Black Messiah.*

CCAC received $109,077.87, according to Cohen's audit; it spent $51,809.30 on operating expenses and sent $46,268.57 on to the Economic Development Corporation, newly formed to research and set up the co-op projects. Most of this corporation's outlay of $83,002.11 was for new property—a two-story building at Livernois and Davison, several miles north of the church, for a day nursery; a one-story office building on Linwood; and similar expenses of the Black Cooperative Services, Inc., the umbrella for a clothing factory on Whitfield, west and north of the church; a service station north of the church; and possibly a new dry-cleaning service. All current CCAC and Economic Development funds are directed to the specific projects and their properties. The Racial Justice Now Committee of the UCC gave the corporation $2,000 in 1968; and $5,000 was given it for 1969 by the Michigan Conference of the UCC, a renewal of support ($4,000) given in 1968.

The diminishing role of CCAC was explained by Cleage in the annual report, which he interspersed with comments as he read it to the fifty persons at the meeting— "We never had a formal membership—all of you who want to participate, do so." With only one technical question about tax exemption, the report was adopted unanimously. Said Cleage, "When it became apparent that CCAC could not attempt large basic community programs requiring substantial funding because of the opposition of the New Detroit Committee, the Ford Foundation, and other funding agencies, the Board of Trustees decided not to fritter away the very limited funds which had already been made available by religious groups in a futile effort to research and plan expensive projects which would only be ridiculed and ignored by funding agencies. The white community seemed at that time, and still is to a degree, paralyzed by a guilt-fear psychosis which found expression in the insane myth that whatever plan or project black militants proposed served only as a screen for the purchase of guns and the instigation of violence.

"CCAC had no alternative but to plan in terms of a one-year operation with paid staff and salaries reduced to a minimum and a carefully planned program of community participation for black self-determination upon the one hand, and a bootstrap economic development program upon the other. The board undertook to set up pilot cooperative projects and to train personnel in cooperation with the Economic Development Corporation of Central Church (Shrine). The church and the Economic Development Corporation guaranteed continuing financial support for the pilot projects even if the white community decided to whiteball the entire undertaking. In this way CCAC hoped to launch a Black Cooperative Movement which could continue after its limited funds would normally have been dissipated in salaries and consultation fees. Most black organizations get funds and after eighteen months, most has been paid out in salaries and consultant fees and little gets to work. I was concerned that we do not whittle away the money in consultant fees."

Raymond O. Hatcher, director of urban affairs for the United Community Services (and a boyhood friend of Cleage), said after the CCAC annual meeting, "This is mighty good accounting; a lot of these organizations are supposed to be grass roots but give no fiscal accounting or explanation."

Initial work of Cleage in the co-op movement for Black Power was the launching of the Black Star Co-op Market early in 1968. Originally "Black Star" applied to a co-op housing program that Cleage had in mind but gave up as the larger program of Accord, Inc., sponsored by big business executives, got underway. Accord, though interracial, has its voting stock in the hands of a black majority. Cleage, as a member of that board, hopes Accord can build sufficient low-income housing and low-priced rehabilitation units. If it comes out with outrageous offerings, he is prepared to resign, but he has faith it has a chance of being a useful housing vehicle. The FHA had turned down a request of the Black Star Co-op to set up a housing cooperative. The store at the outset sold $9,000 in stocks at $25 a share. The cooperative is independent of the church, although Cleage is a founder; most of the stockholders (Cleage is one) are associated with the church, and the president is Ed Vaughn.

I chatted with Vaughn in a rear room of the store as he counted out eggs from a big carton into size-dozen containers. He said the store had averaged $90,000 in a three-month period with 20 percent profit. Above him was a poster with the name and address of the New Republic of Africa and the message, "We are making a new nation — a life of promise without racism or oppression." Vaughn said the eggs had come from the Black Muslim farm at Cassopolis, Michigan, and other products came through a Libby wholesale dealer and a Grosse Pointe foods chain that had given low prices. He explained the name of the Ashanti Co-op, Inc., which runs the store, as coming from the name of an old West African nation of the Middle Ages. The shares in the store do not return a direct dividend; profits go into paying for the building, for further economic expansion, and eventually in rebate with lower prices to customers. Some say the prices should be lower, while others say they are reasonable. I compared their sales prices one weekend, as listed in an area newspaper, with those of a big chain store. Black Star wanted 49 cents for a five-pound bag of Gold Medal flour while Kroger had a ten-pound bag the same week for 85 cents; Black Star, 79 cents for a three-pound can of Crisco shortening, Kroger, 69 cents; chuck-roast — Black Star, 69 cents a pound,

Kroger, 59 cents; head lettuce – Black Star, 25 cents, Kroger, 19 cents. And Black Star had chitterlings, $3.85, and hog maws, 29 cents. The store is not technically part of the Black Cooperative Services, Inc., new umbrella for economic projects, but may come under it eventually.

In Black Cooperative Services, Inc., also selling shares, is the Black Star Shell Service Center, a station at the corner of Linwood at Clairmount, directly west of the corner where the 1967 rebellion started at Clairmount and Twelfth. Open 24 hours a day, offering basic gas station services, the station pumps 55,000 gallons a month compared to 35,000 a month before the cooperative took it over. The goal is to own five franchises, which would entitle the cooperative to become a Shell dealer and thus to wholesale to their own stations and others.

Also in Black Cooperative Services, Inc. is the Black Star Clothing Company, "manufacturers of African-style clothing," making dresses, daishikis, buba suits. The factory is in a blocked-up double storefront painted gray with no identification. You make an appointment and knock on the front door to get in. A half-dozen people sewing – including a young man from Northern High, a young lady from Cincinnati who answered an ad, and Kris, Cleage's daughter studying art at Wayne State University – manned sewing machines in one long room. Karl Bell, 24, tall, energetic, former student of crafts and fashion in Detroit and New York, designed and cut the fabrics in the other long room. Mrs. Barbara Martin, Cleage's sister, managed the operation and ran the front office showing newly made garments to black buyers. Specialties include besides daishikis, buba suits, Western turtle-neck shirts, round felah hats, cashmere and mohair special suits (for music groups, etc.), slack reversible suits – plain on one side, elaborate designs on the other. "Sometimes all African material is too busy and people like a combination," Barbara said. There was durable Dutch-wax cloth from Ghana in exotic design and colorful Kanga cloth with printed sayings in Swahili. Bright baby-doll dresses, a current fad, were mixed in also on the racks. The factory, in rented quarters, was planning a move to the newly purchased Livonois two-story building, with the factory in the basement and showroom on the first floor. The factory and gas station had a combined income of $132,027.83 but showed a slight loss of $5,074.18 after high starting expenses in the first year, "which is pretty good," said Cleage at the annual meeting. "Most businessmen in the first year lose more. We were trying to figure out production methods and ways for discounts. It was good; I give you my opinion. You may think it's bad."

In the economic area Cleage's initial efforts have been repeated by others. The Rev. Otis Saunders' Trinity AME Church laid plans for a "consumers investment" firm with 1,000 persons investing in a small food firm to control it, hoping to trigger similar investments in larger, national corporations to control them. There is ICBIF (Inner City Business Improvement Forum) which operates everything interracially but under black control. ICBIF board chairman is Charles Morton, Baptist minister, Ph.D., former college dean and philosophy professor, and member of the state board of education. (Morton says of Cleage, "He serves a useful function of developing a sense of pride and independence in the general population, which is necessary for significant growth toward self-dignity, although he has a weakness in not enough planning.") ICBIF runs a black-controlled hospital, bank, loan corporation, and supermarket. UCC pastor and councilman Nicholas Hood and also the Linwood Community Organization have both announced plans for black-run supermarkets. So have five young black entrepreneurs, who made $15,000 selling candy, washing cars, and holding raffles. They have acquired six acres in a nearly forgotten borderline black strip, Royal Oak Township, for the food store and other outlets. Even moderate Roy Allen, with the Rev. M. B. Terrell of the Triedstone Baptist Church, are getting into the same action. They announced they have joined with fifty clergy, parishioners, and others in buying a store of Allied Supermarkets. Though controlled predominantly by blacks, the staff of the $530,000 store (with $40,000 from the black ministers and their congregations) will be integrated.

With black-controlled new businesses popping up now all over the ghetto, Cleage is not sitting still with his projects but turning his thoughts to getting blacks into labor unions, red feather efforts, and supply services. He says a black union that "can force white contractors to use black labor (plumbers, electricians, carpenters) is essential in the ghetto. We are moving in that direction in Detroit. If the black church supports this effort it can sweep the country. We must build for ourselves black social agencies controlled by black people. We need a black trucking line to bring food from black farmers in the South to black consumers in the North. The only organization seriously moving in the right direction is the Black Muslim Movement headed by Elijah Mohammed. They are beginning to build farms and to truck their produce into urban centers. This is a move toward genuine Black Power. This is the kind of realistic program being undertaken by the Black Christian Nationalist Movement through the Economic Development Corporation of its shrines and the Black Cooperative Services, Inc. All black people must work together to build Black Power. We are only at the beginning. The black church must lead the way."

Cleage's plans call for the black church to play a key role. Four of the six areas or compartments of his Black Christian Nationalist Movement center in the church directly. Besides the Economic Development Corporation of the Shrine and the Black Cooperative Services, both of which are responsible to the Shrine, with an intermediary board of the wider community, there are four areas which will work through the church: (1) Heritage committee, whose director will be a sort of substitute for the traditional director of education, and would prepare new black curricula, among other things; (2) the regular worship program of the Shrine, which is also to be educative and preparatory for the total movement; (3) the Order of the Black Madonna, covering the benevolence work of the church which involves directing a day nursery, help for the aged, and family services and clinics. "In most cities whites left skeletal agencies which are not adequately related to needs, and blacks do not control these." He

believes these new black services might come under a
United Black Appeal originally charted by IFCO; (4) the
action council and action groups in the church which
tackle specific projects; for example, in local political
action, from working for decentralization of schools to
getting persons registered to vote in a Union Trades Board
election.

Cleage hopes to begin eventually to ordain young men
to the Black Christian Nationalist Movement at the Detroit Shrine and in shrines in other cities that are in the
process of being planned. "If we ordain, we will need our
own training," which he said would consist of giving the
ordinand "enough to do what has to be done. We will encourage young seminarians to come and try something
new." Cleage believes the government would recognize
the ordinations because we would be an "ecclesiastical
incorporation."

"In a sense," he admitted, "it is a new denomination for
black people, but in a peculiar sense, we would have relationship with the UCC; we can do that because of the
autonomy and right to develop within the free church concept of the UCC. The Black Christian Nationalist Movement would be structured here (in Detroit), but if the
UCC can stand us, we can stand them." He sees other
denominations having "fraternal" relationships or associate participation in the movement by involvement in
the various "areas" of the Nation.

Cleage thinks the peculiar arrangement might be a
"milestone ecumenically" in an era that is wearying of
doctrinal approaches to unity. A church or a pastor would
be in the denomination, yet out of it to the point of even
doing ordinations apart from prescribed procedures.

He would combine the full spirit of the Black Revolution
with the Black Christian Nationalist Movement, whose
Christian ties fit in with the Baptist, Methodist, and re-
vivalistic heritage of most blacks. "The Black Muslims demand too much of a break with the past for blacks, most
of whom have grown up in a Christian church of some
sort. We don't demand a break in faith, or customs."

Cleage laid groundwork for a new "black denominational" look with his movement preparing to bring in other churches. The first to join with him was Bishop David Hill, 40, of the House of Israel, Cleveland, who promptly renamed his church also the Shrine of the Black Madonna. Hill, who attended the Churches of Christ conservative "black" Nashville Christian Institute and was ordained by the Church of God in 1959, says he is an agent of "this diocese of Cleveland" under Cleage. Next in line is expected to be the United House of God church in Harlem, which would change its name also. Other churches of the six-church United House of God denomination may also join the Detroit-based Black Christian Nationalist Movement. "In the next five years I see all churches worthy of their name coming into the Black Nation," says Bishop Hill. "Churches as they are, are dying." He says he does not object to continued ties with the UCC if it is deemed necessary and "serves the Nation." He concedes the new movement is a "sort of denomination, but I like the word Nation better."

In recent weeks, Bishop Hill has been preferring the title rabbi, which means teacher, instead of the Greek-Old English term bishop. "It's a way of getting away from white Christianity," he said.

Cleage has tentative plans for a national conference or convention in the spring of 1970 to launch the new national movement at the Shrine. The invitation to join will be general. Early in his planning churches in seven cities had already indicated an interest: Chicago, Cleveland, New York, Philadelphia, Pittsburgh, Milwaukee, and Muncie, Indiana.

Says Cleage, "If they accomplish nothing else than to get the idea of a Black Messiah across, they will be an influence. This form will make other churches change. I am invited to talk all over, but this does not change anything. But when in a community there is truly one black church of the Nation—a shrine of the Black Madonna of the Black Christian Nationalist Movement, there will be an impact in that area on all."

BLACK COMMUNITY

NATIONAL BOARD

BLACK CHRISTIAN NATIONALIST MOVEMENT

```
Field person        Field person    Field person      Field person     Field person
— black heritage    — religious     — social service  — economic       — Black
                                                                         Cooperative Services

Heritage            Shrine — Detroit  Order of          Economic Corp.   Black Cooperative
committee           Worship           Black Madonna                      Services
                    — Action councils — Charity

"                   Shrine —          "                 "                "
                    Cleveland

"                   Shrine —          "                 "                "
                    Philadelphia

"                   Shrine —          "                 "                "
                    Pittsburgh

"                   Shrine —          "                 "                "
                    Harlem

                    Shrine —
                    Chicago
```

CCAC — a catalyst to be recalled in case of emergency.

Notes

INTRODUCTION

1. "Message to the Black Nation," *Michigan Chronicle*, June 29, 1968, p. 16A.

2. *Ibid.*, July 13, 1968, p. 16A.

3. Article by J. Mark Bradley, *Springfield* (Mass.) *Union*, February 20, 1967.

4. "Message to the Black Nation," *op. cit.*, June 1, 1968, p. 16A.

5. Sermon, Palm Sunday, April 7, 1968.

6. "Message to the Black Nation," *op. cit.*, November 25, 1967, p. 16A.

7. Albert B. Cleage, Jr., *The Black Messiah* (New York: Sheed & Ward, Inc., 1968), p. 87.

8. *Ibid.*, p. 92.

9. An attitude ameliorated by a summer education program — "Summer Hope" — piloted by the Archdiocese of Detroit and also ameliorated by the fact that the summer of 1968 was quiet and peaceful except for the horn-honking revelry over the Tigers' baseball pennant.

10. *Daily Press* (interim newspaper during strike), January 17, 1968, p. 3.

11. "Message to the Black Nation," *op. cit.*, December 9, 1967, p. 16A.

12. "Republic of New Africa Minister Hits *Accord* as New Exploitation," *Michigan Chronicle*, July 6, 1968, p. 2B.

13. Profile by Al Dunmore, *Michigan Chronicle*, February 10, 1962, p. 8B.

14. "Cleage Says Black Power Is No Threat to Whites," *Michigan Catholic*, March 21, 1968, p. 1.

15. "Message to the Black Nation," *op. cit.*, December 2, 1967, p. 12A.

CHAPTER 1
PARADOX IN WORSHIP

1. Oscar E. Maurer, editor (Boston: Pilgrim Press, 1947).
2. *Book of Worship for Free Churches*, General Council of Congregational Churches (Oxford Press: New York, 1948).
3. Sterling Gray, "Man of the Year: Rev. Albert B. Cleage, Jr., Architect of a Revolution," *The Liberator Magazine*, December 1963.
4. *Detroit Free Press*, March 25, 1967.

CHAPTER 2
NATION WITHIN A NATION

1. "Message to the Black Nation," *Michigan Chronicle*, August 3, 1968.
2. Leonard Allen, "New York Critic Defines Role of Black Art," *The South End*, Wayne State University, December 5, 1968, p. 3.
3. Also: "Of those who called religion 'extremely important,' only 37 percent had tendencies toward nationalism. Of those who called religion 'very important,' 44 percent were nationalistic. And of those for whom religion was only fairly important or not important at all, 60 percent tended toward nationalism." Philip Meyer, "Black Extremism Blunted," *Detroit Free Press*, Washington Bureau, October 29, 1968.
4. Cf. Eldridge Cleaver, *Soul on Ice* (New York: McGraw-Hill, 1968), p. 30 ff.
5. E. U. Essien-Udom, *Black Nationalism* (New York: Dell, 1965, © University of Chicago Press, 1962), pp. 66, 68, 72.
6. "Mixed Bag of Emotion Exists on Race Issue," *Michigan Chronicle*, August 31, 1968, p. 1.
7. "Abbey Lincoln and Black Nationalism," *The Illustrated News*, December 3, 1962, p. 3.
8. J. Martin Bailey and Charles Cobb, "Interview: Al Cleage on Black Power," *United Church Herald*, February 1968, p. 28.
9. "Rev. Cleage Tells You About Negro Separatism," Bee-line question and answer column, *Detroit Free Press*, September 1, 1968, p. 15A.
10. "The Next Step," *The Illustrated News*, May 4, 1964, p. 6.
11. Dennis Clark, "Urban Violence," *America*, June 1, 1968, pp. 728, 730.
12. From a speech at the American Psychological Association's annual convention, San Francisco, quoted by Royce Rensberger,

"Experts Differ on Black Separatism," *Detroit Free Press,* September 2, 1968.

13. Benjamin E. Mays, "Negroes Still Divided on Black Nationalism," *Michigan Chronicle,* November 30, 1968.

14. "Black Bigotry Is No Better Than White Bigotry," editorial, *Michigan Chronicle,* November 2, 1968, p. 8A.

15. W. H. Ferry, "Farewell to Integration," *The Center Magazine,* a publication of the Center for the Study of Democratic Institutions, March 1968, pp. 39–40.

16. *Ibid.,* p. 40.

CHAPTER 3
SEEDBED OF A MILITANT

1. John M. Green, *Negro History in Michigan,* © John Green, a reprint of the "Michigan Manual of Freedman's Progress," compiled by Francis H. Warren, secretary, Freedman's Progress Commission, 1915, p. 53.

2. Penelope Johnson Allen, chairman of genealogical research, Tennessee Society, D.A.R., "Leaves from the Family Tree: CLEAGE," *The Chattanooga Times,* Sunday, January 21, 1934.

3. "People who knew Rev. Hill as a fiery minister of the 20's and 30's didn't expect him to live to see seventy years. His life has been threatened innumerable times by bigots and police officials. On one occasion during the Sojourner Truth controversy (a project area in which white priests and others were organizing against integration), three carloads of white roughnecks came to his house. Stated Rev. Hill, 'I met them at the door and told them if they crossed the threshold they could prepare to go to the next world.'" — Ofield Dukes, *Michigan Chronicle,* history series, October 5, 1963.

CHAPTER 4
APOSTLE OF YOUTH

1. *Springfield Union,* August 29, 1964.

2. Albert J. Dunmore, "Cleage Cites 'Apathy' of Civic Groups," *Michigan Chronicle,* February 10, 1962, p. 8B.

3. Howard Thurman, *Footprints of a Dream* (New York: Harper & Brothers, 1959), p. 33.

4. *Springfield Union,* April 13, 1950, pp. 20, 24.

5. *The History of St. John's Congregational Church, 1844–1962,* edited by Naomi T. Cummings, et al, © 1962, St. John's Church.

6. *Springfield Union*, July 10, 1948.

7. *The History of St. John's Congregational Church, 1844–1962, op. cit.*

8. *Springfield Union*, March 18, 1949.

9. *The History of St. John's Congregational Church, 1844–1962, op cit.*, p. 85.

10. Cf. James Wise, *The Springfield Plan* (New York: Viking Press, 1945); Clarence Halligan and Alice L. Chatto, *The Story of the Springfield Plan* (New York: Barnes & Noble, 1945); Marie Syrkin, "The Springfield Plan," *Your School, Your Children* (New York: L. B. Fischer, 1944), pp. 208–21; Samuel Tannenbaum, "The Springfield Plan," *Why Men Hate* (New York: The Beechhurst Press, 1947), p. 309 ff.; James E. Pitt, *Adventures in Brotherhood* (New York: Farrar, Straus & Giroux, 1955).

11. J. Mark Bradley, *Springfield Union*, February 20, 1967.

CHAPTER 5
THE MONSTER SCHOOLS

1. Roberta Mackey, education writer, "Outbursts Mar School Meeting," *Detroit Free Press*, June 14, 1967; cf. also Harry Salsinger, education writer, "Shouting Match: Black Schools Demanded," *Detroit News.*

2. "Message to the Black Nation," *Michigan Chronicle*, May 4, 1968.

3. *Ibid.*, June 29, 1968, p. 16A.

4. "Teacher Continues a Northwestern Exposé," *Illustrated News*, February 19, 1962, p. 4.

5. "Detroit's Disgrace," *Newsweek*, July 8, 1968.

6. Albert Cleage, Jr., "Parents Protest Segregation – Court Action Threatened," *The Illustrated News*, January 15, 1962, p. 3.

7. "School Boycott Shaping Up for Fall," *The Illustrated News*, August 27, 1962, p. 1.

8. "School Report Supports Sherrill Parents' Bias Suit," *The Illustrated News*, March 12, 1962, p. 1.

9. "School Board Must Stop Segregated Building Program," *The Illustrated News*, March 19, 1962, p. 4.

10. *The Illustrated News*, April 2, 1962, p. 6.

11. "Race Bias Breeds Hate," *Michigan Chronicle*, April 21, 1962, p. 12.

12. *Michigan Chronicle*, March 23, 1968.

13. *Ibid.*

14. *Michigan Chronicle*, September 14, 1968.

15. "Principal Replies to Chronicle Story," *Michigan Chronicle*, September 9, 1968.

16. *Michigan Chronicle*, September 21, 1968.

17. "Message to the Black Nation," *op. cit.*, September 21, 1968.

18. *Ibid.*

19. "Message to the Black Nation," *op. cit.*, December 14, 1968, p. 12A.

20. *Michigan Chronicle*, editorial, November 2, 1963.

21. "Message to the Black Nation," *op. cit.*, October 26, 1968, p. 12A.

CHAPTER 6
NEOREALISM vs. HOPE

1. *Detroit Free Press*, August 31, 1968.

2. "World Conference on Church and Society—Message to the Conference," *The Ecumenical Review*, XIX, No. 1 (January 1967), pp. 60–61.

3. "Justice and International Development," *Christian Century*, May 17, 1967, pp. 660–62.

4. Reprinted from "Realism and Celebration," *Christianity and Crisis*, November 11, 1968, p. 272, copyright by Christianity and Crisis, Inc., 1968.

5. Reprinted from *Christianity and Crisis*, August 5, 1968, p. 180, copyright by Christianity and Crisis, Inc., 1968.

6. "Message to the Black Nation," *Michigan Chronicle*, May 25, 1968, p. 16A.

CHAPTER 7
THRESHOLD OF FEAR

1. *The South End*, Wayne State University, March 12, 1968.

2. Albert B. Cleage, Jr., *The Black Messiah* (New York: Sheed & Ward, Inc., 1968), p. 31.

3. *Ibid.*, p. 28.

4. *Ibid.*, p. 29.

5. *Ibid.*, p. 66.

6. *Ibid.*, p. 67.

7. *Ibid.*, pp. 74–75.

8. *Ibid.*, p. 258.

9. *Ibid.*, p. 263.

10. "Message to the Black Nation," *Michigan Chronicle*, April 27, 1968, p. 1.

11. *Ibid.*, June 15, 1968, p. 16A.

CHAPTER 8
BLACK GOD, BLACK GOSPEL

1. *The Black Messiah,* (New York: Sheed & Ward, Inc., 1968), pp. 42–43.
2. "Message to the Black Nation," *Michigan Chronicle,* July 20, 1968, p. 16A.
3. Alma Kaufman, "The Jews Were Black," *Cleveland Plain Dealer,* August 31, 1968.
4. The Ishmaelites were parents of tribes east of Palestine in the Syrian desert. The Ishmaelites are also confused with the Midianites to the south, in Arabia. (See Genesis 37: 25 ff.; Judges 8:24 ff.)
5. Rabbi (black) Wentworth A. Matthew, of New York, "The Root and Inception of the House of Israel," *Impact,* October 1968, p. 18.
6. Lerone Bennett, Jr., *Before the Mayflower,* copyright 1962 and 1969, Johnson Publishing Co., Inc., p. 4.
7. *Ibid.,* p. 6.
8. *Ibid.,* p. 7.
9. *Ibid.*
10. *Ibid.,* p. 10.
11. *Ibid.*
12. "Message to the Black Nation," *op. cit.,* March 1, 1969, p. 16A.
13. "Message to the Black Nation," *op. cit.,* December 7, 1968, p. 12A.
14. *The Black Messiah, op. cit.,* p. 88.
15. Alma Kaufman, *Cleveland Plain Dealer, op. cit.*
16. "Message to the Black Nation," *op. cit.,* May 25, 1968, p. 16A.
17. *The Black Messiah, op. cit.,* pp. 89–90.
18. "Message to the Black Nation," *op. cit.,* November 2, 1968, p. 12A.
19. *Ibid.*
20. *Ibid.,* pp. 53–54.
21. Joseph R. Washington, *The Politics of God* (Boston: Beacon Press, 1967), p. 160.
22. *The Black Messiah, op. cit.,* p. 72.
23. *Ibid.,* pp. 92–93.
24. *Ibid.,* pp. 91, 93.

Cleage approaches a secular definition of immortality, still using religious terms. One of the best statements of the immortality of the movement over against individual attainment of heaven is given by Dan Aldridge, SNCC coordinator in Detroit: "One of the ingredients of this black ideology would be the concept of revolutionary immortality. Revolutionary immortality means that we are participants in a perpetual revolution which continues after our physical death. This enables us to rise above the physical death which inevitably greets us all.

"With this new way of looking at ourselves, we begin to see ourselves as links in a long chain of events; i.e., the Revolution.

"This redefinition of ourselves as revolutionaries forces us to redefine our entire existence. As an example, family in the traditional context refers to father, mother, brother, and sister. However, within the context of the 'revolutionary immortality,' both people and events become the new family." Aldridge goes on to describe how all militant black leaders are brothers of one another. "Brother Huey Newton is a fine example. Huey is a brother, real brother; and when he is threatened with death and imprisoned, we are threatened with death and are also imprisoned. . . .

"Imagine what power we would have if the concept of the Expanded New Family were enlarged to include all oppressed people!

"This collective change in our mental attitude revitalizes us with new energy. We no longer fear the police, the army, or any other anti-humanist agents. We are able to rise above our 'old' selves because our concern is now for our brothers and not just the individual self." – Dan Aldridge, "Like It Is" column, *Michigan Chronicle,* September 21, 1968.

25. Stephen Neary, " 'Enemy Is White Man,' Howard Students Told," *Washington Star,* October 28, 1968.

26. "Message to the Black Nation," *op. cit.,* February 10, 1968, p. 16A.

27. Dr. Nathan Wright, Jr., director of urban work for the Episcopal Diocese of Newark, in a statement issued to the National Committee of Black Churchmen: "Ethical religion, in contrast to moral religion, starts with man and not with society. It assumes that life involves continuing growth and interchange. . . . The powerless, the oppressed, in any society provide the natural and historic means for changing moral religion into ethical religion. The oppressed need to have their God-given power developed and utilized. As they work to have their unused power tapped, they change the dynamics of existing power. In this way, moral religion may recapture an ethical character." – "Nathan Wright on Black Power," *The Living Church,* December 1, 1968, p. 5.

CHAPTER 9
STRIFE AT THE SHRINE

1. The two trustees said in their May 5, 1964 memo: "Guilt by association we deplore and reject. But, certainly, one reveals his philosophy by what he supports. Mr. Cleage lends his name to, and appears on the same platform with, extreme militant leadership such as Malcolm X. Most of Malcom X's goals are the civil rights objectives of almost every Negro; but mixed in with his goals is a strategy which, if need be, will use violence and hate.

2. The confrontation and challenge by Central members predated the Easter season tension of 1964. Reports had reached the *Michigan Chronicle,* which on October 26, 1963 carried an item, "Ouster Rumor Fails to Disturb Pastor." It said the Rev. Albert Cleage "seems completely undisturbed by persistent rumors that a move for his dismissal is being considered by certain members of his congregation." Cleage, according to the article, commented, "Such reports have not reached me and the matter has not been officially discussed. I could talk a bit more intelligently about the matter if I knew the source of your information." A Freedom Now rally in the church two weeks previously was cited "by a source close to Cleage" as reason for the ouster rumblings.

3. A *Michigan Chronicle* reporter, Betty De Ramus, visited the church service following the acquittal to try to determine just what Cleage was preaching. She wrote ("Does Cleage Preach Hate?" *Michigan Chronicle,* June 20, 1964): "As he stood before a crowd of attentive worshipers, the Rev. Mr. Cleage thundered:

" 'We don't hate white people; we hate some of the things they do, their ugly ways, their prejudice and discrimination! . . .

" 'Independent black action will force employment for Negroes. We must have economic pressure. It is therapy for us to participate in pickets and boycotts. We must have economic action and black political action.'

"On the specific point of what methods the Negro should use in obtaining his freedom, the Rev. Mr. Cleage said, 'The Negro is now prepared to defend himself against brutality by striking back when knocked down.

" 'But when I speak of independent black action, I am not talking about marching black armies up and down Linwood.'

"Was it hatred and violence he was preaching? Or was it survival?"

In a speech at a Milwaukee (Wisconsin) hotel before 500

UCC leaders from across the nation, in connection with a series of speaking engagements at the University of Wisconsin, February 2, 1969, Cleage said the black struggle could not be equated with a "hate campaign," according to the *Milwaukee Sentinel* (February 3, 1969, p. 9). "There are black people who do hate whites," he said. "That's one step the black man takes in discovering his identity. But it's only temporary, for the black struggle can't be shaped on hate or it will fail." He said blacks oppose the white racist's attitude of superiority. This is a point that Dr. Cone makes — that the black nationalists are not racist, for they do not seek to enslave whites, as white racists seek to do with blacks.

4. "Rev. Cleage Kicks Out Opposition Leaders," *Michigan Chronicle*, June 13, 1964, p. 1.

CHAPTER 10
THE REBEL COMMITTEEMAN

1. "Cleage Resigns from Operation Connection," *The Living Church*, July 14, 1968, p. 6.
2. Religious News Service, *National Catholic Reporter*, July 3, 1968.
3. *American Baptist News Service*, Valley Forge, Pa., July 1, 1968.
4. "Message to the Black Nation," *Michigan Chronicle*, May 18, 1968, p. 16.
5. *Ibid.*
6. *Ibid.*, November 2, 1963.
7. *Michigan Chronicle*, November 2, 1963, p. 1.
8. *Ibid.*, p. 4.

CHAPTER 11
THE CANDIDATE

1. C. C. Douglas, "People, Places and Situations," *Michigan Chronicle*, October 12, 1968.
2. "Ministers Support HHH, Hit Cleage on McCarthy," *Michigan Chronicle*, August 10, 1968, p. 5.
3. "Say Nationalists: We Are Not for McCarthy," *Michigan Chronicle*, August 3, 1968.
4. *Detroit Free Press*, August 16, 1968.
5. "Message to the Black Nation," *Michigan Chronicle*, September 28, 1968, p. 12.
6. *Detroit Free Press*, October 12, 1968.

7. Others: Frank Lovell, Socialist Workers Party, 5,649; James C. Horvath, Socialist Labor, 1,777.

8. *Detroit News*, October 14, 1965.

9. John Millhone, "Vote Drive Is Cited for Racism," *Free Press*, August 4, 1968.

10. Joseph Strickland, "Vote Negro Only Drive Gains Support," *Detroit News*, October 12, 1965.

11. Jo Ann Hardee, "Applaud Poindexter in Debate with Rival," *Detroit News*, July 15, 1965.

12. "Made for Each Other, The Great Poindexter-Cleage 'Debate,'" editorial, *Detroit News*, July 19, 1965, p. 22A.

13. *Detroit Free Press*, June 18, 1966.

14. Ahead of him were the incumbent Remus Robinson, 96, 548; Patrick McDonald, 75,220; Mary Barker, 61,953; Sara Schaden, 48,313.

15. Philip Meyer, "Negroes in Politics Win Praise of Black Community," *Detroit Free Press*, October 31, 1968.

16. C. C. Douglas, "People, Places and Situations," *Michigan Chronicle*, November 9, 1968.

17. C. McCall, "A Free University," *The South End*, Wayne State University, October 1, 1968, p. 1.

18. "Message to the Black Nation," *op. cit.*, April 12, 1969, p. 16A.

CHAPTER 12
STRUCTURE OF THE NATION

1. "To Tell the Truth" column, *West Side Courier*, January 11, 1968, p. 6.

2. "Militants Go It Alone," *Detroit Daily Press* (interim newspaper during newspaper strike), January 6, 1968.

3. "Message to the Black Nation," *Michigan Chronicle*, January 13, 1968.

4. *Ibid.*, December 16, 1967, p. 16A.

5. "Detroit: A Year After the Rebellion," *Detroit Tribune*, August 18, 1968.